DISCARD

An Early Resident of Pittsburgh.

From a statue by T. A. Mills in the Carnegie Museum.

THE WINNING OF THE WEST

BY

THEODORE ROOSEVELT

VOLUME TWO

FROM THE ALLEGHANIES TO THE MISSISSIPPI
1777–1783

WITH MAPS

Introduction to the Bison Book Edition
by Daniel K. Richter

University of Nebraska Press
Lincoln and London

Introduction to the Bison Book Edition © 1995
by the University of Nebraska Press
Manufactured in the United States of America

⊖ The paper in this book meets the minimum requirements of
American National Standard for Information Sciences—
Permanence of Paper for Printed Library Materials,
ANSI Z39.48-1984.

First Bison Book printing: 1995
Most recent printing indicated by the last digit below:
10   9   8   7   6   5   4   3   2   1

Library of Congress Cataloging-in-Publication Data
Roosevelt, Theodore, 1858–1919.
The winning of the West / by Theodore Roosevelt—Presidential
ed.
p.   cm.
Includes index.
Originally published: New York: G. P. Putnam's Sons, 1894.
Contents: v. 1. From the Alleghanies to the Mississippi, 1769–
1776—v. 2. From the Alleghanies to the Mississippi, 1777–
1783—v. 3. The founding of the trans-Alleghany common-
wealths, 1784–1790—v. 4. Louisiana and the Northwest, 1791–
1807.
ISBN 0-8032-8958-8 (set)—ISBN 0-8032-8954-5 (v. 1)—
ISBN 0-8032-8955-3 (v. 2)—ISBN 0-8032-8956-1 (v. 3)—
ISBN 0-8032-8957-X (v. 4)
1. United States—Territorial expansion.   2. Northwest, Old—
History.   3. West (U.S.)—History.   I. Title.
E179.5.R66   1995
976—dc20
94-46645   CIP

The four-volume set of *The Winning of the West* was copyrighted
and published between 1889 and 1896 by G. P. Putnam's Sons,
New York. This Bison Book is a reprint of volume 2, © 1889. The
title-page designation of Presidential Edition and the fron-
tispiece illustration were added later, but in all other respects
this is the original edition.

THIS BOOK IS DEDICATED, WITH HIS PERMISSION

TO

FRANCIS PARKMAN

TO WHOM AMERICANS WHO FEEL A PRIDE IN THE PIONEER HISTORY OF
THEIR COUNTRY ARE SO GREATLY INDEBTED

INTRODUCTION
Daniel K. Richter

"Our more pretentious historians who really did pay some
heed to facts and wrote books that—in addition to their
mortal dulness—were quite accurate, felt it undignified
and beneath them to notice the deeds of mere ignorant Indian fighters," Theodore Roosevelt concluded in Appendix
A to this second volume of *The Winning of the West*. Because of that snobbishness, he continued, early nine-
teenth-century historians "lost all power of doing the best
work; for they passed their lives in a circle of small literary
men, who shrank from any departure from conventional
European standards." If Roosevelt were alive today—more
than a century after he wrote those words—he would no
doubt similarly scorn modern scholars, most of whom still
sniff at the kind of blood-and-guts tales of backcountry
warfare with which this volume abounds.

But mere attention to such tales was not enough for
Roosevelt. With only slightly less contempt, he also dismissed those "who wrote history for the mass of our people,
not for the scholars." Most such writers, he harumphed,
"had not been educated up to the point of appreciating the
value of evidence, and accepted undoubted facts and
absurd traditions with equal good faith" (393). Thus Roosevelt sought a middle way between the "dulness" of prim-
and-proper academic history and the excesses of popu-
larizers who loved a good story about Indian fighters more
than faithfulness to the historical record. He found that
middle way through the careful use of manuscript and
printed sources and through the clear sense of interpretive

purpose that sets a professional historian apart from a curiosity-collecting antiquarian.

Roosevelt's interpretive scheme had first and foremost to provide an intellectual justification for writing about the frontier exploits antiquarians loved but serious historians loathed. With an insight that remains pertinent, this volume gains that justification in nothing less than a redefinition of the nature of the American Revolution. "The revolutionary contest . . . ," Roosevelt concludes, had a "twofold character, making it on the part of the Americans a struggle for independence in the east, and in the west a war of conquest" (373–74). It was not self-evident, he reminds his readers, that the territory "from the Alleghanies to the Mississippi" would become part of the United States should the War for Independence succeed. After all, one of the Parliamentary "Intolerable Acts" of 1774 had declared the region between the Ohio River and the Great Lakes a part of the province of Quebec. Moreover, the trading connections of the area's native peoples and the French culture of its pockets of European inhabitants also oriented it northeastward, through Detroit, toward the St. Lawrence. The western warfare of the Revolutionary period, then, determined who would rule this "*de facto* part of Canada." In Roosevelt's view, "the Americans tried to conquer it exactly as they tried to conquer the rest of Canada; the only difference was that [George Rogers] Clark succeeded, whereas [Benedict] Arnold and [Richard] Montgomery failed" in their 1775 assaults on Quebec and Montreal (373–75).

"What the Westerners Had Done During the Revolution," then, becomes for Roosevelt far more than a summary title for the closing chapter of this volume. It assumes vital importance in his interpretation of American history as a whole, for "had not the backwoodsmen been successful . . . , we would certainly have been cooped up between the sea and the mountains" (374–75). Events of such importance deserve serious study. They are certainly far too significant to leave them in the scribbling hands of "collectors of backwoods anecdotes" ignorant of some "very obvious truths: that with the best intentions in the world the average backwoodsman often has difficulty in describing a confused chain of events exactly as they took place; that when the events are described after a long lapse of years many errors are apt to creep in; and that when they are reported from tradition it is the rarest thing imaginable for the report to be correct" (395).

Rarer still to Roosevelt's imagination would have been the work of turn-of-the-twenty-first-century historians, folklorists, and culture studies specialists who take oral traditions seriously, precisely *because* of the ways in which they mix fact and error, confuse chains of events, and construct narrative fictions about personal or collective pasts. And he would no doubt be horrified at the thought that latter-day "small literary men" and skeptical scholarly women would almost instinctively find *The Winning of the West,* for all its careful scholarship, caught up in a mythic discourse whose "undoubted facts" might better be called "absurd traditions."

The first hints of the discursive world Roosevelt inhabited strike a modern reader through the language he uses to describe Native Americans. Indians are "fickle savages" (19, 127, and passim), whose wars were "waged as relentlessly against the most helpless non-combatants as against the armed solders in the field" (7), with the result that "the defeat of the average white force was usually followed by a merciless slaughter" (124). Indians traveled in a "swarm" or "a huge horde" (52), and were prone "to assail the colonists, just as the wild beasts gathered to prey on the tame herds" (348). When not "tomahawking those, chiefly women and children, who could not keep up with" others they took prisoner (103), they "strutted to and fro in their dirty finery, or lounged round the houses [of French habitants], inquisitive, importunate, and insolent, hardly concealing a lust of bloodshed and plunder that the slightest mishap was certain to render ungovernable" (53). Their "friendship" could only be secured by those willing "continually to give them presents" (3), and their diplomacy embodied "a curious mixture of barbarian cunning and barbarian childishness" suitable to "a page of Græco-Trojan diplomacy" (21). White frontier folk, it is true, harbored some unfortunate stereotypes and, Roosevelt admits, "barely considered an Indian as a human being." But that was because "they knew him for what he was—filthy, cruel, lecherous, and faithless" (147–48). Even their dogs, "by instinct and training . . . mortally hated Indians" (356).

That more than a quaint vocabulary and an unfortunate set of outdated stereotypes was at work in Roosevelt's language is indicated by his attitude toward those who might take exception to his views. "It is indeed a warped, perverse, and silly morality which would forbid a course of conquest that has turned whole continents into the seats of mighty and flourishing civilized nations," he announced early in the third volume of *The Winning of the West* series. Indeed, "All men of sane and wholesome thought must dismiss with impatient contempt the plea that these continents should be reserved for the use of scattered savage tribes, whose life was but a few degrees less meaningless, squalid, and ferocious than that of the wild beasts with whom they held joint ownership." For Roosevelt, then, his story was more than just a history of the "twofold character" of the American Revolution. "Looked at from the standpoint of the ages . . . ," he enthused, "it is of incalculable importance that America, Australia, and Siberia should pass out of the hands of the red, black, and yellow aboriginal owners, and become the heritage of the dominant world races" (vol. 3: 44–46).

Here, stated baldly, are the evolutionary racist assumptions that almost universally infused American social science in the late nineteenth and early twentieth centuries. In the Darwinian struggle for existence, the "civilized" races (of whom those alleged to be of Anglo-Saxon stock were the most "advanced") must triumph over the lesser "savage" races (among whom American Indians were nearly the most "backward"). If anything, the self-confident activism of Progressive-Era reformers such as Roosevelt only reinforced a mythic sense of racial destiny, with an imperative to hurry social evolution along through hard-headed, pragmatic human effort. Anyone who questioned that effort was, according to Roosevelt, "too selfish and indolent, too lacking in imagination, to understand the race-importance of the work" (vol. 3: 44).

Roosevelt's mythic discourse of evolutionary racism—of what the first volume of *The Winning of the West* calls "the spread of the English-speaking peoples over the world's waste spaces" (1)—is seldom explicitly voiced in this second volume. Only the preference for words like *savage*, the occasional remark about the white frontier folk's "race-capacity for self-rule" (342), or the assertion that, by contrast, the French inhabitants of the Illinois country "were utterly unsuited for liberty, as the Americans understood the term" (169) jar the modern ear. Nonetheless, evolutionary racism undergirds the interpretive framework of this and other installments of *The Winning of the West* and explains why the conquest of the trans-Appalachian region was for Roosevelt such an important—indeed necessary—aspect of "What the Westerners Had Done During the Revolution."

Roosevelt's underlying assumptions about the morality of the conquest of a savage race by a civilized one—no matter how bloody the contest—reveal themselves, for instance, in a close reading of his treatment of scalping. Indians almost invariably scalp whites in acts of mindless brutality; to Chickasaws, for example, "the most powerful motive" for attacks on white outposts on the Mississippi "was doubtless simply the desire for scalps and plunder" (348). As members of the civilized English race, British officers who "accompanied the Indians against the frontier and witnessed or shared in their unmentionable atrocities" (87–88) earn special opprobrium. Thus Henry Hamilton, Lieutenant-Governor of Detroit, richly deserved "the ven-

omous hatred of the backwoodsmen, who held him in peculiar abhorrence, and nicknamed him the 'hair-buyer' general, asserting that he put a price on the scalps of the
Americans" (2). Such comments render remarkable the
lack of judgmental remarks that elide Roosevelt's refer-
ences to white Americans, among whom "Every man carried a small-bore rifle, a tomahawk, and a scalping-knife"
(256–57) and whose "higher type" of heroes "frequently
went on scouts alone, either to procure information or to
get scalps" (140). The logic beneath the silences becomes
clear in Roosevelt's third volume, which proclaims that
"the most ultimately righteous of all wars is a war with
savages," because "the rude, fierce settler who drives the
savage from the land lays all civilized mankind under a
debt to him" (vol. 3: 45).

But perhaps the most revealing indicator of Roosevelt's
assumptions about the inevitable evolutionary triumph of
civilized over savage races comes in what appears at first
glance his most sympathetic portrayal of Indians and his
most damning treatment of frontier whites. Chapter 5 of
this volume focuses on what Roosevelt quite rightly calls
"a monument to the cold-blooded and cowardly brutality of
the borderers": the March 1782 massacre of nearly one
hundred pacifist Moravian Delawares at the village of
Gnadenhutten on the Muskingum River in present-day
Ohio. While admitting that "the conduct of the backwoodsmen toward these peaceful and harmless Christian Indians was utterly abhorrent," Roosevelt finds the event
foreordained by broad historical forces. Gnadenhutten and
its neighboring Moravian communities, he asserts, "occupied an utterly untenable position . . . mid-way between
the white settlements southeast of the Ohio, and the towns
of the Indians round Sandusky," whose raiders, the perpetrators of the massacre insisted, found shelter there en
route to and from the Pennsylvania frontier. Under these
circumstances, "the fate of the hapless and peaceful Moravians, if they continued to dwell on the Muskingum, was
absolutely inevitable." And, for Roosevelt, "the obvious

truth" was "that no small share of the blame for their sad end should be put to the credit of the blind folly of their missionary leaders" who—he asserts—refused to let the Indians bow to the inevitable and abandon their villages (142–46).

Such curious exercises in blaming the victim force a modern reader to approach the second volume of *The Winning of the West* with mixed feelings. Roosevelt remains admirable for his literary talents, for his ability to make serious documentary research come alive, for his capacity to place colorful frontier battles in a larger historical context, and for his fundamental insight into the importance of events in the Backcountry during the Revolution. Only very recently, in fact, have professional historians begun to rediscover the centrality of trans-Appalachian events to the story of late eighteenth-century America. Admiration must be balanced, however, against Roosevelt's theory of history as a story of the progressive evolutionary triumph of civilized over savage races. Yet this most appalling characteristic of *The Winning of the West* is itself a reason the work still deserves—or rather needs—to be read. In this light, the volume derives its importance for our time less from its value as a study in historical developments during the 1770s and 1780s than from the insights it provides into interpretations of history during the Progressive Era and into the meaning of words such as *race* and *progress* for white Americans of that generation—and perhaps ours.

CONTENTS.

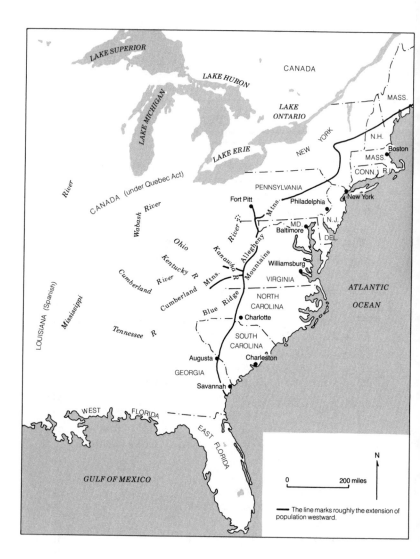

The Colonies in 1774, when the First Continental Congress assembled. The heavy line marks roughly the extension of population westward. Based on a map by G. P. Putnam's Sons, New York and London.

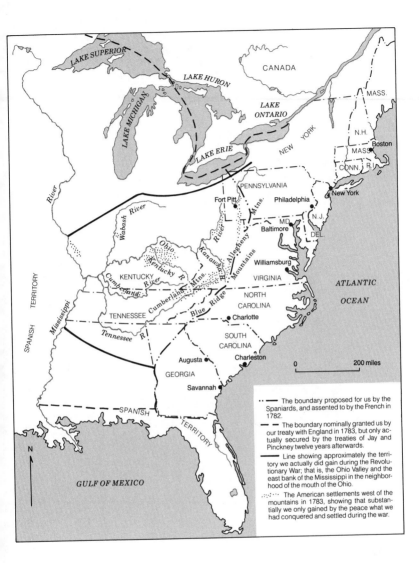

The States in 1783, when peace was declared. Based on a map by G. P. Putnam's Sons, New York and London.

THE WINNING OF THE WEST.

CHAPTER I.

THE WAR IN THE NORTHWEST, 1777–1778.

IN the fall of 1776 it became evident that a formidable Indian war was impending. At Detroit great councils were held by all the northwestern tribes, to whom the Six Nations sent the white belt of peace, that they might cease their feuds and join against the Americans. *The Tribes Hold Councils at Detroit.* The later councils were summoned by Henry Hamilton, the British lieutenant-governor of the northwestern region, whose head-quarters were at Detroit. He was an ambitious, energetic, unscrupulous man, of bold character, who wielded great influence over the Indians; and the conduct of the war in the west, as well as the entire management of frontier affairs, was intrusted to him by the British Government.[1] He had been ordered to enlist the Indians on the British side, and have them ready to act against the Americans in the spring[2]; and accordingly he gathered the tribes together. He himself took part in the war-talks, plying the Indians

[1] Haldimand MSS. Sir Guy Carleton to Hamilton, September 26, 1777.
[2] *Do.*, Carleton to Hamilton, October 6, 1776.

with presents and fire-water no less than with speeches and promises. The headmen of the different tribes, as they grew excited, passed one another black, red or bloody, and tomahawk belts, as tokens of the vengeance to be taken on their white foes. One Delaware chief still held out for neutrality, announcing that if he had to side with either set of combatants it would be with the " buckskins," or backwoodsmen, and not with the red-coats; but the bulk of the warriors sympathized with the Half King of the Wyandots when he said that the Long Knives had for years interfered with the Indians' hunting, and that now at last it was the Indians' turn to threaten revenge.[1]

Hamilton was for the next two years the mainspring of Indian hostility to the Americans in the Lt.-Gov. Henry Hamilton. northwest. From the beginning he had been anxious to employ the savages against the settlers, and when the home government bade him hire them he soon proved himself very expert, as well as very ruthless, in their use.[2] He rapidly acquired the venomous hatred of the backwoodsmen, who held him in peculiar abhorrence, and nicknamed him the " hair-buyer " general, asserting that he put a price on the scalps of the Americans. This allegation may have been untrue

[1] "Am. Archives," 1st Series, Vol. II., p. 517. There were several councils held at Detroit during this fall, and it is difficult—and not very important—to separate the incidents that occurred at each. Some took place before Hamilton arrived, which, according to his " brief account," was November 9th. He asserts that he did not send out war parties until the following June ; but the testimony seems conclusive that he was active in instigating hostility from the time of his arrival.

[2] Haldimand MSS. Germaine to Carlton, March 26, 1777.

as affecting Hamilton personally; he always endeavored to get the war parties to bring in prisoners, and behaved well to the captives when they were in his power; nor is there any direct evidence that he himself paid out money for scalps. But scalps were certainly bought and paid for at Detroit [1]; and the commandant himself was accustomed to receive them with formal solemnity at the councils held to greet the war parties when they returned from successful raids. [2] The only way to keep the friendship of the Indians was continually to give them presents; these presents were naturally given to the most successful warriors; and the scalps were the only safe proofs of a warrior's success. **Scalp Buying.** Doubtless the commandant and the higher British officers generally treated the Americans humanely when they were brought into contact with them; and it is not likely that they knew, or were willing to know, exactly what the savages did in all cases. But they at least connived at the measures of their subordinates. These were hardened, embittered, men who paid for the zeal of their Indian allies accordingly as they received tangible proof thereof; in other words, they hired them to murder non-combatants as well as soldiers, and paid for each life, of any sort, that was taken. The fault lay primarily with the British Government, and with those of its advisers who, like Hamilton, advocated the employment of the savages. They thereby became participants in

[1] See the "American Pioneer," I., 292, for a very curious account of an Indian, who by dividing a large scalp into two got fifty dollars for each half at Detroit.

[2] Haldimand MSS., *passim;* also Heckewelder, etc.

the crimes committed; and it was idle folly for them to prate about having bidden the savages be merciful. The sin consisted in having let them loose on the borders; once they were let loose it was absolutely impossible to control them. More-over, the British sinned against knowledge; for some of their highest and most trusted officers on the frontier had written those in supreme command, relating the cruelties practised by the Indians upon the defenceless, and urging that they should not be made allies, but rather that their neutrality only should be secured.[1] The average American backwoodsman was quite as brutal and inconsiderate a victor as the average British officer; in fact, he was in all likeli-hood the less humane of the two; but the English-man deliberately made the deeds of the savage his own. Making all allowance for the strait in which the British found themselves, and admitting that much can be said against their accusers, the fact remains that they urged on hordes of savages to slaughter men, women, and children along the entire frontier; and for this there must ever rest a dark stain on their national history.

Hamilton organized a troop of white rangers from among the French, British, and tories at Detroit. They acted as allies of the Indians, and furnished leaders to them. Three of these leaders were the tories McKee, Elliot, and Girty, who had fled together from Pittsburg[2]; they all three warred

[1] *E. g.* in Haldimand MSS. Lieut.-Gov. Abbott to General Carleton, June 8, 1778.

[2] Haldimand MSS. Hamilton's letter, April 25, 1778.

" April the 20th—Edward Hayle (who had undertaken to carry a letter

against their countrymen with determined ferocity. Girty won the widest fame on the border by his cunning and cruelty; but he was really a less able foe than the two others. McKee in particular showed himself a fairly good commander of Indians and irregular troops; as did likewise an Englishman named Caldwell, and two French partisans, De Quindre and Lamothe, who were hearty supporters of the British.

Hamilton and his subordinates, both red and white, were engaged in what was essentially an effort to exterminate the borderers. .They were not endeavoring merely to defeat the armed bodies of the enemy. They were explicitly bidden by those in supreme command to push back the frontier, to expel the settlers from the country. Hamilton himself had been ordered by his immediate official superior to assail the borders of Pennsylvania and Virginia with his savages, to destroy the crops and buildings of the settlers who had advanced beyond the moun-

The British Begin a War of Extermination.

from me to the Moravian Minister at Kushayhking) returned, having executed his commission—he brought me a letter & newspapers from Mr. McKee who was Indian Agent for the Crown and has been a long time in the hands of the Rebels at Fort Pitt, at length has found means to make his escape with three other men, two of the name of Girty (mentioned in Lord Dunmore's list) interpreters & Matthew Elliott the young man who was last summer sent down from this place a prisoner.—This last person I am informed has been at New York since he left Quebec, and probably finding the change in affairs unfavourable to the Rebels, has slipp'd away to make his peace here.

" 23d—Hayle went off again to conduct them all safe through the Villages having a letter & Wampum for that purpose. Alexander McKee is a man of good character, and has great influence with the Shawanese is well acquainted with the country & can probably give some useful intelligence, he will probably reach this place in a few days."

tains, and to give to his Indian allies,—the Hurons, Shawnees, and other tribes,—all the land of which they thus took possession.[1] With such allies as Hamilton had this order was tantamount to proclaiming a war of extermination, waged with appalling and horrible cruelty against the settlers, of all ages and sexes. It brings out in bold relief the fact that in the west the war of the Revolution was an effort on the part of Great Britain to stop the westward growth of the English race in America, and to keep the region beyond the Alleghanies as a region where only savages should dwell.

All through the winter of '76–'77 the northwestern Indians were preparing to take up the tomahawk. **All the Northwestern Tribes go to War.** Runners were sent through the leafless, frozen woods from one to another of their winter camps. In each bleak, frail village, each snow-hidden cluster of bark wigwams, the painted, half-naked warriors danced the war dance, and sang the war song, beating the ground with their war clubs and keeping time with their feet to the rhythmic chant as they moved in rings round the peeled post, into which they struck their hatchets. The hereditary sachems, the peace chiefs, could no longer control the young men. The braves made ready their weapons and battle gear; their bodies were painted red and black, the plumes of the war eagle were braided into their long scalp locks, and some put on necklaces of bears' claws, and head-dresses made of panther skin, or of the shaggy and horned frontlet of the buf-

[1] Haldimand MSS. Haldimand to Hamilton, August 6, 1778.

falo.[1]   Before the snow was off the ground the war
parties crossed the Ohio and fell on the frontiers
from the Monongahela and Kanawha to the Kentucky.[2]

On the Pennsylvanian and Virginian frontiers the
panic was tremendous.   The people fled into the already existing forts, or hastily built others; where
there were but two or three families in a place, they
merely gathered into block-houses—stout log-cabins
two stories high, with loop-holed walls, and the upper story projecting a little over the lower.   The
savages, well armed with weapons supplied them
from the British arsenals on the Great Lakes, spread
over the country; and there ensued all the horrors
incident to a war waged as relentlessly against the
most helpless non-combatants as against the armed
soldiers in the field.   Block-houses were surprised
and burnt; bodies of militia were ambushed and
destroyed.   The settlers were shot down as they sat
by their hearth-stones in the evening, or ploughed
the ground during the day; the lurking Indians
crept up and killed them while they still-hunted the
deer, or while they lay in wait for the elk beside the
well-beaten game trails.

The captured women and little ones were driven
off to the far interior.   The weak among them, the
young children, and the women heavy with child,
were tomahawked and scalped as soon as their steps

[1] For instances of an Indian wearing this buffalo cap, with the horns on,
see Kercheval and De Haas.

[2] State Department MSS. for 1777, *passim*.   So successful were the Indian chiefs in hoodwinking the officers at Fort Pitt that some of the latter
continued to believe that only three or four hundred Indians had gone on
the war path.

faltered. The able-bodied, who could stand the terrible fatigue, and reached their journey's end, suffered various fates. Some were burned at the stake, others were sold to the French or British traders, and long afterwards made their escape, or were ransomed by their relatives. Still others were kept in the Indian camps, the women becoming the slaves or wives of the warriors,[1] while the children were adopted into the tribe, and grew up precisely like their little red-skinned playmates. Sometimes, when they had come to full growth, they rejoined the whites; but generally they were enthralled by the wild freedom and fascination of their forest life, and never forsook their adopted tribesmen, remaining inveterate foes of their own color. Among the ever-recurring tragedies of the frontier, not the least sorrowful was the recovery of these long-missing children by their parents, only to find that they had lost all remembrance of and love for their father and mother, and had become irreclaimable savages, who eagerly grasped the first chance to flee from the intolerable irksomeness and restraint of civilized life.[2]

Among others, the stockade at Wheeling [3] was at-

[1] Occasionally we come across records of the women afterwards making their escape ; very rarely they took their half-breed babies with them. De Haas mentions one such case where the husband, though he received his wife well, always hated the copper-colored addition to his family ; the latter, by the way, grew up a thorough Indian, could not be educated, and finally ran away, joined the Revolutionary army, and was never heard of afterwards.

[2] For an instance where a boy finally returned, see " Trans-Alleghany Pioneers," p. 119 ; see also pp. 126, 132, 133, for instances of the capture and treatment of whites by Indians.

[3] Fort Henry. For an account of the siege, see De Haas, pp. 223–340. It took place in the early days of September.

tacked by two or three hundred Indians ; with them
came a party of Detroit Rangers, marshalled by drum
and fife, and carrying the British colors.[1]   The
Most of the men inside the fort were drawn   **Attack on**
out by a stratagem, fell into an ambuscade,   **Wheeling.**
and were slain ; but the remainder made good the defence, helped by the women, who ran the lead into bullets, cooled and loaded the guns, and even, when the
rush was made, assisted to repel it by firing through the
loopholes. After making a determined effort to storm
the stockade, in which some of the boldest warriors
were slain while trying in vain to batter down the gates
with heavy timbers, the baffled Indians were obliged
to retire discomfited. The siege was chiefly memorable because of an incident which is to this day a
staple theme for story-telling in the cabins of the
mountaineers. One of the leading men of the
neighborhood was Major Samuel McColloch, renowned along the border as the chief in a family
famous for its Indian fighters, the dread and terror
of the savages, many of whose most noted warriors
he slew, and at whose hands he himself, in the end,
met his death. When Wheeling was invested, he
tried to break into it, riding a favorite old white

[1] The accounts of the different sieges of Wheeling were first written
down from the statements of the pioneers when they had grown very aged.
In consequence, there is much uncertainty as to the various incidents.
Thus there seems to be a doubt whether Girty did or did not command the
Indians in this first siege. The frontiersmen hated Girty as they did no
other man, and he was credited with numerous actions done by other white
leaders of the Indians ; the British accounts say comparatively little about
him. He seems to have often fought with the Indians as one of their own
number, while his associates led organized bands of rangers ; he was thus
more often brought into contact with the frontiersmen, but was really
hardly as dangerous a foe to them as were one or two of his tory companions..

horse. But the Indians intercepted him, and hemmed him in on the brink of an almost perpendicular slope,[1] some three hundred feet high. So sheer was the descent that they did not dream any horse could go down it, and instead of shooting they advanced to capture the man whom they hated. McColloch had no thought of surrendering, to die by fire at the stake, and he had as little hope of resistance against so many foes. Wheeling short round, he sat back in the saddle, shifted his rifle into his right hand, reined in his steed, and spurred him over the brink. The old horse never faltered, but plunged headlong down the steep, boulder-covered, cliff-broken slope. Good luck, aided by the wonderful skill of the rider and the marvellous strength and sure-footedness of his steed, rewarded, as it deserved, one of the most daring feats of horsemanship of which we have any authentic record. There was a crash, the shock of a heavy body, half springing, half falling, a scramble among loose rocks, and the snapping of saplings and bushes; and in another moment the awe-struck Indians above saw their unharmed foe, galloping his gallant white horse in safety across the plain. To this day the place is known by the name of McColloch's leap.[2]

In Virginia and Pennsylvania the Indian outrages meant only the harassing of the borderers; in Kentucky they threatened the complete destruction of the vanguard of the white advance and, there-

[1] The hill overlooks Wheeling; the slope has now much crumbled away, and in consequence has lost its steepness.

[2] In the west this feat is as well known as is Putnam's similar deed in the north.

fore, the stoppage of all settlement west of the Alleghanies until after the Revolutionary war, when very possibly the soil might not have been ours to settle. Fortunately Hamilton did not yet realize the importance of the Kentucky settlements, nor the necessity of crushing them, and during 1777 the war bands organized at Detroit were sent against the country round Pittsburg; while the feeble forts in the far western wilderness were only troubled by smaller war parties raised among the tribes on their own account. A strong expedition, led by Hamilton in person, would doubtless at this time have crushed them.

The Struggle in Kentucky.

As it was, there were still so few whites in Kentucky that they were greatly outnumbered by the invading Indians. They were, in consequence, unable to meet the enemy in the open field, and gathered in their stations or forted villages. Therefore the early conflicts, for the most part, took the form of sieges of these wooden forts. Such sieges, had little in common with the corresponding operations of civilized armies. The Indians usually tried to surprise a fort; if they failed, they occasionally tried to carry it by open assault, or by setting fire to it, but very rarely, indeed, beleaguered it in form. For this they lacked both the discipline and the commissariat. Accordingly, if their first rush miscarried, they usually dispersed in the woods to hunt, or look for small parties of whites; always, however, leaving some of their number to hover round the fort and watch any thing that took place. Masters in the art of hiding, and able to conceal themselves behind a bush, a stone, or a tuft of weeds, they skulked round the gate before dawn, to shoot the white sentinels; or they ambushed the springs, and killed those who came for water; they slaughtered all of the cattle that had not been driven in, and any one venturing incautiously beyond the walls was certain to be waylaid and murdered. Those who were thus hemmed in the fort were obliged to get game on which to live; the hunters accordingly were accustomed to leave before daybreak, travel eight or ten miles, hunt all day at the risk of their lives, and return after dark. Being of course the picked men of the garrison, they often eluded the Indians, or slew them if an encounter took place, but very frequently indeed they were themselves slain. The Indians always trusted greatly to wiles and feints to draw their foes into their power. As ever in this woodland fighting, their superiority in hiding, or taking advantage of cover, counterbalanced the superiority of the whites as marksmen; and their war parties were thus at least a match, man against man, for the Kentuckians, though the latter, together with the Watauga men, were the best woodsmen and fighters of the frontier. Only a very few of the whites became, like Boon and Kenton, able to beat the best of the savages at their own game.

The innumerable sieges that took place during the long years of Indian warfare differed in detail, but generally closely resembled one another as regards the main points. Those that occurred in 1777 may be considered as samples of the rest; and accounts of these have been preserved by the two chief actors, Boon and Clark.[1] Boonsborough, which was held by twenty-two riflemen, was attacked twice, once in April and again in July, on each occasion by a party of fifty or a hundred warriors.[2] The first time the garrison was taken by surprise; one man lost his scalp, and four were wounded, including Boon himself, who had been commissioned as captain in the county militia.[3] The Indians promptly withdrew when they found they could not carry the fort by a sudden assault. On the second occasion the whites were on their guard, and though they had one man killed and two wounded (leaving but thirteen unhurt men in the fort), they easily beat off the assailants, and slew half a dozen of them. This time the Indians stayed round two days, keeping up a heavy fire, under cover of which they several times tried to burn the fort.[4]

Logan's[5] station at St. Asaphs was likewise at-

---

[1] In Boon's narrative, written down by Filson, and in Clark's diary, as given by Morehead. The McAfee MSS. and Butler's history give some valuable information. Boon asserts that at this time the "Long Knives" proved themselves superior to their foe in almost every battle; but the facts do not seem to sustain him, though the statement was doubtless true as regards a few picked men. His estimates of the Indian numbers and losses must be received with great caution.

[2] Boon says April 15th and July 4th. Clark's diary makes the first date April 24th. Boon says one hundred Indians, Clark "40 or 50." Clark's account of the loss on both sides agrees tolerably well with Boon's. Clark's diary makes the second attack take place on May 23d. His dates are probably correct, as Boon must have written only from memory.

[3] Two of the other wounded men were Captain John Todd and Boon's old hunting companion, Stoner.

[4] Clark's diary.

[5] Boon says July 19th, Clark's diary makes it May 30th: Clark is undoubtedly right; he gives the names of the man who was killed and of the two who were wounded.

tacked; it was held by only fifteen gunmen. When the attack was made the women, guarded by part of

Logan's Adventures. the men, were milking the cows outside the fort. The Indians fired at them from the thick cane that still stood near-by, killing one man and wounding two others, one mortally.[1]   The party, of course, fled to the fort, and on looking back they saw their mortally wounded friend weltering on the ground. His wife and family were within the walls; through the loopholes they could see him yet alive, and exposed every moment to death. So great was the danger that the men refused to go out to his rescue, whereupon Logan alone opened the gate, bounded out, and seizing the wounded man in his arms, carried him back unharmed through a shower of bullets. The Indians continued to lurk around the neighborhood, and the ammunition grew very scarce. Thereupon Logan took two companions and left the fort at night to go to the distant settlements on the Holston, where he might get powder and lead. He knew that the Indians were watching the wilderness road, and trusting to his own hardiness and consummate woodcraft, he struck straight out across the cliff-broken, wood-covered mountains, sleeping wherever night overtook him, and travelling all day long with the tireless speed of a wolf.[2]   He returned with the needed stores in ten days from the time he set out. These tided the people over the warm months.

[1] The name of the latter was Burr Harrison; he died a fortnight afterward. —Clark.

[2] Not a fanciful comparison; the wolf is the only animal that an Indian or a trained frontiersman cannot tire out in several days' travel. Following a deer two days in light snow, I have myself gotten near enough to shoot it without difficulty.

In the fall, when the hickories had turned yellow and the oaks deep red, during the weeks of still, hazy weather that mark the Indian summer, their favorite hunting season,[1] the savages again filled the land, and Logan was obliged to repeat his perilous journey.[2] He also continually led small bands of his followers against the Indian war- and hunting-parties, sometimes surprising and dispersing them, and harassing them greatly. Moreover he hunted steadily throughout the year to keep the station in meat, for the most skilful hunters were, in those days of scarcity, obliged to spend much of their time in the chase. Once, while at a noted game lick,[3] waiting for deer, he was surprised by the Indians, and by their fire was wounded in the breast and had his right arm broken. Nevertheless he sprang on his horse and escaped, though the savages were so close that one, leaping at him, for a moment grasped the tail of the horse. Every one of these pioneer leaders, from Clark and Boon to Sevier and Robertson, was required constantly to expose his life; each lost sons or brothers at the hands of the

[1] Usually early in November.—McAfee MSS.

[2] Marshall, 50.

[3] These game licks were common, and were of enormous extent. Multitudes of game, through countless generations, had tramped the ground bare of vegetation, and had made deep pits and channels with their hoofs and tongues. See McAfee MSS. Sometimes the licks covered acres of ground, while the game trails leading towards them through the wood were as broad as streets, even 100 feet wide. I have myself seen small game licks, the largest not a hundred feet across, in the Selkirks, Cœur d'Alênes, and Bighorns, the ground all tramped up by the hoofs of elk, deer, wild sheep, and white goats, with deep furrows and hollows where the saline deposits existed. In the Little Missouri Bad Lands there is so much mineral matter that no regular licks are needed. As the game is killed off the licks become overgrown and lost.

Indians, and each thinned the ranks of the enemy with his own rifle. In such a primitive state of society the man who led others was expected to show strength of body no less than strength of mind and heart; he depended upon his physical prowess almost as much as upon craft, courage, and headwork. The founder and head of each little community needed not only a shrewd brain and commanding temper, but also the thews and training to make him excel as woodsman and hunter, and the heart and eye to enable him to stand foremost in every Indian battle.

Clark spent most of the year at Harrodstown, taking part in the defence of Kentucky. All the while he was revolving in his bold, ambitious heart a scheme for the conquest of the Illinois country, and he sent scouts thither to spy out the land and report to him what they saw. The Indians lurked round Harrodstown throughout the summer; and Clark and his companions were engaged in constant skirmishes with them. Once, warned by the uneasy restlessness of the cattle (who were sure to betray the presence of Indians if they got sight or smell of them), they were able to surround a party of ten or twelve, who were hidden in a tall clump of weeds. The savages were intent on cutting off some whites who were working in a turnip patch two hundred yards from the fort; Clark's party killed three—he himself killing one,—wounded another, and sold the plunder they took, at auction, for seventy pounds. At other times the skirmishes resulted differently,

Clark Shares in the Defence of Kentucky.

as on the occasion chronicled by Clark in his diary, when they "went out to hunt Indians; one wounded Squire Boon and escaped."[1]

The corn was brought in from the cribs under guard; one day while shelling a quantity, a body of thirty-seven whites were attacked, and seven were killed or wounded, though the Indians were beaten off and two scalps taken. In spite of this constant warfare the fields near the forts were gradually cleared, and planted with corn, pumpkins, and melons; and marrying and mirth-making went on within the walls. One of Clark's scouts, shortly after returning from the Illinois, got married, doubtless feeling he deserved some reward for the hardships he had suffered; on the wedding night Clark remarks that there was "great merriment." The rare and infrequent expresses from Pittsburg or Williamsburg brought letters telling of Washington's campaigns, which Clark read with absorbed interest. On the first of October, having matured his plans for the Illinois campaign, he left for Virginia, to see if he could get the government to help him put them into execution.

During the summer parties of backwoods militia from the Holston settlements—both Virginians and Carolinians—came out to help the Kentuckians in their struggle against the Indians; but they only stayed a few weeks, and then returned home. In the fall, however, several companies of immigrants came out across the mountains; and at the same time the

The Holston Men Help Kentucky.

---

[1] Clark's Diary, entry for July 9th.

small parties of hunters succeeded in pretty well clearing the woods of Indians. Many of the lesser camps and stations had been broken up, and at the end of the year there remained only four—Boonsborough, Harrodstown, Logan's station at St. Asaphs, and McGarry's, at the Shawnee Springs. They contained in all some five or six hundred permanent settlers, nearly half of them being able-bodied riflemen.[1]

Early in 1778 a severe calamity befell the settlements. In January Boon went, with twenty-nine

Boon Captured. other men, to the Blue Licks to make salt for the different garrisons—for hitherto this necessary of life had been brought in, at great trouble and expense, from the settlements.[2] The following month, having sent three men back with loads of salt,

[1] The McAfee MSS. give these four stations ; Boon says there were but three. He was writing from memory, however, and was probably mistaken ; thus he says there were at that time settlers at the Falls, an evident mistake, as there were none there till the following year. Collins, following Marshall, says there were at the end of the year only one hundred and two men in Kentucky,—sixty-five at Harrodstown, twenty-two at Boonsborough, fifteen at Logan's. This is a mistake based on a hasty reading of Boon's narrative, which gives this number for July, and particularly adds that after that date they began to strengthen. In the McAfee MSS. is a census of Harrodstown for the fall of 1777, which sums up : Men in service, 81 ; men not in service, 4 ; women, 24 ; children above ten, 12 ; children under ten, 58 ; slaves above ten, 12 ; slaves under ten, 7 ; total, 198. In October Clark in his diary records meeting fifty men with their families, (therefore permanent settlers), on their way to Boon, and thirty-eight men on their way to Logan's. At the end of the year, therefore, Boonsborough and Harrodstown must have held about two hundred souls apiece ; Logan's and McGarry's were considerably smaller. The large proportion of young children testifies to the prolific nature of the Kentucky women, and also shows the permanent nature of the settlements. Two years previously, in 1775, there had been, perhaps, three hundred people in Kentucky, but very many of them were not permanent residents.

[2] See Clark's Diary, entry for October 25, 1777.

he and all the others were surprised and captured by a
party of eighty or ninety Miamis, led by two Frenchmen, named Baubin and Lorimer.[1]   When surrounded, so that there was no hope of escape, Boon
agreed that all should surrender on condition of
being well treated.   The Indians on this occasion
loyally kept faith.   The two Frenchmen were
anxious to improve their capture by attacking
Boonsborough ; but the fickle savages were satisfied
with their success, and insisted on returning to
their villages.   Boon was taken, first to Old Chillicothe, the chief Shawnee town on the Little Miami,
and then to Detroit, where Hamilton and the other
Englishmen treated him well, and tried to ransom
him for a hundred pounds sterling.   However, the
Indians had become very much attached to him, and
refused the ransom, taking their prisoner back to
Chillicothe.   Here he was adopted into the tribe,
and remained for two months, winning the good-will
of the Shawnees by his cheerfulness and his skill as
a hunter, and being careful not to rouse their jealousy by any too great display of skill at the shooting-
matches.

Hamilton was urging the Indians to repeat their
ravages of the preceding year ; Mingos, Shawnees,
Delawares, and Miamis came to Detroit, bringing
scalps and prisoners.   A great council was held at
that post early in June.[2]   All the northwestern
tribes took part, and they received war-belts from
the Iroquois and messages calling on them to rise as

[1] Haldimand MSS. B., 122, p. 35.   Hamilton to Carleton, April 25,
1778.   He says four-score Miamis.   [2] *Do.*, June 14, 1778.

one man.   They determined forthwith to fall on the
frontier in force.   By their war parties, and the accompanying bands of tories, Hamilton sent placards to be
distributed among the frontiersmen, endeavoring both
by threat and by promise of reward, to make them
desert the patriot cause.[1]

In June a large war party gathered at Chillicothe
to march against Boonsborough, and Boon determined to escape at all hazards, so that he
might warn his friends.   One morning before sunrise he eluded the vigilance of his
Indian companions and started straight
through the woods for his home where he arrived
in four days, having had but one meal during the
whole journey of a hundred and sixty miles.[2]

*Boon Es-
capes and
Makes a
Foray.*

On reaching Boonsborough he at once set about
putting the fort in good condition ; and being tried
by court-martial for the capture at the Blue Licks,
he was not only acquitted but was raised to the rank
of major.   His escape had probably disconcerted the
Indian war party, for no immediate attack was made
on the fort.   After waiting until August he got
tired of the inaction, and made a foray into the Indian country himself with nineteen men, defeating a
small party of his foes on the Sciota.   At the same
time he learned that the main body of the Miamis
had at last marched against Boonsborough.   Instantly
he retraced his steps with all possible speed, passed
by the Indians, and reached the threatened fort a
day before they did.

On the eighth day of the month the savages ap-

[1] *Do.*, April 25, 1778.   [2] Boon's Narrative.

peared before the stockade. They were between
three and four hundred in number, Shawnees and
Miamis, and were led by Captain Daigniau Boonsbor-
de Quindre, a noted Detroit partisan[1]; ough again
with him were eleven other Frenchmen, Besieged.
besides the Indian chiefs. They marched into
view with British and French colors flying, and
formally summoned the little wooden fort to surrender in the name of his Britannic Majesty.
The negotiations that followed showed, on the
part of both whites and reds, a curious mixture
of barbarian cunning and barbarian childishness;
the account reads as if it were a page of Græco-
Trojan diplomacy.[2] Boon first got a respite of two
days to consider de Quindre's request, and occupied
the time in getting the horses and cattle into the fort.
At the end of the two days the Frenchman came
in person to the walls to hear the answer to his
proposition; whereupon Boon jeered at him for his
simplicity, thanking him in the name of the defenders
for having given them time to prepare for defence,
and telling him that now they laughed at his attack.
De Quindre, mortified at being so easily outwitted,
set a trap in his turn for Boon. He assured the
latter that his orders from Detroit were to capture, not to destroy, the garrison, and proposed that
nine of their number should come out and hold a
treaty. The terms of the treaty are not mentioned;
apparently it was to be one of neutrality, Boonsbor-

---

[1] Haldimand MSS. Aug. 17, 1778, Girty reports that four hundred Indians have gone to attack "Fort Kentuck." Hamilton's letter of Sept.
16th speaks of there being three hundred Shawnees with de Quindre
(whom Boon calls Duquesne). [2] See Boon's Narrative.

ough acting as if it were a little independent and sovereign commonwealth, making peace on its own account with a particular set of foes. At any rate, de Quindre agreed to march his forces peaceably off when it was concluded.

Boon accepted the proposition, but, being suspicious of the good-faith of his opponents, insisted upon the conference being held within sixty yards of the fort. After the treaty was concluded the Indians proposed to shake hands with the nine white treaty-makers, and promptly grappled them.[1] However, the borderers wrested themselves free, and fled to the fort under a heavy fire, which wounded one of their number.

The Indians then attacked the fort, surrounding it on every side and keeping up a constant fire at the loop-holes. The whites replied in kind, but the combatants were so well covered that little damage was done. At night the Indians pitched torches of cane and hickory bark against the stockade, in the vain effort to set it on fire,[2] and de Quindre tried to undermine the walls, starting from the water mark. But Boon discovered the attempt, and sunk a trench as a countermine. Then de Quindre gave up and retreated on August 20th, after nine days' fighting, in which the whites had but two killed and four wounded; nor was the loss of the Indians much heavier.[3]

---

[1] Apparently there were eighteen Indians on the treaty ground, but these were probably, like the whites, unarmed.   [2] McAfee MSS.

[3] De Quindre reported to Hamilton that, though foiled, he had but two men killed and three wounded. In Haldimand MSS., Hamilton to Haldimand, October 15, 1778. Often, however, these partisan leaders merely re-

This was the last siege of Boonsborough. Had de Quindre succeeded he might very probably have swept the whites from Kentucky; but he failed, and Boon's successful resistance, taken together with the outcome of Clark's operations at the same time, ensured the permanency of the American occupation. The old-settled region lying around the original stations, or forts, was never afterwards seriously endangered by Indian invasion.

The savages continued to annoy the border throughout the year 1778. The extent of their ravages can be seen from the fact that, during the summer months those around Detroit alone brought in to Hamilton eighty-one scalps and thirty-four prisoners,[1] seventeen of whom they surrendered to the British, keeping the others either to make them slaves or else to put them to death with torture. During the fall they confined themselves mainly to watching the Ohio and the Wilderness road, and harassing the immigrants who passed along them.[2]

Boon, as usual, roamed restlessly over the country, spying out and harrying the Indian war parties, and often making it his business to meet the incoming

ported the loss in their own particular party of savages, taking no account of the losses in the other bands that had joined them—as the Miamis joined the Shawnees in this instance. But it is certain that Boon (or Filson, who really wrote the Narrative) greatly exaggerated the facts in stating that thirty-seven Indians were killed, and that the settlers picked up 125 pounds' weight of bullets which had been fired into the fort.

[1] Haldimand MSS. Letter of Hamilton September 16, 1778. Hamilton was continually sending out small war parties; thus he mentions that on August 25th a party of fifteen Miamis went out; on September 5th, thirty-one Miamis; on September 9th, one Frenchman, five Chippewas, and fifteen Miamis, etc.   [2] McAfee MSS.

bands of settlers, and to protect and guide them on the way to their intended homes.[1]   When not on other duty he hunted steadily, for game was still plentiful in Kentucky, though fast diminishing owing to the wanton slaughter made by some of the more reckless hunters.[2]   He met with many adventures, still handed down by tradition, in the chase of panther, wolf, and bear, of buffalo, elk, and deer.   The latter he killed only when their hides and meat were needed, while he followed unceasingly the dangerous beasts of prey, as being enemies of the settlers.

Throughout these years the obscure strife, made up of the individual contests of frontiersman and Indian, went on almost without a break.   The sieges, surprises, and skirmishes in which large bands took part were chronicled ; but there is little reference in the books to the countless conflicts wherein only one or two men on a side were engaged.   The west could never have been conquered, in the teeth of so formidable and ruthless a foe, had it not been for the personal prowess of the pioneers themselves.   Their natural courage and hardihood, and their long training in forest warfare,[3] made them able to hold their own and to advance step by step, where a peaceable population would have been instantly butchered or driven off.   No regular army could have done what they did.   Only trained woodsmen could have led the white advance into the vast forest-clad regions,

---

[1] Marshall, 55.   [2] McAfee MSS.

[3] The last point is important. No Europeans could have held their own for a fortnight in Kentucky ; nor is it likely that the western men twenty years before, at the time of Braddock's war, could have successfully colonized such a far-off country.

out of which so many fair States have been hewn. The ordinary regular soldier was almost as helpless before the Indians in the woods as he would have been if blindfolded and opposed to an antagonist whose eyes were left uncovered.

Much the greatest loss, both to Indians and whites, was caused by this unending personal warfare. Every hunter, almost every settler, was always in imminent danger of Indian attack, and in return was ever ready, either alone or with one or two companions, to make excursions against the tribes for scalps and horses. One or two of Simon Kenton's experiences during this year may be mentioned less for their own sake than as examples of innumerable similar deeds that were done, and woes that were suffered, in the course of the ceaseless struggle.

Kenton was a tall, fair-haired man of wonderful strength and agility; famous as a runner and wrestler, an unerring shot, and a perfect woodsman. Like so many of these early Indian fighters, he was not at all bloodthirsty. He was a pleasant, friendly, and obliging companion; and it was hard to rouse him to wrath. When once aroused, however, few were so hardy as not to quail before the terrible fury of his anger. He was so honest and unsuspecting that he was very easily cheated by sharpers; and he died a poor man. He was a staunch friend and follower of Boon's.[1] Once, in a fight outside the

Simon Kenton's Adventures.

[1] See McClung's "Sketches of Western Adventure," pp. 86-117; the author had received from Kenton, and other pioneers, when very old, the tales of their adventures as young men. McClung's volume contains very valuable incidental information about the customs of life among the borderers,

stockade at Boonsborough, he saved the life of his leader by shooting an Indian who was on the point of tomahawking him. Boon was a man of few words, cold and grave, accustomed to every kind of risk and hairbreadth escape, and as little apt to praise the deeds of others as he was to mention his own ; but on this occasion he broke through his usual taciturnity to express his thanks for Kenton's help and his admiration for Kenton himself.

Kenton went with his captain on the expedition to the Scioto. Pushing ahead of the rest, he was attracted by the sound of laughter in a canebrake. Hiding himself, he soon saw two Indians approach, both riding on one small pony, and chatting and laughing together in great good-humor. Aiming carefully, he brought down both at once, one dead and the other severely wounded. As he rushed up to finish his work, his quick ears caught a rustle in the cane, and looking around he saw two more Indians aiming at him. A rapid spring to one side on his part made both balls miss. Other Indians came up ; but, at the same time, Boon and his companions appeared, running as fast as they could while still keeping sheltered. A brisk skirmish followed, the Indians retreated, and Kenton got the coveted scalp. When Boon returned to the fort, Kenton stayed behind with another man and

and about Indian warfare ; but he is a very inaccurate and untrustworthy writer ; he could not even copy a printed narrative correctly (see his account of Slover's and McKnight's adventures), and his tales about Kenton must be accepted rather as showing the adventures incident to the life of a peculiarly daring Indian fighter than as being specifically and chronologically correct in Kenton's individual case.

succeeded in stealing four good horses, which he brought back in triumph.

Much pleased with his success he shortly made another raid into the Indian country, this time with two companions. They succeeded in driving off a whole band of one hundred and sixty horses, which they brought in safety to the banks of the Ohio. But a strong wind was blowing, and the river was so rough that in spite of all their efforts they could not get the horses to cross; as soon as they were beyond their depth the beasts would turn round and swim back. The reckless adventurers could not make up their minds to leave the booty; and stayed so long, waiting for a lull in the gale, and wasting their time in trying to get the horses to take to the water in spite of the waves, that the pursuing Indians came up and surprised them. Their guns had become wet and useless; and no resistance could be made. One of them was killed, another escaped, and Kenton himself was captured.

The Indians asked him if "Captain Boon" had sent him to steal horses; and when he answered frankly that the stealing was his own idea, they forthwith proceeded to beat him lustily with their ramrods, at the same time showering on him epithets that showed they had at least learned the profanity of the traders. They staked him out at night, tied so that he could move neither hand nor foot; and during the day he was bound on an unbroken horse, with his hands tied behind him so that he could not protect his face from the trees and bushes. This was repeated every day. After three days he reached the town of Chillicothe, stiff, sore, and bleeding.

Next morning he was led out to run the gauntlet. A row of men, women, and boys, a quarter of a mile long, was formed, each with a tomahawk, switch, or club; at the end of the line was an Indian with a big drum, and beyond this was the council-house, which, if he reached, would for the time being protect him. The moment for starting arrived; the big drum was beaten; and Kenton sprang forward in the race.[1] Keeping his wits about him he suddenly turned to one side and darted off with the whole tribe after him. His wonderful speed and activity enabled him to keep ahead, and to dodge those who got in his way, and by a sudden double he rushed through an opening in the crowd, and reached the council-house, having been struck but three or four blows.

He was not further molested that evening. Next morning a council was held to decide whether he should be immediately burnt at the stake, or should first be led round to the different villages. The warriors sat in a ring to pass judgment, passing the war club from one to another; those who passed it in silence thereby voted in favor of sparing the prisoner for the moment, while those who struck it violently on the ground thus indicated their belief that he should be immediately put to death. The former prevailed, and Kenton was led from town to town. At each place he was tied to the stake, to be

[1] For this part of Kenton's adventures compare the "Last of the Mohicans."

switched and beaten by the women and boys; or else was forced to run the gauntlet, while sand was thrown in his eyes and guns loaded with powder fired against his body to burn his flesh.

Once, while on the march, he made a bold rush for liberty, all unarmed though he was; breaking out of the line and running into the forest. His speed was so great and his wind so good that he fairly outran his pursuers; but by ill-luck, when almost exhausted, he came against another party of Indians. After this he abandoned himself to despair. He was often terribly abused by his captors; once one of them cut his shoulder open with an axe, breaking the bone.

His face was painted black, the death color, and he was twice sentenced to be burned alive, at the Pickaway Plains and at Sandusky. But each time he was saved at the last moment, once through a sudden spasm of mercy on the part of the renegade Girty, his old companion in arms at the time of Lord Dunmore's war, and again by the powerful intercession of the great Mingo chief, Logan. At last, after having run the gauntlet eight times and been thrice tied to the stake, he was ransomed by some traders. They hoped to get valuable information from him about the border forts, and took him to Detroit. Here he stayed until his battered, wounded body was healed. Then he determined to escape, and formed his plan in concert with two other Kentuckians, who had been in Boon's party that was captured at the Blue Licks. They managed to secure some guns, got safely off, and came straight down through the great forests to the Ohio, reaching their homes in safety.[1]

Boon and Kenton have always been favorite heroes of frontier story,—as much so as ever were Robin Hood and Little John in England. Both lived to a great age, and did and saw many strange things, and in the backwoods cabins the tale of their deeds has been handed down in traditional form from father to son and to son's son. They were known to be honest, fearless, adventurous, mighty men of their hands; fond of long, lonely wanderings; renowned as woodsmen and riflemen, as hunters and Indian fighters. In course of time it naturally came about that all notable incidents of the chase and woodland warfare were incorporated into their lives by the story-tellers. The facts were altered and added to by tradition year after year; so that the two old frontier warriors already stand in that misty group of heroes whose rightful title to fame has been partly overclouded by the haze of their mythical glories and achievements.

[1] McClung gives the exact conversations that took place between Kenton, Logan, Girty, and the Indian chiefs. They are very dramatic, and may possibly be true; the old pioneer would probably always remember even the words used on such occasions; but I hesitate to give them because McClung is so loose in his statements. In the account of this very incident he places it in '77, and says Kenton then accompanied Clark to the Illinois. But in reality —as we know from Boon—it took place in '78, and Kenton must have gone with Clark first.

CHAPTER II.

KENTUCKY had been settled, chiefly through Boon's instrumentality, in the year that saw the first fighting of the Revolution, and it had been held ever since, Boon still playing the greatest part in the defence. Clark's more far-seeing and ambitious soul now prompted him to try and use it as a base from which to conquer the vast region northwest of the Ohio.

The country beyond the Ohio was not, like Kentucky, a tenantless and debatable hunting-ground. It was the seat of powerful and warlike Indian confederacies, and of clusters of ancient French hamlets which had been founded generations before the Kentucky pioneers were born; and it also contained posts that were garrisoned and held by the soldiers of the British king. Virginia, and other colonies as well, made, it is true, vague claims to some of this territory.[1] But their titles were as unreal and shadowy

The Country beyond the Ohio.

---

[1] Some of the numerous land speculation companies, which were so prominent about this time, both before and after the Revolution, made claims to vast tracts of territory in this region, having bought them for various trinkets from the Indian chiefs. Such were the "Illinois Land Company" and "Wabash Land Company," that, in 1773 and 1775, made purchases from the Kaskaskias and Piankeshaws. The companies were composed of British, American, and Canadian merchants and traders, of London, Philadelphia,

as those acquired by the Spanish and Portuguese kings when the Pope, with empty munificence, divided between them the Eastern and the Western hemispheres. For a century the French had held adverse possession; for a decade and a half the British, not the colonial authorities, had acted as their unchallenged heirs; to the Americans the country was as much a foreign land as was Canada. It could only be acquired by force, and Clark's teeming brain and bold heart had long been busy in planning its conquest. He knew that the French villages, the only settlements in the land, were the seats of the British power, the head-quarters whence their commanders stirred up, armed, and guided the hostile Indians. If these settled French districts were conquered, and the British posts that guarded them captured, the whole territory would thereby be won for the Federal Republic, and added to the heritage of its citizens; while the problem of checking and subduing the northwestern Indians would be greatly simplified, because the source of much of both their power and hostility would be cut off at the springs. The friendship of the French was invaluable, for they had more influence than any other people with the Indians.

In 1777 Clark sent two young hunters as spies

Baltimore, Quebec, etc. Lord Dunmore was in the Wabash Company. The agents of the companies, in after years, made repeated but unsuccessful efforts to get Congress to confirm their grants. Although these various companies made much noise at the time, they introduced no new settlers into the land, and, in fact, did nothing of lasting effect; so that it is mere waste of time to allude to most of them. See, however, the "History of Indiana," by John B. Dillon (Indianapolis, 1859), pp. 102–109, etc.

to the Illinois country and to the neighborhood of Vincennes, though neither to them nor to any one else did he breathe a hint of the plan that was in his mind. They brought back word Clark Sends that, though some of the adventurous Spies to the young men often joined either the Brit- Illinois. ish or the Indian war parties, yet that the bulk of the French population took but little interest in the struggle, were lukewarm in their allegiance to the British flag, and were somewhat awed by what they had heard of the backwoodsmen.[1] Clark judged from this report that it would not be difficult to keep the French neutral if a bold policy, strong as well as conciliatory, was pursued towards them; and that but a small force would be needed to enable a resolute and capable leader to conquer at least the southern part of the country. It was impossible to raise such a body among the scantily garrisoned forted villages of Kentucky. The pioneers, though warlike and fond of fighting, were primarily settlers; their soldiering came in as a purely secondary occupation. They were not a band of mere adventurers, living by the sword and bent on nothing but conquest. They were a group of hard-working, hard-fighting freemen, who had come in with their wives and children to possess the land. They were obliged to use all their wit and courage to defend what they had already won without wasting their strength by grasping at that which lay beyond. The very con-

---

[1] The correctness of this account is amply confirmed by the Haldimand MSS., letters of Hamilton, *passim ;* also Rocheblave to Carleton, July 4, 1778 ; and to Hamilton, April 12, 1778.

ditions that enabled so small a number to make a permanent settlement forbade their trying unduly to extend its bounds.

Clark knew he could get from among his fellow-settlers some men peculiarly suited for his purpose, but he also realized that he would **He Goes to** have to bring the body of his force from **Virginia to** Virginia. Accordingly he decided to lay **Raise** the case before Patrick Henry, then Gov-**Troops.** ernor of the State of which Kentucky was only a frontier county.

On October 1, 1777, he started from Harrodsburg,[1] to go over the Wilderness road. The brief entries of his diary for this trip are very interesting and sometimes very amusing. Before starting he made a rather shrewd and thoroughly characteristic speculation in horseflesh, buying a horse for £12, and then "swapping" it with Isaac Shelby and getting £10 to boot. He evidently knew how to make a good bargain, and had the true backwoods passion for barter. He was detained a couple of days by that commonest of frontier mischances, his horses straying; a natural incident when the animals were simply turned loose on the range and looked up when required.[2] He travelled in company with a large party of men, women, and children who, disheartened by the Indian ravages, were going back to the settlements. They marched from fifteen to

[1] In the earlier MSS. it is called sometimes Harrodstown and sometimes Harrodsburg ; but from this time on the latter name is in general use.

[2] This, like so many other incidents in the every-day history of the old pioneers, is among the ordinary experiences of the present sojourner in the far west.

twenty miles a day, driving beeves along for food. In addition the scouts at different times killed three buffalo [1] and a few deer, so that they were not stinted for fresh meat.

When they got out of the wilderness he parted from his companions and rode off alone. He now stayed at the settler's house that was nearest when night overtook him. At a large house, such as that of the Campbell's, near Abingdon, he was of course welcomed to the best, and treated with a generous hospitality, for which it would have been an insult to offer money in return. At the small cabins he paid his way; usually a shilling and threepence or a shilling and sixpence for breakfast, bed, and feed for the horse; but sometimes four or five shillings. He fell in with a Captain Campbell, with whom he journeyed a week, finding him "an agreable companion." They had to wait over one stormy day, at a little tavern, and probably whiled away the time by as much of a carouse as circumstances allowed; at any rate, Clark's share of the bill when he left was £1 4s. [2] Finally, a month after leaving Harrodsburg, having travelled six hundred and twenty miles, he reached his father's house. [3]

After staying only a day at his old home, he set

[1] One at Rockcastle River, two at Cumberland Ford.

[2] The items of expense jotted down in the diary are curious. For a night's lodging and board they range from 1s. 3d. to 13s. In Williamsburg, the capital, they were for a fortnight £9 18s.

[3] Seventy miles beyond Charlottesville; he gives an itinerary of his journey, making it six hundred and twenty miles in all, by the route he travelled. On the way he had his horse shod and bought a pair of shoes for himself; apparently he kept the rest of his backwoods apparel. He sold his gun for £15 and swapped horses again—this time giving £7 10s. to boot.

out for Williamsburg, where he was detained a fortnight before the State auditors would settle the accounts of the Kentucky militia, which he had brought with him. The two things which he deemed especially worthy of mention during this time were his purchase of a ticket in the State lottery, for three pounds, and his going to church on Sunday—the first chance he had had to do so during the year.[1] He was overjoyed at the news of Burgoyne's surrender; and with a light heart he returned to his father's house, to get a glimpse of his people before again plunging into the wilds.

After a week's rest he went back to the capital, laid his plans before Patrick Henry, and urged their **Clark and** adoption with fiery enthusiasm.[2] Henry's **Patrick** ardent soul quickly caught flame; but the **Henry.** peril of sending an expedition to such a wild and distant country was so great, and Virginia's resources were so exhausted, that he could do little beyond lending Clark the weight of his name and influence. The matter could not be laid before the Assembly, nor made public in any way; for the hazard would be increased tenfold if the strictest secrecy were not preserved. Finally Henry author-

---

[1] When his accounts were settled he immediately bought " a piece of cloth for a jacket; price, £4 15*s.*; buttons, etc., 3*s.*"

[2] Clark has left a full MS. memoir of the events of 1777, 1778, and 1779. It was used extensively by Mann Butler, the first historian who gave the campaign its proper prominence, and is printed almost complete by Dillon, on pp. 115–167 of his " Indiana." It was written at the desire of Presidents Jefferson and Madison; and therefore some thirty or forty years after the events of which it speaks. Valuable though it is, as the narrative of the chief actor, it would be still more valuable had it been written earlier; it undoubtedly contains some rather serious errors.

ized Clark to raise seven companies, each of fifty men, who were to act as militia and to be paid as such.[1] He also advanced him the sum of twelve hundred pounds (presumably in depreciated paper), and gave him an order on the authorities at Pittsburg for boats, supplies, and ammunition; while three of the most prominent Virginia gentlemen[2] agreed in writing to do their best to induce the Virginia Legislature to grant to each of the adventurers three hundred acres of the conquered land, if they were successful. He was likewise given the commission of colonel, with instructions to raise his men solely from the frontier counties west of the Blue Ridge,[3] so as not to weaken the people of the seacoast region in their struggle against the British.

Thus the whole burden of making ready the expedition was laid on Clark's shoulders. The hampered Virginian authorities were able to give him little beyond their good-will. He is rightfully entitled to the whole glory; the plan and the execution were both his. *Clark alone Organizes the Expedition.* It was an individual rather than a state or national enterprise.

Governor Henry's open letter of instructions merely ordered Clark to go to the relief of Kentucky. He carried with him also the secret letter which bade him attack the Illinois regions; for he had decided to assail this first, because, if defeated, he would then be able to take refuge in the Spanish

[1] Henry's private letter of instructions, January 2, 1778.

[2] Thomas Jefferson, George Mason, and George Wythe.

[3] Butler, p. 48 ; but Henry's public instructions authorized Clark to raise his men in any county.

dominions beyond the Mississippi.   He met with the
utmost difficulty in raising men.   Some were to be
sent to him from the Holston overland, to meet him
in Kentucky; but a combination of accidents resulted in his getting only a dozen or so from this
source.[1]   Around Pittsburg the jealousy between
the Virginians and Pennsylvanians hampered him
greatly.   Moreover, many people were strongly
opposed to sending any men to Kentucky at all,
deeming the drain on their strength more serious
than the value of the new land warranted; for they
were too short-sighted rightly to estimate what the
frontiersmen had really done.   When he had finally
raised his troops he was bothered by requests from
the different forts to aid detachments of the local
militia in expeditions against bands of marauding
Indians.

But Clark never for a moment wavered nor lost
sight of his main object.   He worked steadily on,
He Starts heedless of difficulty and disappointment,
Down and late in the spring at last got together
the Ohio. four small companies of frontiersmen from
the clearings and the scattered hunters' camps.   In
May, 1778, he left the Redstone settlements, taking
not only his troops—one hundred and fifty in all [2]—
but also a considerable number of private adventurers
and settlers with their families.   He touched at
Pittsburg and Wheeling to get his stores.   Then the

[1] Four companies were to be raised on the Holston; but only one actually
went to Kentucky; and most of its members deserted when they found out
about the true nature of the expedition.

[2] Clark's letter to George Mason, Nov. 19, 1779.   Given in "Clark's
Campaign in the Illinois" (Cincinnati, 1869), for the first time; one of
Robert Clarke's excellent Ohio Valley Historical Series.

flotilla of clumsy flatboats, manned by tall riflemen, rowed and drifted cautiously down the Ohio between the melancholy and unbroken reaches of Indian-haunted forest. The presence of the families shows that even this expedition had the usual peculiar western character of being undertaken half for con-quest, half for settlement.

He landed at the mouth of the Kentucky, but rightly concluded that as a starting-point against the British posts it would be better to choose a place farther west, so he drifted on down the stream, and on the 27th of May [1] reached the Falls of the Ohio, where the river broke into great rapids or riffles of swift water. This spot he chose, both because from it he could threaten and hold in check the dif-ferent Indian tribes, and because he deemed it wise to have some fort to protect in the future the craft that might engage in the river trade, when they stopped to prepare for the passage of the rapids. Most of the families that had come with him had gone off to the interior of Kentucky, but several were left, and these settled on an island near the falls, where they raised a crop of corn; and in the autumn they moved to the mainland. On the site thus chosen by the clear-eyed frontier leader there afterwards grew up a great city, named in honor of the French king, who was then our ally. Clark may fairly be called its founder.[2]

[1] This is the date given in the deposition, in the case of Floyd's heirs, in 1815 ; see MSS. in Col. Durrett's library at Louisville. Clark's dates, given from memory, are often a day or two out. His " Memoir " is of course less accurate than the letter to Mason.

[2] It was named Louisville in 1780, but was long known only as the Falls. Many other men had previously recognized the advantages of the place ; hunters and surveyors had gone there, but Clark led thither the first per-

Here Clark received news of the alliance with France, which he hoped would render easier his task **Clark at** of winning over the habitants of the Illinois. **the Falls.** He was also joined by a few daring Kentuckians, including Kenton, and by the only Holston company that had yet arrived. He now disclosed to his men the real object of his expedition. The Kentuckians, and those who had come down the river with him, hailed the adventure with eager enthusiasm, pledged him their hearty support, and followed him with staunch and unflinching loyalty. But the Holston recruits, who had not come under the spell of his personal influence, murmured against him. They had not reckoned on an expedition so long and so dangerous, and in the night most of them left the camp and fled into the woods. The Kentuckians, who had horses, pursued the deserters, with orders to kill any who resisted; but all save six or eight escaped. Yet they suffered greatly for their crime, and endured every degree of hardship and fatigue, for the Kentuckians spurned them from the gates of the wooden forts, and would not for a long time suffer them to enter, hounding them back to the homes they had dishonored. They came from among a bold and adventurous people, and their action was due rather to wayward and sullen disregard of authority than to cowardice.

manent settlers. Conolly had laid out at the Falls a grant of two thousand acres, of which he afterwards surrendered half. His grant, covering much of the present site of the city, was on July 1, 1780, declared to be forfeited by a jury consisting of Daniel Boon and eleven other good men and true, empanelled by the sheriff of the county. See Durrett MSS. in " Papers Relating to Louisville, Ky."

When the pursuing horsemen came back a day of mirth and rejoicing was spent between the troops who were to stay behind to guard Kentucky and those who were to go onward to conquer Illinois. On the 24th of June Clark's boats put out from shore, and shot the falls at the very moment that there was a great eclipse of the sun, at which the frontiersmen wondered greatly, but for the most part held it to be a good omen.

Clark had weeded out all those whom he deemed unable to stand fatigue and hardship; his four little companies were of picked men, each with a good captain.[1] His equipment was as light as that of an Indian war party, for he knew better than to take a pound of baggage that could possibly be spared.

He intended to land some three leagues below the entrance of the Tennessee River,[2] thence to march on foot against the Illinois towns; for he feared discovery if he should attempt to ascend the Mississippi, the usual highway by which the fur traders went up to the quaint French hamlets that lay between the Kaskaskia and the Illinois rivers. Accordingly he double-manned his oars and rowed night and day until he reached a small island off the mouth of the Tennessee, where he halted to make his final preparations, and was there joined by a little party of

He Meets a Party of Hunters.

[1] The names of the four captains were John Montgomery, Joseph Bowman, Leonard Helm, and William Harrod. Each company nominally consisted of fifty men, but none of them was of full strength.

[2] At the old Fort Massac, then deserted. The name is taken from that of an old French commander; it is not a corruption of Fort Massacre, as has been asserted.

American hunters,[1] who had recently been in the French settlements. The meeting was most fortunate. The hunters entered eagerly into Clark's plans, joining him for the campaign, and they gave him some very valuable information. They told him that the royal commandant was a Frenchman, Rocheblave, whose head-quarters were at the town of Kaskaskia; that the fort was in good repair, the militia were well drilled and in constant readiness to repel attack, while spies were continually watching the Mississippi, and the Indians and the coureurs des bois were warned to be on the look-out for any American force. If the party were discovered in time the hunters believed that the French would undoubtedly gather together instantly to repel them, having been taught to hate and dread the backwoodsmen as more brutal and terrible than any Indians; and in such an event the strength of the works and the superiority of the French in numbers would render the attack very hazardous. But they thought that a surprise would enable Clark to do as he wished, and they undertook to guide him by the quickest and shortest route to the towns.

Clark was rather pleased than otherwise to learn of the horror with which the French regarded the backwoodsmen. He thought it would render them more apt to be panic-struck when surprised, and also more likely to feel a strong revulsion of gratitude when they found that the Americans meant them

[1] In his " Memoir " he says " from the States " ; in his letter to Mason he calls them " Englishmen," probably to show that they were not French, as they had just come from Kaskaskia. He almost always spoke of the English proper as British.

well and not ill.   Taking their new allies for guides, the little body of less than two hundred men started north across the wilderness, scouts being scattered out well ahead of them, both to kill game for their subsistence and to see that their march was not discovered by any straggling Frenchman or Indian.   The first fifty miles led through tangled and pathless forest, the toil of travelling being very great.   After that the work was less difficult as they got out among the prairies, but on these great level meadows they had to take extra precautions to avoid being seen. Once the chief guide got bewildered and lost himself; he could no longer tell the route, nor whither it was best to march.[1]   The whole party was at once cast into the utmost confusion; but Clark soon made the guide understand that he was himself in greater jeopardy than any one else, and would forfeit his life if he did not guide them straight.   Not knowing the man, Clark thought he might be treacherous; and, as he wrote an old friend, he was never in his life in such a rage as when he found his troops wandering at random in a country where, at any moment, they might blunder on several times their number of hostile Indians; while, if they were discovered by any one at all, the whole expedition was sure to miscarry.   However, the guide proved to be faithful; after a couple of hours he found his bearings once more, and guided the party straight to their destination.

The March to Kaskaskia.

[1] Even experienced woodsmen or plainsmen sometimes thus become lost or "turned round," if in a country of few landmarks, where they have rarely been before.

On the evening of the fourth of July [1] they reached the river Kaskaskia, within three miles of the town, which lay on the farther bank. They kept in the woods until after it grew dusk, and then marched silently to a little farm on the hither side of the river, a mile from the town. The family were taken prisoners, and from them Clark learned that some days before the townspeople had been alarmed at the rumor of a possible attack; but that their suspicions had been lulled, and they were then off their guard. There were a great many men in the town, but almost all French, the Indians having for the most part left. The account proved correct. Rocheblave, the creole commandant, was sincerely attached to the British interest. He had been much alarmed early in the year by the reports brought to him by Indians that the Americans were in Kentucky and elsewhere beyond the Alleghanies. He had written repeatedly to Detroit, asking that regulars could be sent him, and that he might himself be replaced by a commandant of English birth; for though the French were well-disposed towards the crown, they had been frightened by the reports of the ferocity of the backwoodsmen, and the Indians were fickle. In his letters he mentioned that the French were much more loyal than the men of English parentage. Ham-

The Surprise of Kaskaskia.

---

[1] So says Clark; and the Haldimand MSS. contains a letter of Rocheblave of July 4th. For these campaigns of 1778 I follow where possible Clark's letter to Mason as being nearly contemporary; his "Memoir," as given by Dillon, comes next in authority; while Butler, who was very accurate and painstaking, also got hold of original information from men who had taken part in the expedition, or from their descendants, besides making full use of the "Memoir."

ilton found it impossible to send him reinforcements however, and he was forced to do the best he could without them; but he succeeded well in his endeavors to organize troops, as he found the creole militia very willing to serve, and the Indians extremely anxious to attack the Americans.[1] He had under his orders two or three times as many men as Clark, and he would certainly have made a good fight if he had not been surprised. It was only Clark's audacity and the noiseless speed of his movements that gave him a chance of success with the odds so heavily against him.

Getting boats the American leader ferried his men across the stream under cover of the darkness and in profound silence; the work occupying about two hours. He then approached Kaskaskia under cover of the night, dividing his force into two divisions, one being spread out to surround the town so that none might escape, while he himself led the other up to the walls of the fort.

Inside the fort the lights were lit, and through the windows came the sounds of violins. The officers of the post had given a ball, and the mirth-loving creoles, young men and girls, were dancing and revelling within, while the sentinels had left their posts. One of his captives showed Clark a postern-gate by the river-side, and through this he entered the fort, having placed his men round about at the entrance. Advancing to the great hall where the revel was held, he leaned silently with folded arms against the

[1] Haldimand MSS. Carleton to Hamilton, May 16, 1777 ; Rocheblave to Carleton, February 8, 1778 ; Rocheblave to Hamilton, April 12, 1778 ; Rocheblave to Carleton, July 4, 1778.

door-post, looking at the dancers. An Indian, lying on the floor of the entry, gazed intently on the stranger's face as the light from the torches within flickered across it, and suddenly sprang to his feet uttering the unearthly war-whoop. Instantly the dancing ceased ; the women screamed, while the men ran towards the door. But Clark, standing unmoved and with unchanged face, grimly bade them continue their dancing, but to remember that they now danced under Virginia and not Great Britain.[1] At the same time his men burst into the fort, and seized the French officers, including the commandant, Rocheblave.[2]

Immediately Clark had every street secured, and sent runners through the town ordering the people to keep close to their houses on pain of death ; and by daylight he had them all disarmed. The backwoodsmen patrolled the town in little squads ; while the French in silent terror cowered within their low-roofed houses. Clark was quite willing that they should fear the worst ; and their panic was very

[1] Memoir of Major E. Denny, by Wm. H. Denny, p. 217. In "Record of the Court of Upland and Military Journal of Major E. Denny," Philadelphia, 1860 (Historical Society of Penn.). The story was told to Major Denny by Clark himself, some time in '87 or '88 ; in process of repetition it evidently became twisted, and, as related by Denny, there are some very manifest inaccuracies, but there seems no reason to reject it entirely.

[2] It is worth noting that these Illinois French, and most of the Indians with whom the French fur traders came in contact, called the Americans "Bostonnais." (In fact the fur traders have taught this name to the northern tribes right across to the Pacific. While hunting in the Selkirk Mountains last fall, the Kootenai Indian who was with me always described me as a "Boston man.") Similarly the Indians round the upper Ohio and thence southward often called the backwoodsmen "Virginians." In each case the French and Indians adopted the name of their leading and most inveterate enemies as the title by which to call all of them.

great. The unlooked-for and mysterious approach and sudden onslaught of the backwoodsmen, their wild and uncouth appearance, and the ominous silence of their commander, all combined to fill the French with fearful forebodings for their future fate.[1]

Next morning a deputation of the chief men waited upon Clark; and thinking themselves in the hands of mere brutal barbarians, all they dared to do was to beg for their lives, which they did, says Clark, " with the greatest servancy [saying] they were willing to be slaves to save their families," though the bolder spirits could not refrain from cursing their fortune that they had not been warned in time to defend themselves. Now came Clark's chance for his winning stroke. He knew it was hopeless to expect his little band permanently to hold down a much more numerous hostile population, that was closely allied to many surrounding tribes of warlike Indians; he wished above all things to convert the inhabitants into ardent adherents of the American Government.

So he explained at length that, though the Americans came as conquerors, who by the laws of war could treat the defeated as they wished, yet it was ever their principle to free, not to enslave, the people with whom they came in contact. If the French

[1] In his "Memoir" Clark dwells at length on the artifices by which he heightened the terror of the French ; and Butler enlarges still further upon them. I follow the letter to Mason, which is much safer authority, the writer having then no thought of trying to increase the dramatic effect of the situation—which in Butler, and indeed in the " Memoir " also, is strained till it comes dangerously near bathos.

chose to become loyal citizens, and to take the oath of fidelity to the Republic, they should be welcomed to all the privileges of Americans; those who did not so choose should be allowed to depart from the land in peace with their families.

The mercurial creoles who listened to his speech passed rapidly from the depth of despair to the height of joy. Instead of bewailing their fate they now could not congratulate themselves enough on their good-fortune. The crowning touch to their happiness was given by Clark when he told the priest, Pierre Gibault, in answer to a question as to whether the Catholic Church could be opened, that an American commander had nothing to do with any church save to defend it from insult, and that by the laws of the Republic his religion had as great privileges as any other. With that they all returned in noisy joy to their families, while the priest, a man of ability and influence, became thenceforth a devoted and effective champion of the American cause. The only person whom Clark treated harshly was M. Rocheblave, the commandant, who, when asked to dinner, responded in very insulting terms. Thereupon Clark promptly sent him as a prisoner to Virginia (where he broke his parole and escaped), and sold his slaves for five hundred pounds, which was distributed among the troops as prize-money.

The Creoles Espouse the American Cause.

A small detachment of the Americans, accompanied by a volunteer company of French militia, at once marched rapidly on Cahokia. The account of what had happened in Kaskaskia, the news of the alliance between France and America, and the enthusiastic advocacy of Clark's new friends, soon converted Cahokia; and all of its inhabitants, like those of Kaskaskia, took the oath of allegiance to America. Almost at the same time the priest Gibault volunteered to go, with a few of his compatriots, to Vincennes, and there endeavor to get the people to join the Americans, as being their natural friends and allies. He started on his mission at once, and on the first of August returned to Clark with the news that he had been completely successful, that the entire population, after having gathered in the church to hear him, had taken the oath of allegiance, and that the American flag floated over their fort.[1] No garrison could be spared to go to Vincennes; so one of the captains[2] was sent thither alone to take command.

The priest Gibault had given convincing proof of his loyalty. He remarked to Clark rather dryly that he had, properly speaking, nothing to do with the temporal affairs of his flock, but that now and then he was able to give them such hints in a spiritual way as would tend to increase their devotion to their new friends.

Clark now found himself in a position of the utmost difficulty. With a handful of unruly backwoodsmen, imperfectly disciplined and **Clark's** kept under control only by his own per- **Difficulties.** sonal influence, he had to protect and govern a region as large as any European kingdom. More-

---

[1] Judge John Law's "Address on the Colonial History of Vincennes," p. 25. [2] Leonard Helm.

over, he had to keep content and loyal a population of alien race, creed, and language, while he held his own against the British and against numerous tribes of Indians, deeply imbittered against all Americans and as blood-thirsty and treacherous as they were warlike. It may be doubted if there was another man in the west who possessed the daring and resolution, the tact, energy, and executive ability necessary for the solution of so knotty a series of problems.

He was hundreds of miles from the nearest post containing any American troops; he was still farther from the seat of government. He had no hope whatever of getting reinforcements or even advice and instruction for many months, probably not for a year; and he was thrown entirely on his own resources and obliged to act in every respect purely on his own responsibility.

Governor Patrick Henry, although leaving every thing in the last resort to Clark's discretion, had evidently been very doubtful whether a permanent occupation of the territory was feasible,[1] though both he, and especially Jefferson, recognized the important bearing that its acquisition would have upon the settlement of the northwestern boundary, when the time came to treat for peace. Probably

---

[1] In his secret letter of instructions he orders Clark to be especially careful to secure the artillery and military stores at Kaskia, laying such stress upon this as to show that he regarded the place itself as of comparatively little value. In fact, all Henry's order contemplated was an attack on "the British post at Kaskasky." However, he adds, that if the French are willing to become American citizens, they shall be fully protected against their foes. The letter earnestly commands Clark to treat not only the inhabitants, but also all British prisoners, with the utmost humanity.

Clark himself had not at first appreciated all the possibilities that lay within his conquest, but he was fully alive to them now and saw that, provided he could hold on to it, he had added a vast and fertile territory to the domain of the Union. To the task of keeping it he now bent all his energies.

The time of service of his troops had expired, and they were anxious to go home. By presents and promises he managed to enlist one hundred of them for eight months longer. Then, to color his staying with so few men, he made a feint of returning to the Falls, alleging as a reason his entire confidence in the loyalty of his French friends and his trust in their capacity to defend themselves. He hoped that this would bring out a remonstrance from the inhabitants, who, by becoming American citizens, had definitely committed themselves against the British. The result was such as he expected. On the rumor of his departure, the inhabitants in great alarm urged him to stay, saying that otherwise the British would surely retake the post. He made a show of reluctantly yielding to their request, and consented to stay with two companies; and then finding that many of the more adventurous young creoles were anxious to take service, he enlisted enough of them to fill up all four companies to their original strength. His whole leisure was spent in drilling the men, Americans and French alike, and in a short time he turned them into as orderly and well disciplined a body as could be found in any garrison of regulars.

He also established very friendly relations with

the Spanish captains of the scattered creole villages across the Mississippi, for the Spaniards were very hostile to the British, and had not yet begun to realize that they had even more to dread from the Americans. Clark has recorded his frank surprise at finding the Spanish commandant, who lived at St. Louis, a very pleasant and easy companion, instead of haughty and reserved, as he had supposed all Spaniards were.

The most difficult, and among the most important, of his tasks, was dealing with the swarm of fickle **Dealings** and treacherous savage tribes that sur- **with the** rounded him. They had hitherto been **Indians.** hostile to the Americans ; but being great friends of the Spaniards and French they were much confused by the change in the sentiments of the lat- ter, and by the sudden turn affairs had taken.

Some volunteers—Americans, French, and friendly Indians—were sent to the aid of the American cap- tain at Vincennes, and the latter, by threats and prom- ises, and a mixture of diplomatic speech-making with a show of force, contrived, for the time being, to pacify the immediately neighboring tribes.

Clark took upon himself the greater task of deal- ing with a huge horde of savages, representing every tribe between the Great Lakes and the Mississippi, who had come to the Illinois, some from a distance of five hundred miles, to learn accurately all that had happened, and to hear for themselves what the Long Knives had to say. They gathered to meet him at Cahokia, chiefs and warriors of every grade ; among them were Ottawas and Chippewas, Pottawatomies, Sacs, and Foxes, and others belonging to tribes whose very names have perished. The straggling streets of the dismayed little town were thronged with many hundreds of dark-browed, sullen-looking savages, grotesque in look and terrible in possibility. They strutted to and fro in their dirty finery, or lounged round the houses, inquisitive, importunate, and insolent, hardly concealing a lust for bloodshed and plunder that the slightest mishap was certain to render ungovernable.

Fortunately Clark knew exactly how to treat them. He thoroughly understood their natures, and was always on his guard, while seemingly perfectly confident; and he combined conciliation with firmness and decision, and above all with prompt rapidity of action.

For the first two or three days no conclusion was reached, though there was plenty of speech-making. But on the night of the third a party of turbulent warriors [1] endeavored to force their way into the house where he was lodging, and to carry him off. Clark, who, as he records, had been " under some apprehensions among such a number of Devils," was anticipating treachery. His guards were at hand, and promptly seized the savages ; while the townspeople took the alarm and were under arms in a couple of minutes, thus convincing the Indians that their friendship for the Americans was not feigned.

Clark instantly ordered the French militia to put the captives, both chiefs and warriors, in irons. He had treated the Indians well, and had not angered them by the harshness and brutality that so often

---

[1] " A party of Puans and others."—Clark's letter to Mason.

made them side against the English or Americans
and in favor of the French; but he knew that any
signs of timidity would be fatal. His boldness and
Clark decision were crowned with complete
and the success. The crestfallen prisoners humbly
Savages. protested that they were only trying to
find out if the French were really friendly to Clark,
and begged that they might be released. He answered with haughty indifference, and refused to
release them, even when the chiefs of the other
tribes came up to intercede. Indians and whites
alike were in the utmost confusion, every man dis-
trusting what the moment might bring forth. Clark
continued seemingly wholly unmoved, and did not
even shift his lodgings to the fort, remaining in a
house in the town, but he took good care to secretly
fill a large room adjoining his own with armed men,
while the guards were kept ready for instant action.
To make his show of indifference complete, he
"assembled a Number of Gentlemen and Ladies
and danced nearly the whole Night." The per-
plexed savages, on the other hand, spent the hours of
darkness in a series of councils among themselves.

Next morning he summoned all the tribes to a
grand council, releasing the captive chiefs, that he
might speak to them in the presence of their friends
and allies. The preliminary ceremonies were carefully executed in accordance with the rigid Indian
etiquette. Then Clark stood up in the midst of
the rings of squatted warriors, while his riflemen
clustered behind him in their tasselled hunting-shirts,
travel-torn and weather-beaten. He produced the

bloody war-belt of wampum, and handed it to the chiefs whom he had taken captive, telling the assembled tribes that he scorned alike their treachery and their hostility; that he would be thoroughly justified in putting them to death, but that instead he would have them escorted safely from the town, and after three days would begin war upon them. He warned them that if they did not wish their own women and children massacred, they must stop killing those of the Americans. Pointing to the war-belt, he challenged them, on behalf of his people, to see which would make it the most bloody; and he finished by telling them that while they stayed in his camp they should be given food and strong drink,[1] and that now he had ended his talk to them, and he wished them to speedily depart.

Not only the prisoners, but all the other chiefs in turn forthwith rose, and in language of dignified submission protested their regret at having been led astray by the British, and their determination thenceforth to be friendly with the Americans.

[1] " Provisions and Rum." Letter to Mason. This is much the best authority for these proceedings. The " Memoir," written by an old man who had squandered his energies and sunk into deserved obscurity, is tedious and magniloquent, and sometimes inaccurate. Moreover, Dillon has not always chosen the extracts judiciously. Clark's decidedly prolix speeches to the Indians are given with intolerable repetition. They were well suited to the savages, drawing the causes of the quarrel between the British and Americans in phrases that could be understood by the Indian mind ; but their inflated hyperbole is not now interesting. They describe the Americans as lighting a great council-fire, sharpening tomahawks, striking the war-post, declining to give " two bucks for a blanket," as the British wanted them to, etc. ; with incessant allusions to the Great Spirit being angry, the roads being made smooth, refusing to listen to the bad birds who flew through the woods, and the like. Occasional passages are fine ; but it all belongs to the study of Indians and Indian oratory, rather than to the history of the Americans.

In response Clark again told them that he came
not as a counsellor but as a warrior, not begging for
a truce but carrying in his right hand peace and in
his left hand war; save only that to a few of their
worst men he intended to grant no terms whatever.
To those who were friendly he, too, would be a
friend, but if they chose war, he would call from the
Thirteen Council Fires [1] warriors so numerous that
they would darken the land, and from that time on
the red people would hear no sound but that of the
birds that lived on blood. He went on to tell them
that there had been a mist before their eyes, but that
he would clear away the cloud and would show them
the right of the quarrel between the Long Knives
and the King who dwelt across the great sea; and
then he told them about the revolt in terms which
would almost have applied to a rising of Hurons or
Wyandots against the Iroquois. At the end of his
speech he offered them the two belts of peace and
war.

They eagerly took the peace belt, but he declined
to smoke the calumet, and told them he would not
enter into the solemn ceremonies of the peace treaty
The In- with them until the following day. He
dians Make likewise declined to release all his prisoners,
Peace. and insisted that two of them should be put
to death. They even yielded to this, and surrendered
to him two young men, who advanced and sat down
before him on the floor, covering their heads with their

[1] In his speeches, as in those of his successors in treaty-making, the United
States were sometimes spoken of as the Thirteen Fires, and sometimes as the
Great Fire.

blankets, to receive the tomahawk.[1] Then he granted
them full peace and forgave the young men their
doom, and the next day, after the peace council, there
was a feast, and the friendship of the Indians was won.
Clark ever after had great influence over them; they
admired his personal prowess, his oratory, his address
as a treaty-maker, and the skill with which he led
his troops. Long afterwards, when the United
States authorities were endeavoring to make treaties
with the red men, it was noticed that the latter
would never speak to any other white general or
commissioner while Clark was present.

After this treaty there was peace in the Illinois
country; the Indians remained for some time friendly,
and the French were kept well satisfied.

[1] I have followed the contemporary letter to Mason rather than the more
elaborate and slightly different account of the " Memoir." The account written by Clark in his old age, like Shelby's similar autobiography, is, in many
respects, not very trustworthy. It cannot be accepted for a moment where
it conflicts with any contemporary accounts.

CHAPTER III.

CLARK'S CAMPAIGN AGAINST VINCENNES, 1779.

HAMILTON, at Detroit, had been so encouraged by the successes of his war parties that, in 1778, he began to plan an attack on Fort Pitt[1]; but his plans were forestalled by Clark's movements, and he, of course, abandoned them when the astounding news reached him that the rebels had themselves invaded the Illinois country, captured the British commandant, Rocheblave, and administered to the inhabitants the oath of allegiance to Congress.[2] Shortly afterwards he learned that Vincennes likewise was in the hands of the Americans.

He was a man of great energy, and he immediately began to prepare an expedition for the reconquest of the country. French emissaries who were loyal to the British crown were sent to the Wabash to stir up the Indians against the Americans; and though the Piankeshaws remained friendly to the latter, the Kickapoos and Weas, who were more powerful, announced their readiness to espouse the British cause if they received support, while the neighboring Miamis were already on the war-path. The com-

Hamilton Prepares to Reconquer the Country.

---

[1] Haldimand MSS. Hamilton to Carleton, January, 1778.
[2] *Do.* Hamilton's letter of August 8th.

mandants at the small posts of Mackinaw and St. Josephs were also notified to incite the Lake Indians to harass the Illinois country.[1]

He led the main body in person, and throughout September every soul in Detroit was busy from morning till night in mending boats, baking biscuit, packing provisions in kegs and bags, preparing artillery stores, and in every way making ready for the expedition. Fifteen large bateaux and pirogues were procured, each capable of carrying from 1,800 to 3,000 pounds; these were to carry the ammunition, food, clothing, tents, and especially the presents for the Indians. Cattle and wheels were sent ahead to the most important portages on the route that would be traversed; a six-pounder gun was also forwarded. Hamilton had been deeply exasperated by what he regarded as the treachery of most of the Illinois and Wabash creoles in joining the Americans; but he was in high spirits and very confident of success. He wrote to his superior officer that the British were sure to succeed if they acted promptly, for the Indians were favorable to them, knowing they alone could give them supplies; and he added "the Spaniards are feeble and hated by the French, the French are fickle and have no man of capacity to advise or lead them, and the Rebels are enterprising and brave, but want resources." The bulk of the Detroit French, including all their leaders, remained staunch supporters of the crown, and the militia eagerly volunteered to go on the expedition. Feasts were held with the Ottawas, Chippewas, and Pottawatomies,

[1] Hamilton to Haldimand, September 17, 1778.

at which oxen were roasted whole, while Hamilton and the chiefs of the French rangers sang the war-song in solemn council, and received pledges of armed assistance and support from the savages.[1]

On October 7th the expedition left Detroit; before starting the venerable Jesuit missionary gave the Catholic French who went along his solemn blessing **He Starts** and approval, conditionally upon their strict-**against** ly keeping the oath they had taken to be **Vincennes.** loyal and obedient servants of the crown.[2] It is worthy of note that, while the priest at Kaskaskia proved so potent an ally of the Americans, the priest at Detroit was one of the staunchest supporters of the British. Hamilton started with thirty-six British regulars, under two lieutenants, forty-five Detroit volunteers (chiefly French), who had been carefully drilled for over a year, under Captain Lamothe; seventy-nine Detroit militia, under a major and two captains; and seventeen members of the Indian Department (including three captains and four lieutenants) who acted with the Indians. There were thus in all one hundred and seventy-seven whites.[3] Sixty Indians started with the troops from Detroit, but so many bands joined him on the route that when he reached Vincennes his entire force amounted to five hundred men.[4]

---

[1] *Do.* Hamilton to Haldimand, September 23, October 3, 1778.

[2] Haldimand MSS., Series B., Vol. 123, p. 53. Hamilton's letter of July 6, 1781, containing a "brief account" of the whole expedition, taken from what he calls a "diary of transactions" that he had preserved.

[3] *Do.*, Series B., Vol. 122, p. 253, return of forces on Dec. 24th.

[4] *Do.* Hamilton's letter of July 6, 1781, the "brief account." Clark's estimate was very close to the truth; he gave Hamilton six hundred men, four hundred of them Indians. See State Department MSS., No. 71, Vol. I., p. 247. Papers Continental Congress. Letter of G. R. Clark to Gov.

Having embarked, the troops and Indians paddled down stream to Lake Erie, reaching it in a snow-storm, and when a lull came they struck boldly across the lake, making what bateau men still call a "traverse" of thirty-six miles to the mouth of the Maumee. Darkness overtook them while still on the lake, and the head boats hung out lights for the guidance of those astern; but about midnight a gale came up, and the whole flotilla was nearly swamped, being beached with great difficulty on an oozy flat close to the mouth of the Maumee. The waters of the Maumee were low, and the boats were poled slowly up against the current, reaching the portage point, where there was a large Indian village, on the 24th of the month. Here a nine miles' carry was made to one of the sources of the Wabash, called by the voyageurs "la petite rivière." This stream was so low that the boats could not have gone down it had it not been for a beaver dam four miles below the land-ing-place, which backed up the current. An opening was made in the dam to let the boats pass. The traders and Indians thoroughly appreciated the help given them at this difficult part of the course by the engineering skill of the beavers—for Hamilton was following the regular route of the hunting, trading, and war parties,—and none of the beavers of this particular dam were ever molested, being left to keep their dam in order, and repair it, which they always speedily did whenever it was damaged.[1]

> Margin note: Difficulties of the Route.

Henry, April 29, 1779.   This letter was written seven months before that to Mason, and many years before the "Memoir," so I have, where possible, followed it as being better authority than either.

[1] Haldimand's MSS.   Hamilton's "brief account."

It proved as difficult to go down the Wabash as to get up the Maumee. The water was shallow, and once or twice in great swamps dykes had to be built that the boats might be floated across. Frost set in heavily, and the ice cut the men as they worked in the water to haul the boats over shoals or rocks. The bateaux often needed to be beached and caulked, while both whites and Indians had to help carry the loads round the shoal places. At every Indian village it was necessary to stop, hold a conference, and give presents. At last the Wea village—or Ouiatanon, as Hamilton called it—was reached. Here the Wabash chiefs, who had made peace with the Americans, promptly came in and tendered their allegiance to the British, and a reconnoitring party seized a lieutenant and three men of the Vincennes militia, who were themselves on a scouting expedition, but who nevertheless were surprised and captured without difficulty.[1] They had been sent out by Captain Leonard Helm, then acting as commandant at Vincennes. He had but a couple of Americans with him, and was forced to trust to the creole militia, who had all embodied themselves with great eagerness, having taken the oath of allegiance to Congress. Having heard rumors of the British advance, he had dispatched a little party to keep watch, and in consequence of their capture he was taken by surprise.

From Ouiatanon Hamilton dispatched Indian parties to surround Vincennes and intercept any

[1] *Do.* The French officer had in his pocket one British and one American commission ; Hamilton debated in his mind for some time the advisability of hanging him.

messages sent either to the Falls or to the Illinois; they were completely successful, capturing a messenger who carried a hurried note written by Helm to Clark to announce what had happened. An advance guard, under Major Hay, was sent forward to take possession, but Helm showed so good a front that nothing was attempted until the next day, the 17th of December, just seventy-one days after the expedition had left Detroit, when Hamilton came up at the head of his whole force and entered Vincennes. Poor Helm was promptly deserted by all the creole militia. The latter had been loud in their boasts until the enemy came in view, but as soon as they caught sight of the red-coats they began to slip away and run up to the British to surrender their arms.[1] He was finally left with only one or two men, Americans. Nevertheless he refused the first summons to surrender; but Hamilton, who knew that Helm's troops had deserted him, marched up to the fort at the head of his soldiers, and the American was obliged to surrender, with no terms granted save that he and his associates should be treated with humanity.[2] The instant the fort was surrendered

Hamilton Captures Vincennes.

[1] *Do.* Intercepted letter of Captain Helm, Series B., Vol. 122, p. 280.

[2] Letter of Hamilton, Dec. 18–30, 1778. The story of Helm's marching out with the honors of war is apparently a mere invention. Even Mann Butler, usually so careful, permits himself to be led off into all sorts of errors when describing the incidents of the Illinois and Vincennes expeditions, and the writers who have followed him have generally been less accurate. The story of Helm drinking toddy by the fire-place when Clark retook the fort, and of the latter ordering riflemen to fire at the chimney, so as to knock the mortar into the toddy, may safely be set down as pure—and very weak—fiction. When Clark wrote his memoirs, in his old age, he took delight in writing down among his exploits all sorts of childish stratagems; the marvel

the Indians broke in and plundered it; but they committed no act of cruelty, and only plundered a single private house.

The French inhabitants had shown pretty clearly that they did not take a keen interest in the struggle, on either side. They were now summoned to the church and offered the chance—which **Measures to Secure his Conquest.** they for the most part eagerly embraced —of purging themselves of their past misconduct by taking a most humiliating oath of repentance, acknowledging that they had sinned against God and man by siding with the rebels, and promising to be loyal in the future. Two hundred and fifty of the militia, being given back their arms, appeared with their officers, and took service again under the British king, swearing a solemn oath of allegiance. They certainly showed throughout the most light-hearted indifference to chronic perjury and treachery; nor did they in other respects appear to very good advantage. Clark was not in the least surprised at the news of their conduct; for he had all along realized that the attachment of the French would prove but a slender reed on which to lean in the moment of trial.

Hamilton had no fear of the inhabitants themselves, for the fort completely commanded the town. To keep them in good order he confiscated all their spirituous liquors, and in a rather amusing burst of Puritan feeling destroyed two billiard tables, which he announced were "sources of immorality

is that any sane historian should not have seen that these were on their face as untrue as they were ridiculous.

and dissipation in such a settlement." [1] He had no idea that he was in danger of attack from without, for his spies brought him word that Clark had only a hundred and ten men in the Illinois county [2]; and the route between was in winter one of extraordinary difficulty.

He had five hundred men and Clark but little over one hundred. He was not only far nearer his base of supples and reinforcements at Detroit, than Clark was to his at Fort Pitt, but he was also actually across Clark's line of communications. Had he pushed forward at once to attack the Americans, and had he been able to overcome the difficulties of the march, he would almost certainly have conquered. But he was daunted by the immense risk and danger of the movement. The way was long and the country flooded, and he feared the journey might occupy so much time that his stock of provisions would be exhausted before he got half-way. In such a case the party might starve to death or perish from exposure. Besides he did not know what he should do for carriages; and he dreaded the rigor of the winter weather. [3] There were undoubtedly appalling difficulties in the way of a mid-winter march and attack; and the fact that Clark attempted and performed the feat which Hamilton dared not try, marks just the difference between a man of genius and a good, brave, ordinary commander.

He Goes into Winter Quarters.

[1] *Do.*

[2] *Do.* " Fourscore at Kaskaskia and thirty at Cahokia."

[3] Haldimand MSS.; in his various letters Hamilton sets forth the difficulties at length.

Having decided to suspend active operations during the cold weather, he allowed the Indians to scatter back to their villages for the winter, and sent most of the Detroit militia home, retaining in garrison only thirty-four British regulars, forty French volunteers, and a dozen white leaders of the Indians[1]; in all eighty or ninety whites, and a probably larger number of red auxiliaries. The latter were continually kept out on scouting expeditions; Miamis and Shawnees were sent down to watch the Ohio, and take scalps in the settlements, while bands of Kickapoos, the most warlike of the Wabash Indians, and of Ottawas, often accompanied by French partisans, went towards the Illinois country.[2] Hamilton intended to undertake a formidable campaign in the spring. He had sent messages to Stuart, the British Indian agent in the south, directing him to give war-belts to the Chickasaws, Cherokees, and Creeks, that a combined attack on the frontier might take place as soon as the weather opened. He himself was to be joined by reinforcements from Detroit, while the Indians were to gather round him as soon as the winter broke. He would then have had probably over a thousand men, and light cannon with which to batter down the stockades. He rightly judged that with this force he could not only reconquer the Illinois, but also sweep Kentucky, where the outnumbered riflemen could not have met him in the field, nor the wooden forts have withstood his artillery.

He Plans a Great Campaign in the Spring.

---

[1] *Do.* B. Vol. 122, p. 287. Return of Vincennes garrison for Jan. 30, 1779.

[2] Hamilton's "brief account," and his letter of December 18th.

Undoubtedly he would have carried out his plan, and have destroyed all the settlements west of the Alleghanies, had he been allowed to wait until the mild weather brought him his hosts of Indian allies and his reinforcements of regulars and militia from Detroit.

But in Clark he had an antagonist whose far-sighted daring and indomitable energy raised him head and shoulders above every other frontier leader. This backwoods colonel was perhaps the one man able in such a crisis to keep the land his people had gained. When the news of the loss of Vincennes reached the Illinois towns, and especially when there followed a rumor that Hamilton himself was on his march **Panic among the Illinois French.** thither to attack them,[1] the panic became tremendous among the French. They frankly announced that though they much preferred the Americans, yet it would be folly to oppose armed resistance to the British ; and one or two of their number were found to be in communication with Hamilton and the Detroit authorities. Clark promptly made ready for resistance, tearing down the buildings near the fort at Kaskaskia—his head-quarters—and sending out scouts and runners ; but he knew that it was hopeless to try to withstand such a force as Hamilton could gather. He narrowly escaped being taken prisoner by a party of Ottawas and Canadians, who had come from Vincennes early in January, when

[1] The rumor came when Clark was attending a dance given by the people of the little village of La Prairie du Rocher. The Creoles were passionately fond of dancing and the Kentuckians entered into the amusement with the utmost zest.

the weather was severe and the travelling fairly good.[1] He was at the time on his way to Cahokia, to arrange for the defence ; several of the wealthier Frenchmen were with him in " chairs "—presumably creaking wooden carts,—and one of them " swampt," or mired down, only a hundred yards from the ambush. Clark and his guards were so on the alert that no attack was made.

In the midst of his doubt and uncertainty he received some news that enabled him immediately to **Clark** decide on the proper course to follow. He **Receives** had secured great influence over the bolder, **News** **concerning** and therefore the leading, spirits among **Vincennes.** the French. One of these was a certain Francis Vigo, a trader in St. Louis. He was by birth an Italian, who had come to New Orleans in a Spanish regiment, and having procured his discharge, had drifted to the creole villages of the frontier, being fascinated by the profitable adventures of the Indian trade. Journeying to Vincennes, he was thrown into prison by Hamilton ; on being released, he returned to St. Louis. Thence he instantly crossed over to Kaskaskia, on January 27, 1779,[2] and told Clark that Hamilton had at the time only eighty men in garrison, with three pieces of cannon and some swivels mounted, but that as soon as the winter broke, he intended to gather a very large force and take the offensive.[3]

[1] Haldimand MSS. Hamilton's letter January 24, 1779.

[2] State Department MSS. Letters to Washington, 33, p. 90.

[3] State Department MSS. Papers of Continental Congress, No. 71, Vol I., p. 267.

Clark instantly decided to forestall his foe, and to make the attack himself, heedless of the almost impassable nature of the ground and of the icy severity of the weather. Not only had he received no reinforcements from Virginia but he had not had so much as "a scrip of a pen" from Governor Henry since he had left him, nearly twelve months before.[1] So he was forced to trust entirely to his own energy and power. He first equipped a row-galley with two four-pounders and four swivels, and sent her off with a crew of forty men, having named her the *Willing*.[2] She was to patrol the Ohio, and then to station herself in the Wabash so as to stop all boats from descending it. She was the first gun-boat ever afloat on the western waters.

Clark Determines to Strike the First Blow.

Then he hastily drew together his little garrisons of backwoodsmen from the French towns, and prepared for the march overland against Vincennes. His bold front and confident bearing, and the prompt decision of his measures, had once more restored confidence among the French, whose spirits rose as readily as they were cast down ; and he was especially helped by the creole girls, whose enthusiasm for the expedition roused many of the more daring young men to volunteer under Clark's banner. By these means he gathered together a band of one hundred and seventy men, at whose head he marched out of Kaskaskia on the 7th of February.[3] All the inhabitants escorted them out of the village,

His March against Vincennes.

---

[1] *Do.*

[2] Under the command of Clark's cousin, Lt. John Rogers.

[3] Letter to Henry. The letter to Mason says it was the 5th.

and the Jesuit priest, Gibault, gave them absolution at parting.

The route by which they had to go was two hundred and forty miles in length. It lay through a beautiful and well watered country, of groves and prairies ; but at that season the march was necessarily attended with the utmost degree of hardship and fatigue. The weather had grown mild, so that there was no suffering from cold ; but in the thaw the ice on the rivers melted, great freshets followed, and all the lowlands and meadows were flooded. Clark's great object was to keep his troops in good spirits. Of course he and the other officers shared every hardship and led in every labor. He encouraged the men to hunt game ; and to " feast on it like Indian war-dancers," [1] each company in turn inviting the others to the smoking and plentiful banquets. One day they saw great herds of buffaloes and killed many of them. They had no tents [2] ; but

[1] Clark's " Memoir."

[2] State Department MSS. Letters to Washington, Vol. 33, p. 90. " A Journal of Col. G. R. Clark. Proceedings from the 29th Jan'y 1779 to the 26th March Inst." [by Captain Bowman]. This journal has been known for a long time. The original is supposed to have been lost ; but either this is it or else it is a contemporary MS. copy. In the " Campaign in the Illinois " (Cincinnati, Robert Clarke and Co., 1869), p. 99, there is a printed copy of the original. The Washington MS. differs from it in one or two particulars. Thus, the printed diary in the " Campaign," on p. 99, line 3, says " fifty volunteers " ; the MS. copy says " 50 French volunteers." Line 5 in the printed copy says " and such other Americans " ; in the MS. it says " and several other Americans." Lines 6 and 7 of the printed copy read as follows in the MS. (but only make doubtful sense) : " These with a number of horses designed for the settlement of Kantuck &c. Jan. 30th, on which Col. Clark," etc. Lines 10 and 11 of the printed copy read in the MS. : " was let alone till spring that he with his Indians would undoubtedly cut us all off." Lines 13 and 14, of the printed copy read in the MS. " Jan. 31st, sent an express to Cahokia for volunteers. Nothing extraordinary this day."

at nightfall they kindled huge camp-fires, and spent the evenings merrily round the piles of blazing logs, in hunter fashion, feasting on bear's ham and buffalo hump, elk saddle, venison haunch, and the breast of the wild turkey, some singing of love and the chase and war, and others dancing after the manner of the French trappers and wood-runners.

Thus they kept on, marching hard but gleefully and in good spirits until after a week they came to the drowned lands of the Wabash. They first struck the two branches of the Little Wabash. Their channels were a league apart, but the flood was so high that they now made one great river five miles in width, the overflow of water being three feet deep in the shallowest part of the plains between and alongside them.

Clark instantly started to build a pirogue; then crossing over the first channel he put up a scaffold on the edge of the flooded plain. He ferried his men over, and brought the baggage across and placed it on the scaffold; then he swam the pack-horses over, loaded them as they stood belly-deep in the water beside the scaffold, and marched his men on through the water until they came to the second channel, which was crossed as the first had been. The building of the pirogue and the ferrying took three days in all.

They had by this time come so near Vincennes that they dared not fire a gun for fear of being discovered; besides, the floods had driven the game all away; so that they soon began to feel hunger, while their progress was very slow, and they suffered much from the fatigue of travelling all day long through deep mud or breast-high water. On the 17th they reached the Embarras River, but could not cross, nor could they find a dry spot on which to camp; at last they found the water falling off a small, almost submerged hillock, and on this they huddled through the night. At daybreak they heard Hamilton's morning gun from the fort, that was but three leagues distant; and as they could not find a ford across the Embarras, they followed it down and camped by the Wabash. There Clark set his drenched, hungry, and dispirited followers to building some pirogues; while two or three unsuccessful attempts were made to get men across the river that they might steal boats. He determined to leave his horses at this camp; for it was almost impossible to get them further.[1]

On the morning of the 20th the men had been without food for nearly two days. Many of the creole volunteers began to despair, and talked of returning. Clark **Hardship and Suffering.** knew that his Americans, veterans who had been with him for over a year, had no idea of abandoning the enterprise, nor yet of suffering the last extremities of hunger while they had horses along. He paid no heed to the request of the creoles, nor did he even forbid their going back; he only laughed at them, and told them to go out and try to kill a deer. He knew that without any violence he could yet easily detain the volunteers for a few days longer; and he kept up the spirits of

[1] This is not exactly stated in the " Memoir "; but it speaks of the horses as being with the troops on the 20th; and after they left camp, on the evening of the 21st, states that he " would have given a good deal . . . for one of the horses."

the whole command by his undaunted and confident mien. The canoes were nearly finished; and about noon a small boat with five Frenchmen from Vincennes was captured. From these Clark gleaned the welcome intelligence that the condition of affairs was unchanged at the fort, and that there was no suspicion of any impending danger. In the evening the men were put in still better heart by one of the hunters killing a deer.

It rained all the next day. By dawn Clark began to ferry the troops over the Wabash in the canoes he had built, and they were soon on the eastern bank of the river, the side on which Vincennes stood. They now hoped to get to town by nightfall; but there was no dry land for leagues round about, save where a few hillocks rose island-like above the flood. The Frenchmen whom they had captured said they could not possibly get along; but Clark led the men in person, and they waded with infinite toil for about three miles, the water often up to their chins; and they then camped on a hillock for the night. Clark kept the troops cheered up by every possible means, and records that he was much assisted by "a little antic drummer," a young boy who did good service by making the men laugh with his pranks and jokes.[1]

Next morning they resumed their march, the

---

[1] Law, in his " Vincennes " (p. 32), makes the deeds of the drummer the basis for a traditional story that is somewhat too highly colored. Thus he makes Clark's men at one time mutiny, and refuse to go forwards. This they never did; the creoles once got dejected and wished to return, but the Americans, by Clark's own statement, never faltered at all. Law's " Vincennes " is an excellent little book, but he puts altogether too much confidence in mere tradition. For another instance besides this, see page 68, where he describes Clark as entrapping and killing " upwards of fifty Indians," instead of only eight or nine, as was actually the case.

strongest wading painfully through the water, while the weak and famished were carried in the canoes, which were so hampered by the bushes that they could hardly go even as fast as the toiling footmen. The evening and morning guns of the fort were heard plainly by the men as they plodded onward, numbed and weary. Clark, as usual, led them in person. Once they came to a place so deep that there seemed no crossing, for the canoes could find no ford. It was hopeless to go back or stay still, and the men huddled together, apparently about to despair. But Clark suddenly blackened his face with gunpowder, gave the war-whoop, and sprang forwards boldly into the ice-cold water, wading out straight towards the point at which they were aiming; and the men followed him, one after another, without a word. Then he ordered those nearest him to begin one of their favorite songs; and soon the whole line took it up, and marched cheerfully onward. He intended to have the canoes ferry them over the deepest part, but before they came to it one of the men felt that his feet were in a path, and by carefully following it they got to a sugar camp, a hillock covered with maples, which once had been tapped for sugar. Here they camped for the night, still six miles from the town, without food, and drenched through. The prisoners from Vincennes, sullen and weary, insisted that they could not possibly get to the town through the deep water; the prospect seemed almost hopeless even to the iron-willed, steel-sinewed backwoodsmen[1]; but their leader never lost courage for a moment.

[1] Bowman ends his entry for the day with : "No provisions yet. Lord help us !"

That night was bitterly cold, for there was a heavy frost, and the ice formed half an inch thick round the edges and in the smooth water. But the sun rose bright and glorious, and Clark, in burning words, told his stiffened, famished, half-frozen followers that the evening would surely see them at the goal of their hopes. Without waiting for an answer, he plunged into the water, and they followed him with a cheer, in Indian file. Before the third man had entered the water he halted and told one of his officers [1] to close the rear with twenty-five men, and to put to death any man who refused to march; and the whole line cheered him again.

Then came the most trying time of the whole march. Before them lay a broad sheet of water, covering what was known as the Horse Shoe Plain; the floods had made it a shallow lake four miles across, unbroken by so much as a handsbreadth of dry land. On its farther side was a dense wood. Clark led breast high in the water with fifteen or twenty of the strongest men next him. About the middle of the plain the cold and exhaustion told so on the weaker men that the canoes had to take them aboard and carry them on to the land; and from that time on the little dug-outs plied frantically to and fro to save the more helpless from drowning. Those, who, though weak, could still move onwards, clung to the stronger, and struggled ahead, Clark animating them in every possible way. When they at last reached the woods the water became so deep that it was to the shoulders of the tallest, but the weak and those of low stature

[1] Bowman.

could now cling to the bushes and old logs, until the canoes were able to ferry them to a spot of dry land, some ten acres in extent, that lay near-by. The strong and tall got ashore and built fires. Many on reaching the shore fell flat on their faces, half in the water, and could not move farther. It was found that the fires did not help the very weak, so every such a one was put between two strong men who ran him up and down by the arms, and thus soon made him recover.[1]

Fortunately at this time an Indian canoe, paddled by some squaws, was discovered and overtaken by one of the dug-outs. In it was half a quarter of a buffalo, with some corn, tallow and kettles. This was an invaluable prize. Broth was immediately made, and was served out to the most weakly with great care; almost all of the men got some, but very many gave their shares to the weakly, rallying and joking them to put them in good heart. The little refreshment, together with the fires and the bright weather, gave new life to all. They set out again in the afternoon, crossed a deep, narrow lake in their canoes, and after marching a short distance came to a copse of timber from which they saw the fort and town not two miles away. Here they halted, and looked to their rifles and ammunition, making ready for the fight. Every man now feasted his eyes with the sight of what he had so long labored to reach, and forthwith forgot that he had suffered any thing; making light of what had been gone through, and passing from dogged despair to the most exultant self-confidence.

[1] Clark's "Memoir."

Between the party and the town lay a plain, the hollows being filled with little pools, on which were many water-fowl, and some of the townspeople were in sight, on horseback, shooting ducks. Clark sent out a few active young creoles, who succeeded in taking prisoner one of these fowling horsemen. From him it was learned that neither Hamilton nor any one else had the least suspicion that any attack could possibly be made at that season, but that a couple of hundred Indian warriors had just come to town.

Clark was rather annoyed at the last bit of information. The number of armed men in town, including British, French, and Indians about quadrupled his own force. This made heavy odds to face, even with the advantage of a surprise, and in spite of the fact that his own men were sure to fight to the last, since failure meant death by torture. Moreover, if he made the attack without warning, some of the Indians and Vincennes people would certainly be slain, and the rest would be thereby made his bitter enemies, even if he succeeded. On the other hand, he found out from the prisoner that the French were very lukewarm to the British, and would certainly not fight if they could avoid it; and that half of the Indians were ready to side with the Americans. Finally, there was a good chance that before dark some one would discover the approach of the troops and would warn the British, thereby doing away with all chance of a surprise.

After thinking it over Clark decided, as the less of two evils, to follow the hazardous course of himself announcing his approach. He trusted that the

boldness of such a course, together with the shock
of his utterly unexpected appearance, would para-
lyze his opponents and incline the wavering to
favor him. So he released the prisoner and sent him
in ahead, with a letter to the people of Vincennes.
By this letter he proclaimed to the French that
he was that moment about to attack the town; that
those townspeople who were friends to the Americans were to remain in their houses, where they
would not be molested; that the friends of the king
should repair to the fort, join the "hair-buyer
general," and fight like men; and that those who
did neither of these two things, but remained armed
and in the streets, must expect to be treated as
enemies.[1]

Having sent the messenger in advance, he waited
until his men were rested and their rifles and powder
Surprise of dry, and then at sundown marched straight
the Town. against the town. He divided his force into
two divisions, leading in person the first, which consisted of two companies of Americans and of the Kaskaskia creoles; while the second, led by Bowman,
contained Bowman's own company and the Cahokians.
His final orders to the men were to march with the
greatest regularity, to obey the orders of their officers, and, above all, to keep perfect silence.[2] The

[1] Clark's "Memoir."

[2] In the Haldimand MSS., Series B., Vol. 122, p. 289, there is a long
extract from what is called "Col. Clark's Journal." This is the official
report which he speaks of as being carried by William Moires, his express,
who was taken by the Indians (see his letter to Henry of April 29th; there
seems, by the way, to be some doubt whether this letter was not written to
Jefferson; there is a copy in the Jefferson MSS. Series I., Vol. I.). This is
not only the official report, but also the earliest letter Clark wrote on the

rapidly gathering dusk prevented any discovery of his real numbers.

In sending in the messenger he had builded even better than he knew; luck which had long been against him now at last favored him. Hamilton's runners had seen Clark's camp-fires the night before; and a small scouting party of British regulars, Detroit volunteers, and Indians had in consequence been sent to find out what had caused them.[1] These men were not made of such stern stuff as Clark's followers, nor had they such a commander; and after going some miles they were stopped by the floods, and started to return. Before they got back, Vincennes was assailed. Hamilton trusted so completely to the scouting party, and to the seemingly

subject and therefore the most authoritative. The paragraph relating to the final march against Vincennes is as follows :

" I order'd the march in the first division Capt. Williams, Capt. Worthingtons Company & the Cascaskia Volunteers, in the 2d commanded by Capt. Bowman his own Company & the Cohos Volunteers. At sun down I put the divisions in motion to march in the greatest order & regularity & observe the orders of their officers. Above all to be silent—the 5 men we took in the canoes were our guides. We entered the town on the upper part leaving detached Lt. Bayley & 15 rifle men to attack the Fort & keep up a fire to harrass them untill we took possession of the town & they were to remain on that duty till relieved by another party, the two divisions marched into the town & took possession of the main street, put guards &c without the least molestation."

This effectually disposes of the account, which was accepted by Clark himself in his old age, that he ostentatiously paraded his men and marched them to and fro with many flags flying, so as to impress the British with his numbers. Instead of indulging in any such childishness (which would merely have warned the British, and put them on their guard), he in reality made as silent an approach as possible, under cover of the darkness.

Hamilton, in his narrative, speaks of the attack as being made on the 22d of February, not the 23d as Clark says.

[1] Hamilton's "brief account" in the Haldimand MSS. The party was led by Lt. Schieffelin of the regulars and the French captains Lamothe and Maisonville.

impassable state of the country, that his watch was very lax. The creoles in the town, when Clark's proclamation was read to them, gathered eagerly to discuss it; but so great was the terror of his name, and so impressed and appalled were they by the mysterious approach of an unknown army, and the confident and menacing language with which its coming was heralded, that none of them dared show themselves partisans of the British by giving warning to the garrison. The Indians likewise heard vague rumors of what had occurred and left the town; a number of the inhabitants who were favorable to the British, followed the same course.[1] Hamilton, attracted by the commotion, sent down his soldiers to find out out what had occurred; but before they succeeded, the Americans were upon them.

About seven o'clock[2] Clark entered the town, and at once pushed his men on to attack the fort. Had he charged he could probably have taken it at once; for so unprepared were the garrison that the first rifle shots were deemed by them to come from drunken Indians. But of course he had not counted on such a state of things. He had so few men that he dared not run the risk of suffering a heavy loss. Moreover, the backwoodsmen had neither swords nor bayonets.

Most of the creole townspeople received Clark

[1] Haldimand MSS. Series B., Vol. 122, p. 337. Account brought to the people of Detroit of the loss of Vincennes, by a Captain Chêne, who was then living in the village. As the Virginians entered it he fled to the woods with some Huron and Ottawa warriors; next day he was joined by some French families and some Miamis and Pottawatomies.

[2] Clark's letter to Henry.

joyfully, and rendered him much assistance, especially by supplying him with powder and ball, his own stock of ammunition being scanty. One of the Indian chiefs [1] offered to bring his tribe to the support of the Americans, but Clark answered that all he asked of the red men was that they should for the moment remain neutral. A few of the young creoles were allowed to join in the attack, however, it being deemed good policy to commit them definitely to the American side.

Fifty of the American troops were detached to guard against any relief from without, while the rest attacked the fort; yet Hamilton's scouting party crept up, lay hid all night in an old barn, and at daybreak rushed into the fort.[2] Firing was kept up with very little intermission throughout the night. At one o'clock the moon set, and Clark took advantage of the

The Attack on the Fort.

[1] A son of the Piankeshaw head-chief Tabac.

[2] Hamilton's Narrative. Clark in his " Memoir" asserts that he designedly let them through, and could have shot them down as they tried to clamber over the stockade if he had wished. Bowman corroborates Hamilton, saying : " We sent a party to intercept them, but missed them. However, we took one of their men, . . . the rest making their escape under the cover of the night into the fort." Bowman's journal is for this siege much more trustworthy than Clark's " Memoir." In the latter, Clark makes not a few direct misstatements, and many details are colored so as to give them an altered aspect. As an instance of the different ways in which he told an event at the time, and thirty years later, take the following accounts of the same incident. The first is from the letter to Henry (State Department MSS.), the second from the " Memoir." 1. " A few days ago I received certain intelligence of Wm. Moires my express to you being killed near the Falls of Ohio, news truly disagreeable to me, as I fear many of my letters will fall into the hands of the enemy at Detroit." 2. " Poor Myres the express, who set out on the 15th, got killed on his passage, and his packet fell into the hands of the enemy ; but I had been so much on my guard that there was not a sentence in it that could be of any disadvantage to us for the enemy to know ; and there were private letters from soldiers

darkness to throw up an intrenchment within rifle-shot of the strongest battery, which consisted of two guns. All of the cannon and swivels in the fort were placed about eleven feet above the ground, on the upper floors of the strong block-houses that formed the angles of the palisaded walls. At sunrise on the 24th the riflemen from the intrenchment opened a hot fire into the port-holes of the battery, and speedily silenced both guns.[1] The artillery and musketry of the defenders did very little damage to the assailants, who lost but one man wounded, though some of the houses in the town were destroyed by the cannon-balls. In return, the backwoodsmen, by firing into the ports, soon rendered it impossible for the guns to be run out and served, and killed or severely wounded six or eight of the garrison ; for the Americans showed themselves much superior, both in marksmanship and in the art of sheltering themselves, to the British regulars and French Canadians against whom they were pitted.

Early in the forenoon Clark summoned the fort to surrender, and while waiting for the return of the flag his men took the opportunity of getting breakfast, the first regular meal they had had for six days.

to their friends designedly wrote to deceive in cases of such accidents." His whole account of the night attack and of his treating with Hamilton is bombastic. If his account of the incessant " blaze of fire " of the Americans is true, they must have wasted any amount of ammunition perfectly uselessly. Unfortunately, most of the small western historians who have written about Clark have really damaged his reputation by the absurd inflation of their language ; They were adepts in the forcible-feeble style of writing, a sample of which is their rendering him ludicrous by calling him " the Hannibal of the West," and the " Washington of the West." Moreover, they base his claims to greatness not on his really great deeds, but on the half-imaginary feats of childish cunning he related in his old age.

[1] Clark's letter to Henry.

Hamilton declined to surrender, but proposed a three days' truce instead. This proposition Clark instantly rejected, and the firing again began, the backwoodsmen beseeching Clark to let them storm the fort; he refused. While the negotiations were going on a singular incident occurred. A party of Hamilton's Indians returned from a successful scalping expedition against the frontier, and being ignorant of what had taken place, marched straight into the town. Some of Clark's backwoodsmen instantly fell on them and killed or captured nine, besides two French partisans who had been out with them.[1] One of the latter was the son of a creole lieutenant in Clark's troops, and after much pleading his father and friends procured the release of himself and his comrade.[2] Clark determined to make a signal example of the six captured Indians, both to strike terror into the rest and to show them how powerless the British were to protect them; so he had them led within sight of the fort and there tomahawked and thrown into the river.[3] The sight

[1] *Do.* In the letter to Mason he says two scalped, six captured and afterwards tomahawked. Bowman says two killed, three wounded, six captured ; and calls the two partisans " prisoners." Hamilton and Clark say they were French allies of the British, the former saying there were two, the latter mentioning only one. Hamilton says there were fifteen Indians.

[2] The incident is noteworthy as showing how the French were divided ; throughout the Revolutionary war in the west they furnished troops to help in turn whites and Indians, British and Americans. The Illinois French, however, generally remained faithful to the Republic, and the Detroit French to the crown.

[3] Hamilton, who bore the most vindictive hatred to Clark, implies that the latter tomahawked the prisoners himself ; but Bowman explicitly says that it was done while Clark and Hamilton were meeting at the church. Be it noticed in passing, that both Clark and Hamilton agree that though the Vincennes people favored the Americans, only a very few of them took active part on Clark's side.

did not encourage the garrison. The English troops remained firm and eager for the fight, though they had suffered the chief loss; but the Detroit volunteers showed evident signs of panic.

In the afternoon Hamilton sent out another flag, and he and Clark met in the old French church to **Surrender** arrange for the capitulation. Helm, who **of the Fort.** was still a prisoner on parole, and was told by Clark that he was to remain such until recaptured, was present; so were the British Major Hay and the American Captain Bowman. There was some bickering and recrimination between the leaders, Clark reproaching Hamilton with having his hands dyed in the blood of the women and children slain by his savage allies; while the former answered that he was not to blame for obeying the orders of his superiors, and that he himself had done all he could to make the savages act mercifully. It was finally agreed that the garrison, seventy-nine men in all,[1] should surrender as prisoners of war. The British commander has left on record his bitter mortification at having to yield the fort " to a set of uncivilized Virginia woodsmen armed with rifles." In truth, it was a most notable achievement. Clark had taken, without artillery, a heavy stockade, protected by cannon and swivels, and garrisoned by trained soldiers. His superiority in numbers was very far from being in itself sufficient to bring about the result, as witness the almost invariable success with which the similar but smaller

---

[1] Letter to Henry. Hamilton's letter says sixty rank and file of the 8th regiment and Detroit volunteers; the other nineteen were officers and under-officers, artillerymen, and French partisan leaders. The return of the garrison already quoted shows he had between eighty and ninety white troops.

Kentucky forts, unprovided with artillery and held
by fewer men, were defended against much larger
forces than Clark's. Much credit belongs to Clark's
men, but most belongs to their leader. The boldness of his plan and the resolute skill with which he
followed it out, his perseverance through the intense
hardships of the midwinter march, the address with
which he kept the French and Indians neutral, and
the masterful way in which he controlled his own
troops, together with the ability and courage he displayed in the actual attack, combined to make his
feat the most memorable of all the deeds done west
of the Alleghanies in the Revolutionary war.[1] It was
likewise the most important in its results, for had he
been defeated we would not only have lost the Illinois, but in all probability Kentucky also.

Immediately after taking the fort Clark sent
Helm and fifty men, in boats armed with swivels,
up the Wabash to intercept a party of forty
French volunteers from Detroit, who were
bringing to Vincennes bateaux heavily
laden with goods of all kinds, to the value
of ten thousand pounds sterling.[2] In a few days
Helm returned successful, and the spoils, together

*Capture of
a Convoy
from
Detroit.*

[1] Hamilton himself, at the conclusion of his "brief account," speaks as
follows in addressing his superiors : "The difficulties and dangers of Colonel
Clark's march from the Illinois were such as required great courage to encounter and great perseverance to overcome. In trusting to traitors he was
more fortunate than myself ; whether, on the whole, he was entitled to success is not for me to determine." Both Clark and Hamilton give minute
accounts of various interviews that took place between them ; the accounts do
not agree, and it is needless to say that in the narration of each the other
appears to disadvantage, being quoted as practically admitting various acts
of barbarity, etc.

[2] Letter to Henry.

with the goods taken at Vincennes, were distributed among the soldiers, who " got almost rich." [1]   The officers kept nothing save a few needed articles of clothing.   The gun-boat *Willing* appeared shortly after the taking of the fort, the crew bitterly disappointed that they were not in time for the fighting. The long-looked-for messenger from the governor of Virginia also arrived, bearing to the soldiers the warm thanks of the Legislature of that State for their capture of Kaskaskia and the promise of more substantial reward. [2]

Clark was forced to parole most of his prisoners, but twenty-seven, including Hamilton himself, were **Disposal** sent to .Virginia.   The backwoodsmen re- **of the** garded Hamilton with revengeful hatred, **Prisoners.** and he was not well treated while among them, [3] save only by Boon—for the kind-hearted, fearless old pioneer never felt any thing but pity for a fallen enemy.   All the borderers, including Clark, [4] believed that the British commander him-

[1] "Memoir."

[2] One hundred and fifty thousand acres of land opposite Louisville were finally allotted them.   Some of the Piankeshaw Indians ceded Clark a tract of land for his own use, but the Virginia Legislature very properly disallowed the grant.

[3] In Hamilton's " brief account " he says that their lives were often threatened by the borderers, but that " our guard behaved very well, protected us, and hunted for us."   At the Falls he found " a number of settlers who lived in log-houses, in eternal apprehension from the Indians," and he adds : " The people at the forts are in a wretched state, obliged to enclose the cattle every night within the fort, and carry their rifles to the field when they go to plough or cut wood."   He speaks of Boon's kindness in his short printed narrative in the *Royal Gazette.*

[4] Clark, in his letter to Mason, alludes to Hamilton's " known barbarity " ; but in his memoir he speaks very well of Hamilton, and attributes the murderous forays to his subordinates, one of whom, Major Hay, he particularly specifies.

self gave rewards to the Indians for the American scalps they brought in; and because of his alleged behavior in this regard he was kept in close confinement by the Virginia government until, through the intercession of Washington, he was at last released and exchanged. Exactly how much he was to blame it is difficult to say. Certainly the blame rests even more with the crown, and the ruling class in Britain, than with Hamilton, who merely carried out the orders of his superiors; and though he undoubtedly heartily approved of these orders, and executed them with eager zest, yet it seems that he did what he could—which was very little—to prevent unnecessary atrocities.

The crime consisted in employing the savages at all in a war waged against men, women, and children alike. Undoubtedly the British at Detroit followed the example of the French[1] in paying money to the Indians for the scalps of their foes. It is equally beyond question that the British acted with much more humanity than their French predecessors had shown. Apparently the best officers utterly disapproved of the whole business of scalp buying; but it was eagerly followed by many of the reckless agents and partisan leaders, British, tories, and Canadians, who themselves often accompanied the Indians against the frontier and witnessed or

---

[1] See Parkman's "Montcalm and Wolfe," II., 421, for examples of French payments, some of a peculiarly flagrant sort. A certain kind of American pseudo-historian is especially fond of painting the British as behaving to us with unexampled barbarity ; yet nothing is more sure than that the French were far more cruel and less humane in their contests with us than were the British.

shared in their unmentionable atrocities. It is impossible to acquit either the British home government or its foremost representatives at Detroit of a large share in the responsibility for the appalling brutality of these men and their red allies; but the heaviest blame rests on the home government.

Clark soon received some small reinforcements, and was able to establish permanent garrisons at Vincennes, Kaskaskia, and Cahokia. With the Indian tribes who lived round about he made firm peace; against some hunting bands of Delawares who came in and began to commit ravages, he waged ruthless and untiring war, sparing the women and children, but killing all the males capable of bearing arms, and he harried most of them out of the territory, while the rest humbly sued for peace. His own men worshipped him; the French loved and stood in awe of him. while the Indians respected and feared him greatly. During the remainder of the Revolutionary war the British were not able to make any serious effort to shake the hold he had given the Americans on the region lying around and between Vincennes and the Illinois. Moreover he so effectually pacified the tribes between the Wabash and the Mississippi that they did not become open and formidable foes of the whites until, with the close of the war against Britain, Kentucky passed out of·the stage when Indian hostilities threatened her very life.

The fame of Clark's deeds and the terror of his prowess spread to the southern Indians, and the British at Natchez trembled lest they should share the fate that had come on Kaskaskia and Vincennes.[1] Flat-boats from the Illinois went down to New Orleans, and keel-boats returned from that city with arms and munitions, or were sent up to Pittsburg[2]; and the following spring Clark built a fort on the east bank of the Mississippi below the Ohio.[3] It was in the Chickasaw territory, and these warlike Indians soon assaulted it, making a determined effort to take it by storm, and though they were repulsed with very heavy slaughter, yet, to purchase their neutrality, the Americans were glad to abandon the fort.

Clark himself, towards the end of 1779, took up his abode at the Falls of the Ohio, where he served in some sort as a shield both for the Illinois and for Kentucky, and from whence he hoped some day to march against Detroit. This was his darling scheme, which he never ceased to cherish. Through no fault of his own, the day never came when he could put it in execution.

Clark Moves to the Falls of the Ohio.

He was ultimately made a brigadier-general of the Virginian militia, and to the harassed settlers in Kentucky his mere name was a tower of strength. He was the sole originator of the plan for the conquest of the northwestern lands, and, almost unaided, he had executed his own scheme. For a

[1] State Department MSS. [Intercepted Letters], No. 51, Vol. II., pp. 17 and 45. Letter of James Colbert, a half-breed in the British interest, resident at that time among the Chickasaws, May 25, 1779, etc.

[2] The history of the early navigation of the Ohio and Mississippi begins many years before the birth of any of our western pioneers, when the French went up and down them. Long before the Revolutionary war occasional hunters, in dug-outs, or settlers going to Natchez in flat-boats, descended these rivers, and from Pittsburg craft were sent to New Orleans to open negotiations with the Spaniards as soon as hostilities broke out ; and ammunition was procured from New Orleans as soon as Independence was declared.

[3] In lat. 36° 30' ; it was named Fort Jefferson. Jefferson MSS., 1st Series, Vol. 19. Clark's letter.

year he had been wholly cut off from all communication with the home authorities, and had received no
help of any kind. Alone, and with the very slenderest means, he had conquered and held a vast and
beautiful region, which but for him would have
formed part of a foreign and hostile empire [1]; he had
clothed and paid his soldiers with the spoils of his
enemies ; he had spent his own fortune as carelessly
as he had risked his life, and the only reward that
he was destined for many years to receive was the
sword voted him by the Legislature of Virginia.[2]

[1] It is of course impossible to prove that but for Clark's conquest the Ohio
would have been made our boundary in 1783, exactly as it is impossible to
prove that but for Wolfe the English would not have taken Quebec.   But
when we take into account the determined efforts of Spain and France to
confine us to the land east of the Alleghanies, and then to the land southeast
of the Ohio, the slavishness of Congress in instructing our commissioners to
do whatever France wished, and the readiness shown by one of the commissioners, Franklin, to follow these instructions, it certainly looks as if there
would not even have been an effort made by us to get the northwestern territory had we not already possessed it, thanks to Clark.   As it was, it was
only owing to Jay's broad patriotism and stern determination that our western
boundaries were finally made so far-reaching.   None of our early diplomats did
as much for the west as Jay, whom at one time the whole west hated and reviled ;
Mann Butler, whose politics are generally very sound, deserves especial credit
for the justice he does the New Yorker.
     It is idle to talk of the conquest as being purely a Virginian affair.   It was
conquered by Clark, a Virginian, with some scant help from Virginia, but it
was retained only owing to the power of the United States and the patriotism
of such northern statesmen as Jay, Adams, and Franklin, the negotiators of
the final treaty.   Had Virginia alone been in interest, Great Britain would
not have even paid her claims the compliment of listening to them.   Virginia's
share in the history of the nation has ever been gallant and leading ; but the
Revolutionary war was emphatically fought by Americans for America ; no
part could have won without the help of the whole, and every victory was
thus a victory for all, in which all alike can take pride.
     [2] A probably truthful tradition reports that when the Virginian commis-
sioners offered Clark the sword, the grim old fighter, smarting under the
sense of his wrongs, threw it indignantly from him, telling the envoys that he
demanded from Virginia his just rights and the promised reward of his services, not an empty compliment.

CHAPTER IV.

CONTINUANCE OF THE STRUGGLE IN KENTUCKY AND THE NORTHWEST, 1779-1781.

CLARK's successful campaigns against the Illinois towns and Vincennes, besides giving the Americans a foothold north of the Ohio, were of the utmost importance to Kentucky. Until this time, the Kentucky settlers had been literally fighting for life and home, *Clark's Conquests Benefit Kentucky.* and again and again their strait had been so bad, that it seemed—and was—almost an even chance whether they would be driven from the land. The successful outcome of Clark's expedition temporarily overawed the Indians, and, moreover, made the French towns outposts for the protection of the settlers; so that for several years thereafter the tribes west of the Wabash did but little against the Americans. The confidence of the backwoodsmen in their own ultimate triumph was likewise very much increased; while the fame of the western region was greatly spread abroad. From all these causes it resulted that there was an immediate and great increase of immigration thither, the bulk of the immigrants of course stopping in Kentucky, though a very few, even thus early, went to Illinois. Every settlement in Kentucky was still in jeopardy, and there came moments of dejection, when some of her bravest leaders spoke gloomily of the possibility of the Americans being driven from the land. But these were merely words such as even strong men utter when sore from fresh disaster. After the spring of 1779, there was never any real danger that the whites would be forced to abandon Kentucky.

The land laws which the Virginia Legislature enacted about this time [1] were partly a cause, partly **The Land Laws.** a consequence, of the increased emigration to Kentucky, and of the consequent rise in the value of its wild lands. Long before the Revolution, shrewd and far-seeing speculators had organized land companies to acquire grants of vast stretches of western territory; but the land only acquired an actual value for private individuals after the incoming of settlers. In addition to the companies, many private individuals had acquired rights to tracts of land; some, under the royal proclamation, giving bounties to the officers and soldiers in the French war; others by actual payment into the public treasury.[2] The Virginia Legislature now ratified all titles to regularly surveyed ground claimed under charter, military bounty, and old treasury rights, to the extent of four hundred acres each. Tracts of land were reserved

[1] May, 1779; they did not take effect nor was a land court established until the following fall, when the land office was opened at St. Asaphs, Oct. 13th. Isaac Shelby's claim was the first one considered and granted. He had raised a crop of corn in the country in 1776.

[2] The Ohio Company was the greatest of the companies. There were " also, among private rights, the ancient importation rights, the Henderson Company rights, etc." See Marshall, I., 82.

as bounties for the Virginia troops, both Continentals and militia. Each family of actual settlers
was allowed a settlement right to four hundred
acres for the small sum of nine dollars, and, if very
poor, the land was given them on credit. Every such
settler also acquired a preëmptive right to purchase
a thousand acres adjoining, at the regulation State
price, which was forty pounds, paper money, or forty
dollars in specie, for every hundred acres. One
peculiar provision was made necessary by the system
of settling in forted villages. Every such village was
allowed six hundred and forty acres, which no outsider
could have surveyed or claim, for it was considered
the property of the townsmen, to be held in common
until an equitable division could be made; while
each family likewise had a settlement right to four
hundred acres adjoining the village. The vacant
lands were sold, warrants for a hundred acres costing
forty dollars in specie; but later on, towards the
close of the war, Virginia tried to buoy up her mass
of depreciated paper currency by accepting it nearly
at par for land warrants, thereby reducing the cost
of these to less than fifty cents for a hundred
acres. No warrant applied to a particular spot; it
was surveyed on any vacant or presumably vacant
ground. Each individual had the surveying done
wherever he pleased, the county surveyor usually
appointing some skilled woodsman to act as his
deputy.

In the end the natural result of all this was to
involve half the people of Kentucky in lawsuits
over their land, as there were often two or three

titles to each patch,[1] and the surveys crossed each other in hopeless tangles. Immediately, the system gave a great stimulus to immigration, for it made it easy for any incoming settler to get title to his farm, and it also strongly attracted all land speculators. Many well-to-do merchants or planters of the seaboard sent agents out to buy lands in Kentucky; and these agents either hired the old pioneers, such as Boon and Kenton, to locate and survey the lands, or else purchased their claims from them outright. The advantages of following the latter plan were of course obvious; for the pioneers were sure to have chosen fertile, well-watered spots; and though they asked more than the State, yet, ready money was so scarce, and the depreciation of the currency so great, that even thus the land only cost a few cents an acre.[2]

[1] McAfee MSS.

[2] From the Clay MSS. "Virginia, Frederick Co. to wit: This day came William Smith of [illegible] before me John A. Woodcock, a Justice of the peace of same county, who being of full age deposeth and saith that about the first of June 1780, being in Kentuckey and empowered to purchase Land, for Mr. James Ware, he the deponent agreed with a certain Simon Kenton of Kentucky for 1000 Acres of Land about 2 or 3 miles from the big salt spring on Licking, that the sd. Kenton on condition that the sd. Smith would pay him £100 in hand and £100 more when sd. Land was surveyed, . . . sd. Kenton on his part wou'd have the land surveyed, and a fee Simple made there to. . . . sd. Land was first rate Land and had a good Spring thereon. . . . he agreed to warrant and defend the same . . . against all persons whatsoever. . . . sworn too before me this 17th day of Nov. 1789." Later on, the purchaser, who did not take possession of the land for eight or nine years, feared it would not prove as fertile as Kenton had said, and threatened to sue Kenton; but Kenton evidently had the whip-hand in the controversy, for the land being out in the wilderness, the purchaser did not know its exact location, and when he threatened suit, and asked to be shown it, Kenton "swore that he would not shoe it at all." Letter of James Ware, Nov. 29, 1789.

Thus it came about that with the fall of 1779 a
strong stream of emigration set towards Kentucky,
from the backwoods districts of Pennsyl-   **Inrush of**
vania, Virginia, and North Carolina. In   **Settlers.**
company with the real settlers came many land
speculators, and also many families of weak, ir-
resolute, or shiftless people, who soon tired of the
ceaseless and grinding frontier strife for life, and
drifted back to the place whence they had come.[1]
Thus there were ever two tides—the larger setting
towards Kentucky, the lesser towards the old States;
so that the two streams passed each other on the
Wilderness road—for the people who came down
the Ohio could not return against the current.
Very many who did not return nevertheless found
they were not fitted to grapple with the stern
trials of existence on the border. Some of these
succumbed outright; others unfortunately survived,
and clung with feeble and vicious helplessness to the
skirts of their manlier fellows; and from them have
descended the shiftless squatters, the "mean whites,"
the listless, uncouth men who half-till their patches

---

[1] Thus the increase of population is to be measured by the net gain of
immigration over emigration, not by immigration alone. It is probably
partly neglect of this fact, and partly simple exaggeration, that make the early
statements of the additions to the Kentucky population so very untrustworthy. In 1783, at the end of the Revolution, the population of Kentucky
was probably nearer 12,000 than 20,000, and it had grown steadily each year.
Yet Butler quotes Floyd as saying that in the spring of 1780 three hundred
large family boats arrived at the Falls, which would mean an increase of
perhaps four or five thousand people; and in the McAfee MSS. occurs the
statement that in 1779 and 1780 nearly 20,000 people came to Kentucky.
Both of these statements are probably mere estimates, greatly exaggerated;
any westerner of to-day can instance similar reports of movements to western
localities, which under a strict census dwindled wofully.

of poor soil, and still cumber the earth in out-of-the-way nooks from the crannies of the Alleghanies to the canyons of the southern Rocky Mountains.

In April, before this great rush of immigration began, but when it was clearly foreseen that it would immediately take place, the county court of Kentucky issued a proclamation to the new settlers, recommending them to keep as united and compact as possible, settling in "stations" or forted towns; and likewise advising each settlement to choose three or more trustees to take charge of their public affairs.[1] Their recommendations and advice were generally followed.

During 1779 the Indian war dragged on much as usual. The only expedition of importance was that **Bowman** undertaken in May by one hundred and **Attacks** sixty Kentuckians, commanded by the **Chillicothe.** county lieutenant, John Bowman,[2] against the Indian town of Chillicothe. Logan, Harrod, and other famous frontier fighters went along. The town was surprised, several cabins burned, and a

[1] Durrett MSS., in the bound volume of "Papers relating to Louisville and Kentucky." On May 1, 1780, the people living at the Falls, having established a town, forty-six of them signed a petition to have their title made good against Conolly. On Feb. 7, 1781, John Todd and five other trustees of Louisville met; they passed resolutions to erect a grist mill and make surveys.

[2] MS. "Notes on Kentucky," by George Bradford, who went there in 1779; in the Durrett collection. Haldimand MSS., Letter of Henry Bird, June 9, 1779. As this letter is very important, and gives for the first time the Indian side, I print it in the Appendix almost in full. The accounts of course conflict somewhat; chiefly as to the number of cabins burnt—from five to forty, and of horses captured—from thirty to three hundred. They agree in all essential points. But as among the whites themselves there is one serious question. Logan's admirers, and most Kentucky historians, hold Bowman responsible for the defeat; but in reality (see Butler, p. 110) there seems strong reason to believe that it was simply due to the unexpectedly strong

number of horses captured. But the Indians rallied, and took refuge in a central block-house and a number of strongly built cabins surrounding it, from which they fairly beat off the whites. They then followed to harass the rear of their retreating foes, but were beaten off in turn. Of the whites, nine were killed and two or three wounded; the Indians' loss was two killed and five or six wounded.

The defeat caused intense mortification to the whites; but in reality the expedition was of great service to Kentucky, though the Kentuckians never knew it. The Detroit people had been busily organizing expeditions against Kentucky. Captain Henry Bird had been given charge of one, and he had just collected two hundred Indians at the Mingo town when news of the attack on Chillicothe arrived. Instantly the Indians dissolved in a panic, some returning to defend their towns; others were inclined to beg peace of the Americans. So great was their terror that it was found impossible to persuade them to make any inroad as long as they deemed themselves menaced by a counter attack of the Kentuckians.[1]

It is true that bands of Mingos, Hurons, Delawares, and Shawnees made occasional successful raids against the frontier, and brought their scalps and prisoners in triumph to Detroit,[2] where they drank such astonishing quantities of rum as to incite the indignation

resistance of the Indians. Bird's letter shows, what the Kentuckians never suspected, that the attack was a great benefit to them in frightening the Indians and stopping a serious inroad. It undoubtedly accomplished more than Clark's attack on Piqua next year, for instance.

[1] Haldimand MSS. De Peyster to Haldimand, Nov. 20, 1779.
[2] Haldimand MSS. De Peyster to Haldimand, Oct. 20, 1779.

of the British commander-in-chief.[1] But instead of
being able to undertake any formidable expedition
against the settlers, the Detroit authorities were
during this year much concerned for their own
safety, taking every possible means to provide for
the defence, and keeping a sharp look-out for any
hostile movement of the Americans.[2]

The incoming settlers were therefore left in comparative peace. They built many small palisaded
towns, some of which proved permanent, while
others vanished utterly when the fear of the Indians
was removed and the families were able to scatter
out on their farms. At the Falls of the Ohio a
regular fort was built, armed with cannon and garrisoned by Virginia troops,[3] who were sent down the
river expressly to reinforce Clark. The Indians
never dared assail this fort; but they ravaged up to
its walls, destroying the small stations on Bear Grass
Creek and scalping settlers and soldiers when they
wandered far from the protection of the stockade.

The new-comers of 1779 were destined to begin
with a grim experience, for the ensuing winter [4] was
The Hard the most severe ever known in the west, and
Winter.   was long recalled by the pioneers as the
"hard winter." Cold weather set in towards the end
of November, the storms following one another in
unbroken succession, while the snow lay deep until
the spring. Most of the cattle, and very many of the

[1] Haldimand MSS. Haldimand's letter, July 23, 1779.

[2] Haldimand MSS., April 8, 1779.

[3] One hundred and fifty strong, under Col. George Slaughter.

[4] Boon, in his Narrative, makes a mistake in putting this hard winter a year
later; all the other authorities are unanimous against him.

horses, perished; and deer and elk were likewise found dead in the woods, or so weak and starved that they would hardly move out of the way, while the buffalo often came up at nightfall to the yards, seeking to associate with the starving herds of the settlers.[1] The scanty supply of corn gave out, until there was not enough left to bake into johnny-cakes on the long boards in front of the fire.[2]   Even at the Falls, where there were stores for the troops, the price of corn went up nearly fourfold,[3] while elsewhere among the stations of the interior it could not be had at any price, and there was an absolute dearth both of salt and of vegetable food, the settlers living for weeks on the flesh of the lean wild game,[4] especially of the buffalo.[5] The hunters searched with especial eagerness for the bears in the hollow trees, for they alone among the animals kept fat; and the breast of the wild turkey served for bread.[6]   Nevertheless, even in the midst of this season of cold and famine, the settlers began to take the first steps for the education of their children. In this year Joseph Doniphan, whose son long afterwards won fame in the Mexican war, opened the first

[1] McAfee MSS. Of the McAfees' horses ten died, and only two survived, a brown mare and "a yellow horse called Chickasaw."   Exactly a hundred years later, in the hard winter of 1879-80, and the still worse winter of 1880-81, the settlers on the Yellowstone and the few hunters who wintered on the Little Missouri had a similar experience.   The buffalo crowded with the few tame cattle round the hayricks and log-stables; the starving deer and antelope gathered in immense bands in sheltered places.   Riding from my ranch to a neighbor's I have, in deep snows, passed through herds of antelope that would barely move fifty or a hundred feet out of my way.

[2] *Do.*

[3] From fifty dollars (Continental money) a bushel in the fall to one hundred and seventy-five in the spring.

[4] McAfee MSS.   [5] Boon's Narrative.   [6] McAfee MSS.

regular school at Boonsborough,[1] and one of the Mc-
Afees likewise served as a teacher through the winter.[2] But from the beginning some of the settlers'
wives had now and then given the children in the
forts a few weeks' schooling.

Through the long, irksome winter, the frontiersmen remained crowded within the stockades. The
men hunted, while the women made the clothes, of
tanned deer-hides, buffalo-wool cloth, and nettle-
bark linen. In stormy weather, when none could
stir abroad, they turned or coopered the wooden
vessels; for tin cups were as rare as iron forks, and
the "noggin" was either hollowed out of the knot
of a tree, or else made with small staves and hoops.[3]
Every thing was of home manufacture—for there
was not a store in Kentucky,—and the most expensive domestic products seem to have been the hats,
made of native fur, mink, coon, fox, wolf, and beaver.
If exceptionally fine, and of valuable fur, they cost
five hundred dollars in paper money, which had not
at that time depreciated a quarter as much in outlying Kentucky as at the seat of government.[4]

As soon as the great snow-drifts began to melt,
and thereby to produce freshets of unexampled
height, the gaunt settlers struggled out to their
clearings, glad to leave the forts. They planted
corn, and eagerly watched the growth of the crop;
and those who hungered after oatmeal or wheaten
bread planted other grains as well, and apple-seeds
and peach-stones.[5]

[1] *Historical Magazine*, Second Series, Vol. VIII.
[2] McAfee MSS. [3] McAfee MSS. [4] Marshall, p. 124. [5] McAfee MSS.

As soon as the spring of 1780 opened, the immigrants began to arrive more numerously than ever.
Some came over the Wilderness road; Many New
among these there were not a few hag- Settlers Ar-
gard, half-famished beings, who, having rive in the
started too late the previous fall, had Spring.
been overtaken by the deep snows, and forced to
pass the winter in the iron-bound and desolate
valleys of the Alleghanies, subsisting on the carcasses
of their stricken cattle, and seeing their weaker
friends starve or freeze before their eyes. Very
many came down the Ohio, in flat-boats. A good-
sized specimen of these huge unwieldly scows was
fifty-five feet long, twelve broad, and six deep,
drawing three feet of water[1]; but the demand was
greater than the supply, and a couple of dozen people, with half as many horses, and all their effects,
might be forced to embark on a flat-boat not
twenty-four feet in length.[2] Usually several families came together, being bound by some tie of
neighborhood or purpose. Not infrequently this tie
was religious, for in the back setlements the few
churches were almost as much social as religious
centres. Thus this spring, a third of the congregation of a Low Dutch Reformed Church came
to Kentucky bodily, to the number of fifty heads
of families, with their wives and children, their
beasts of burden and pasture, and their household goods; like most bands of new immigrants,

[1] Lettres d'un Cultivateur Américain, St. John de Creve Cœur, Paris, 1787.
p. 407. He visited Kentucky in 1784.

[2] MS. Journals of Rev. James Smith. Tours in western country in 1785–
1795 (in Col. Durrett's library).

they suffered greatly from the Indians, much more than did the old settlers.[1] The following year a Baptist congregation came out from Virginia, keeping up its organization even while on the road, the preacher holding services at every long halt.

Soon after the rush of spring immigration was at its height, the old settlers and the new-comers alike **De Peyster** were thrown into the utmost alarm by a **at Detroit.** formidable inroad of Indians, accompanied by French partisans, and led by a British officer. De Peyster, a New York tory of old Knickerbocker family, had taken command at Detroit. He gathered the Indians around him from far and near, until the expense of subsidizing these savages became so enormous as to call forth serious complaints from head-quarters.[2] He constantly endeavored to equip and send out different bands, not only to retake the Illinois and Vincennes, but to dislodge Clark from the Falls[3]; he was continually receiving scalps and prisoners, and by May he had fitted out two thousand warriors to act along the Ohio and the Wabash.[4] The rapid growth of Kentucky especially excited his apprehension,[5] and his main stroke was directed against the clusters of wooden forts that were springing up south of the Ohio.[6]

Late in May, some six hundred Indians and a few Canadians, with a couple of pieces of light field

---

[1] State Department MSS. No. 41, Vol. V., Memorials K, L, 1777–1787, pp. 95–97, Petition of Low Dutch Reformed Church, etc.

[2] Haldimand MSS. Haldimand to Guy Johnson, June 30, 1780.

[3] *Do.* Haldimand to De Peyster, Feb. 12 and July 6, 1780.

[4] *Do.* De Peyster to Haldimand, June 1, 1780.

[5] *Do.* March 8, 1780.   [6] *Do.* May 17 to July 19, 1780.

artillery, were gathered and put under the command
of Captain Henry Bird. Following the rivers where
practicable, that he might the easier carry   **Bird's**
his guns, he went down the Miami, and   **Inroad.**
on the 22d of June, surprised and captured without
resistance Ruddle's and Martin's stations, two small
stockades on the South Fork of the Licking.[1]   But
Bird was not one of the few men fitted to command
such a force as that which followed him ; and con-
tenting himself with the slight success he had won,
he rapidly retreated to Detroit, over the same path
by which he had advanced. The Indians carried off
many horses, and loaded their prisoners with the
plunder, tomahawking those, chiefly women and
children, who could not keep up with the rest ; and
Bird could not control them nor force them to show
mercy to their captives.[2] He did not even get his
cannon back to Detroit, leaving them at the British
store in one of the upper Miami towns, in charge of
a bombardier. The bombardier did not prove a very
valorous personage, and on the alarm of Clark's advance, soon afterwards, he permitted the Indians to
steal his horses, and was forced to bury his ordnance
in the woods.[3]

[1] He marched overland from the forks of the Licking.   Marshall says the
season was dry and the waters low; but the Bradford MSS. particularly declare
that Bird only went up the Licking at all because the watercourses were so
full, and that he had originally intended to attack the settlements at the Falls.

[2] Collins, Butler, etc. Marshall thinks that if the force could have been
held together it would have depopulated Kentucky ; but this is nonsense,
for within a week Clark had gathered a very much larger and more efficient
body of troops.

[3] Haldimand MSS.   Letter of Bombardier Wm. Homan, Aug. 18, 1780.
He speaks of "the gun" and "the smaller ordnance," presumably swivels.
It is impossible to give Bird's numbers correctly, for various bands of
Indians kept joining and leaving him.

Before this inroad took place Clark had been planning a foray into the Indian country, and the news only made him hasten his prepara-tions. In May this adventurous leader had performed one of the feats which made him the darling of the backwoodsmen. Painted and dressed like an Indian so as to deceive the lurking bands of savages, he and two companions left the fort he had built on the bank of the Missis-sippi, and came through the wilderness to Harrods-burg. They lived on the buffaloes they shot, and when they came to the Tennessee River, which was then in flood, they crossed the swift torrent on a raft of logs bound together with grapevines. At Harrodsburg they found the land court open, and thronged with an eager, jostling crowd of settlers and speculators, who were waiting to enter lands in the surveyor's office. Even the dread of the Indians could not overcome in these men's hearts the keen and selfish greed for gain. Clark instantly grasped the situation. Seeing that while the court remained open he could get no volunteers, he on his own responsibility closed it off-hand, and proclaimed that it would not be opened until after he came back from his expedition. The speculators grumbled and clamored, but this troubled Clark not at all, for he was able to get as many volunteers as he wished. The discontent, and still more the panic over Bird's inroad, made many of the settlers determine to flee from the country, but Clark sent a small force to Crab Orchard, at the mouth of the Wilderness road, the only outlet from Kentucky, with instructions to

Clark Hears the News.

stop all men from leaving the country, and to take away their arms if they persisted; while four fifths of all the grown men were drafted, and were bidden to gather instantly for a campaign.[1]

He appointed the mouth of the Licking as the place of meeting. Thither he brought the troops from the Falls in light skiffs he had built for the pur-
pose, leaving behind scarce a handful of men to garrison the stockade. Logan went with him as second in command. He carried with him a light three-pounder gun; and those of the men who had horses marched along the bank beside the flotilla. The only mishap that befell the troops happened to McGarry, who had a subordinate command. He showed his usual foolhardy obstinacy by persisting in landing with a small squad of men on the north bank of the river, where he was in consequence surprised and roughly handled by a few Indians. Nothing was done to him because of his disobedience, for the chief of such a backwoods levy was the leader, rather than the commander, of his men.

His Campaign against Piqua.

At the mouth of the Licking Clark met the riflemen from the interior stations, among them being Kenton, Harrod, and Floyd, and others of equal note. They had turned out almost to a man, leaving the women and boys to guard the wooden forts until they came back, and had come to the appointed place, some on foot or on horseback, others floating and paddling down the Licking in canoes. They left scanty provisions with their families, who had to subsist during their absence on what game the boys shot, on nettle,

[1] Bradford MSS.

tops, and a few early vegetables; and they took with them still less. Dividing up their stock, each man had a couple of pounds of meal and some jerked venison or buffalo meat.[1]

All his troops having gathered, to the number of nine hundred and seventy, Clark started up the Ohio on the second of August.[2] The skiffs, laden with men, were poled against the current, while bodies of footmen and horsemen marched along the bank. After going a short distance up stream the horses and men were ferried to the farther bank, the boats were drawn up on the shore and left, with a guard of forty men, and the rest of the troops started overland against the town of Old Chillicothe, fifty or sixty miles distant. The three-pounder was carried along on a pack-horse. The march was hard, for it rained so incessantly that it was difficult to keep the rifles dry. Every night they encamped in a hollow square, with the baggage and horses in the middle.

Chillicothe, when reached, was found to be deserted. It was burned, and the army pushed on to Piqua, a town a few miles distant, on the banks of the Little Miami,[3] reaching it about ten in the morning of the 8th of August.[4] Piqua was substantially

---

[1] McAfee MSS.; the Bradford MS. says six quarts of parched corn.

[2] This date and number are those given in the Bradford MS. The McAfee MSS. say July 1st; but it is impossible that the expedition should have started so soon after Bird's inroad. On July 1st, Bird himself was probably at the mouth of the Licking.

[3] The Indians so frequently shifted their abode that it is hardly possible to identify the exact location of the successive towns called Piqua or Pickaway.

[4] "Papers relating to G. R. Clark." In the Durrett MSS. at Louisville. The account of the death of Joseph Rogers. This settles, by the way, that the march was made in August, and not in July.

built, and was laid out in the manner of the French villages. The stoutly built log-houses stood far apart, surrounded by strips of corn-land, and fronting the stream ; while a strong block-house with loop-holed walls stood in the middle. Thick woods, broken by small prairies, covered the rolling country that lay around the town.

Clark divided his army into four divisions, taking the command of two in person. Giving the others to Logan, he ordered him to cross the river **The Fight** above the town [1] and take it in the rear, **at Piqua.** while he himself crossed directly below it and assailed it in front. Logan did his best to obey the orders, but he could not find a ford, and he marched by degrees nearly three miles up stream, making repeated and vain attempts to cross ; when he finally succeeded the day was almost done, and the fighting was over.

Meanwhile Clark plunged into the river, and crossed at the head of one of his own two divisions ; the other was delayed for a short time. Both Simon Girty and his brother were in the town, together with several hundred Indian warriors ; exactly how many cannot be said, but they were certainly fewer in number than the troops composing either wing of Clark's army. [2] They were surprised by Clark's swift

[1] There is some conflict as to whether Logan went up or down stream.

[2] Haldimand MSS. McKee to De Peyster, Aug. 22, 1780. He was told of the battle by the Indians a couple of days after it took place. He gives the force of the whites correctly as nine hundred and seventy, forty of whom had been left to guard the boats. He says the Indians were surprised, and that most of the warriors fled, so that all the fighting was done by about seventy, with the two Girtys. This was doubtless not the case ; the beaten party in all these encounters was fond of relating the valorous deeds of some of its

advance just as a scouting party of warriors, who had been sent out to watch the whites, were returning to the village. The warning was so short that the squaws and children had barely time to retreat out of the way. As Clark crossed the stream, the warriors left their cabins and formed in some thick timber behind them. At the same moment a cousin of Clark's, who had been captured by the Indians, and was held prisoner in the town, made his escape and ran towards the Americans, throwing up his hands, and calling out that he was a white man. He was shot, whether by the Americans or the Indians none could say. Clark came up and spoke a few words with him before he died.[1] A long-range skirmish ensued with the warriors in the timber ; but on the approach of Clark's second division the Indians fell back. The two divisions followed in pursuit, becoming mingled in disorder. After a slight running fight of two hours the whites lost sight of their foes, and, wondering what had become of Logan's wing, they gathered to-

members, who invariably state that they would have conquered, had they not been deserted by their associates. McKee reported that the Indians could find no trace of the gun-wheels—the gun was carried on a pack-horse,—and so he thought that the Kentuckians were forced to leave it behind on their retreat. He put the killed of the Kentuckians at the modest number of forty-eight ; and reported the belief of Girty and the Indians that " three hundred [of them] would have given [Clark's men] a total rout." A very common feat of the small frontier historian was to put high praise of his own side in the mouth of a foe. Withers, in his " Chronicles of Border Warfare," in speaking of this very action, makes Girty withdraw his three hundred warriors on account of the valor of Clark's men, remarking that it was "useless to fight with fools or madmen." This offers a comical contrast to Girty's real opinion, as shown in McKee's letter.

[1] Durrett MSS. Volume : " Papers referring to G. R. Clark." The cousin's name was Joseph Rogers, a brother of the commander of the galley.

gether and marched back towards the river. One
of the McAfees, captain over a company of riflemen from Salt River, was leading, when he discovered an Indian in a tree-top. He and one of his
men sought shelter behind the same tree; whereupon
he tried to glide behind another, but was shot and
mortally wounded by the Indian, who was himself
instantly killed. The scattered detachments now sat
down to listen for the missing wing. After half an
hour's silent waiting, they suddenly became aware of
the presence of a body of Indians, who had slipped
in between them and the town. The backwoodsmen
rushed up to the attack, while the Indians whooped
and yelled defiance. There was a moment's heavy
firing; but as on both sides the combatants carefully
sheltered themselves behind trees, there was very little loss; and the Indians steadily gave way until they
reached the town, about two miles distant from the
spot where the whites had halted. They then made a
stand, and, for the first time, there occurred some real
fighting. The Indians stood stoutly behind the loop-
holed walls of the cabins, and in the block-house;
the Americans, advancing cautiously and gaining
ground inch by inch, suffered much more loss than
they inflicted. Late in the afternoon Clark managed
to bring the three-pounder into action, from a point
below the town; while the riflemen fired at the red
warriors as they were occasionally seen running from
the cabins to take refuge behind the steep bank of
the river. A few shots from the three-pounder dis-
lodged the defenders of the block-house; and about
sunset the Americans closed in, but only to find

that their foes had escaped under cover of a noisy fire from a few of the hindmost warriors. They had run up stream, behind the banks, until they came to a small "branch" or brook, by means of which they gained the shelter of the forest, where they at once scattered and disappeared. A few of their stragglers exchanged shots with the advance guard of Logan's wing as it at last came down the bank ; this was the only part Logan was able to take in the battle. Of the Indians six or eight were slain, whereas the whites lost seventeen killed, and a large number wounded.[1] Clark destroyed all the houses and a very large quantity of corn ; and he sent out detachments which destroyed another village, and the stores of some British and French Canadian traders. Then the army marched back to the mouth of the Licking and disbanded, most of the volunteers having been out just twenty-five days.[2]

The Indians were temporarily cowed by their loss and the damage they had suffered,[3] and especially by the moral effect of so formidable a retaliatory

[1] Bradford MS. ; the McAfee MSS. make the loss " 15 or 20 Indians " in the last assault, and " nearly as many " whites. Boon's narrative says seventeen on each side. But McKee says only six Indians were killed and three wounded ; and Bombardier Homan, in the letter already quoted, says six were killed and two captured, who were afterwards slain. The latter adds from hearsay that the Americans cruelly slew an Indian woman ; but there is not a syllable in any of the other accounts to confirm this, and it may be set down as a fiction of the by-no-means-valorous bombardier. The bombardier mentions that the Indians in their alarm and anger immediately burnt all the male prisoners in their villages.

The Kentucky historians give very scanty accounts of this expedition ; but as it was of a typical character it is worth while giving in full. The McAfee MSS. contain most information about it.

[2] Bradford MS.

[3] See Haldimand MSS. De Peyster to Haldimand, Aug. 30, 1780.

foray following immediately on the heels of Bird's inroad. Therefore, thanks to Clark, the settlements south of the Ohio were but little molested   **Effect of** for the remainder of the year.[1]   The bulk **the Victory.** of the savages remained north of the river, hovering about their burned towns, planning to take vengeance in the spring.[2]

Nevertheless small straggling bands of young braves occasionally came down through the woods; and though they did not attack any fort or any large body of men, they were ever on the watch to steal horses, burn lonely cabins, and waylay travellers between the stations. They shot the solitary settlers who had gone out to till their clearings by stealth, or ambushed the boys who were driving in the milk cows or visiting their lines of traps. It was well for the victim if he was killed at once; otherwise he was bound with hickory withes and driven to the distant Indian towns, there to be tortured with hideous cruelty and burned to death at the stake.[3] Boon himself suffered at the hands of one of these parties. He had gone with his brother to the Blue Licks, to him a spot always fruitful of evil; and being ambushed by the Indians, his brother was killed, and he himself was only saved by his woodcraft and speed of foot. The Indians had with them a tracking dog, by the aid of which they followed his trail for three miles; until he halted, shot the dog, and thus escaped.[4]

[1] McAfee MSS.   [2] Virginia State Papers, I., 451.
[3] McAfee MSS.   The last was an incident that happened to a young man named McCoun on March 8, 1781.   [4] Boon's Narrative.

During this comparatively peaceful fall the settlers fared well; though the men were ever on the
Life watch for Indian war parties, while the
of the mothers, if their children were naughty,
Settlers. frightened them into quiet with the threat
that the Shawnees would catch them. The widows
and the fatherless were cared for by the other
families of the different stations. The season of
want and scarcity had passed for ever; from thenceforth on there was abundance in Kentucky. The
crops did not fail; not only was there plenty of
corn, the one essential, but there was also wheat,
as well as potatoes, melons, pumpkins, turnips, and
the like. Sugar was made by tapping the maple
trees; but salt was bought at a very exorbitant price
at the Falls, being carried down in boats from the
old Redstone Fort. Flax had been generally sown
(though in the poorer settlements nettle bark still
served as a substitute), and the young men and girls
formed parties to pick it, often ending their labor
by an hour or two's search for wild plums. The men
killed all the game they wished, and so there was
no lack of meat. They also surveyed the land and
tended the stock—cattle, horses, and hogs, which
throve and multiplied out on the range, fattening
on the cane, and large white buffalo-clover. At odd
times the men and boys visited their lines of traps.
Furs formed almost the only currency, except a little
paper money; but as there were no stores west of
the mountains, this was all that was needed, and
each settlement raised most things for itself, and
procured the rest by barter.

The law courts were as yet very little troubled, each small community usually enforcing a rough-and-ready justice of its own. On a few of the streams log-dams were built, and tub-mills started. In Harrodsburg a toll mill was built in 1779. The owner used to start it grinding, and then go about his other business; once on returning he found a large wild turkey-gobbler so busily breakfasting out of the hopper that he was able to creep quietly up and catch him with his hands. The people all worked together in cultivating their respective lands; coming back to the fort before dusk for supper. They would then call on any man who owned a fiddle and spend the evening, with interludes of singing and story-telling, in dancing—an amusement they considered as only below hunting. On Sundays the stricter parents taught their children the catechism; but in spite of the presence of not a few devout Baptists and Presbyterians there was little chance for general observance of religious forms. Ordinary conversation was limited to such subjects as bore on the day's doings; the game that had been killed, the condition of the crops, the plans of the settlers for the immediate future, the accounts of the last massacre by the savages, or the rumor that Indian sign had been seen in the neighborhood; all interspersed with much banter, practical joking, and rough, good-humored fun. The scope of conversation was of necessity narrowly limited even for the backwoods; for there was little chance to discuss religion and politics, the two subjects that the average backwoodsman regards as the staples of deep conversation. The deeds of the Indians of course formed the one absorbing topic.[1]

An abortive separatist movement was the chief political sensation of this summer. Many hundreds **An Abortive** and even thousand of settlers from the **Separatist** backwoods districts of various States, had **Movement.** come to Kentucky, and some even to Illinois, and a number of them were greatly discontented with the Virginian rule. They deemed it too difficult to get justice when they were so far from the seat of government; they objected to the land being granted to any but actual settlers; and they protested against being taxed, asserting that they did not know whether the country really belonged to Virginia or the United States. Accordingly, they petitioned the Continental Congress that Kentucky and Illinois combined might be made into a separate State;[2] but no heed was paid to their request, nor did their leading men join in making it.

In November the Virginia Legislature divided Kentucky into the three counties of Jefferson, **Kentucky** Lincoln, and Fayette, appointing for each **Divided into** a colonel, a lieutenant-colonel, and a **Counties.** surveyor. The three colonels, who were also justices of the counties,[3] were, in their order, John Floyd—whom Clark described as "a soldier, a gentleman and a scholar,"[4]—Benjamin Logan, and John Todd. Clark, whose station was at the

---

[1] For all this see McAfee MSS.

[2] State Department MSS. No. 48. See Appendix G. As containing an account of the first, and hitherto entirely unnoticed, separatist movement in Kentucky, I give the petition entire.

[3] Calendar of Virginia State Papers, Vol. II., p. 47. [4] *Do.*, Vol. I., p. 452.

Falls of the Ohio, was brigadier-general and commander over all. Boon was lieutenant-colonel under Todd; and their county of Fayette had for its surveyor Thomas Marshall, [1] the father of the great chief-justice, whose services to the United States stand on a plane with those of Alexander Hamilton. [2]

The winter passed quietly away, but as soon as the snow was off the ground in 1781, the Indians renewed their ravages. Early in the winter Clark went to Virginia to try to get an army for an expedition against Detroit. He likewise applied to Washington for assistance. Washington fully entered into his plans, and saw their importance. He would gladly have rendered him every aid. But he could do nothing, because of the impotence to which the central authority, the Continental Congress, had been reduced by the selfishness and supine indifference of the various States—Virginia among the number. He wrote Clark : " It is out of my power to send any reinforcements to the westward. If the States would fill their continental battalions we should be able to oppose a regular and permanent force to the enemy in every quarter. If they will not, they must certainly take measures to defend themselves by their militia, however expensive and ruinous the system." [3]   It was impossible to state

Clark's Plans to Attack Detroit.

---

[1] Collins, I., 20.

[2] Roughly, Fayette embraced the territory north and northeast of the Kentucky River, Jefferson that between Green River and the lower Kentucky, and Lincoln the rest of the present State.

[3] State Department MSS., No. 147, Vol. V.   Reports of Board of War. Letter of Washington, June 8, 1781. It is impossible to study any part of the Revolutionary struggle without coming to the conclusion that Washington would have ended it in half the time it actually lasted, had the jangling

with more straightforward clearness the fact that Kentucky owed the unprotected condition in which she was left, to the divided or States-rights system of government that then existed; and that she would have had ample protection—and incidentally greater liberty—had the central authority been stronger.

At last, Clark was empowered to raise the men he wished, and he passed and repassed from Fort Pitt to **Why his** the Falls of the Ohio and thence to the **Efforts were** Illinois in the vain effort to get troops. **Baffled.** The inertness and shortsightedness of the frontiersmen, above all the exhaustion of the States, and their timid selfishness and inability to enforce their commands, baffled all of Clark's efforts. In his letters to Washington he bitterly laments his enforced dependence upon "persuasive arguments to draw the inhabitants of the country into the field."[1] The Kentuckians were anxious to do all in their power, but of course only a comparatively small number could be spared for so long a campaign from their scattered stockades. Around Pittsburg, where he hoped to raise the bulk of his forces, the frontiersmen were split into little factions by their petty local rivalries, the envy their

States and their governments, as well as the Continental Congress, backed him up half as effectively as the Confederate people and government backed up Lee, or as the Northerners and the Washington administration backed up McClellan—still more as they backed up Grant. The whole of our Revolutionary history is a running commentary on the anarchic weakness of disunion, and the utter lack of liberty that follows in its train.

[1] State Department MSS. Letters to Washington, Vol. 49, p. 235, May 21, 1781. The entire history of the western operations shows the harm done by the weak and divided system of government that obtained at the time of the Revolution, and emphasizes our good fortune in replacing it by a strong and permanent Union.

leaders felt of Clark himself, and the never-ending jealousies and bickerings between the Virginians and Pennsylvanians.[1]

The fort at the Falls, where Clark already had some troops, was appointed as a gathering-place for the different detachments that were to join him; but from one cause or another, all save one or two failed to appear. Most of them did not even start, and one body of Pennsylvanians that did go met with an untoward fate. This was a party of a hundred Westmoreland men under their county-lieutenant, Col. Archibald Loughry. They started down the Ohio in flat-boats, but having landed on a sand bar to butcher and cook a buffalo that they had killed, they were surprised by an equal number of Indians under Joseph Brant, and being huddled together, were all slain or captured with small loss to their assailants.[2] Many of the prisoners, including Loughry himself, were afterwards murdered in cold blood by the Indians.

During this year the Indians continually harassed the whole frontier, from Pennsylvania to Kentucky, ravaging the settlements and assailing the forts in great bands of five or six hundred warriors.[3] The

[1] Calendar of Virginia State Papers, I., pp. 502, 597, etc.; II., pp. 108, 116, 264, 345. The Kentuckians were far more eager for action than the Pennsylvanians.

[2] At Loughry's Creek, some ten miles below the mouth of the Miami, on August 24, 1781. Diary of Captain Isaac Anderson, quoted in "Indiana Hist. Soc. Pamphlets, No. 4," by Charles Martindale, Indianapolis, 1888. Collins, whose accuracy by no means equals his thirst for pure detail, puts this occurrence just a year too late. Brant's force was part of a body of several hundred Indians gathered to resist Clark.

[3] It is most difficult to get at the number of the Indian parties; they were sometimes grossly exaggerated and sometimes hopelessly underestimated.

Continental troops stationed at Fort Pitt were reduced to try every expedient to procure supplies.
Fighting on the Frontier. Though it was evident that the numbers of the hostile Indians had largely increased, and that even such tribes as the Delawares, who had been divided, were now united against the Americans, nevertheless, because of the scarcity of food, a party of soldiers had to be sent into the Indian country to kill buffalo, that the garrison might have meat.[1] The Indians threatened to attack the fort itself, as well as the villages it protected; passing around and on each side, their war parties ravaged the country in its rear, distressing greatly the people; and from this time until peace was declared with Great Britain, and indeed until long after that event, the westernmost Pennsylvanians knew neither rest nor safety.[2] Among many others the forted village at Wheeling was again attacked. But its most noteworthy siege occurred during the succeeding summer, when

The commanders at the unmolested forts and the statesmen who stayed at home only saw those members of the tribes who claimed to be peaceful, and invariably put the number of warriors on the warpath at far too low a figure. Madison's estimates, for instance, were very much out of the way, yet many modern critics follow him.

[1] State Department MSS., No. 147, Vol. VI. Reports of Board of War. March 15, 1781.

[2] *Do.*, No. 148, Vol. I., January 4, 1781 ; No. 149, Vol. I., August 6, 1782 ; No. 149, Vol. II., p. 461 ; No. 149, Vol. III., p. 183. Federal garrisons were occasionally established at, or withdrawn from, other posts on the upper Ohio besides Fort Pitt ; but their movements had no permanent value, and only require chronicling by the local, State, or county historians. In 1778 Fort McIntosh was built at Beaver Creek, on the north bank of the Ohio, and Fort Laurens seventy miles towards the interior. The latter was soon abandoned ; the former was in Pennsylvania, and a garrison was kept there.

Simon Girty, with fife and drum, led a large band of
Indians and Detroit rangers against it, only to be
beaten off. The siege was rendered memorable by
the heroism of a girl, who carried powder from the
stockade to an outlying log-house, defended by four
men ; she escaped unscathed because of her very
boldness, in spite of the fire from so many rifles, and
to this day the mountaineers speak of her deed.[1]

It would be tiresome and profitless to so much as
name the many different stations that were attacked.
In their main incidents all the various assaults were
alike, and that made this summer on McAfee's station may be taken as an illustration.

The McAfees brought their wives and children to
Kentucky in the fall of '79, and built a little stockaded hamlet on the banks of Salt River, six or seven
miles from Harrodsburg. Some relatives **The Attack**
and friends joined them, but their station **on McAfee's**
was small and weak. The stockade, on **Station.**
the south side, was very feeble, and there were but
thirteen men, besides the women and children, in

[1] See De Haas, 263–281, for the fullest, and probably most accurate, account
of the siege ; as already explained he is the most trustworthy of the border
historians. But it is absolutely impossible to find out the real facts concerning the sieges of Wheeling ; it is not quite certain even whether there were
two or three. The testimony as to whether the heroine of the powder feat
was Betty Zane or Molly Scott is hopelessly conflicting ; we do not know
which of the two brothers Girty was in command, nor whether either was
present at the first attack. Much even of De Haas' account is, to put it
mildly, greatly embellished ; as for instance his statement about the cannon
(a small French gun, thrown into the Monongahela when Fort Du Quesne
was abandoned, and fished up by a man named Naly, who was in swimming),
which he asserts cut "a wide passage" through the "deep columns" of the
savages. There is no reason to suppose that the Indians suffered a serious
loss. Wheeling was a place of little strategic importance, and its fall
would not have produced any far-reaching effects.

garrison; but they were strong and active, good woodsmen, and excellent marksmen. The attack was made on May 4, 1781.[1]

The Indians lay all night at a corn-crib three-quarters of a mile distant from the stockade. The settlers, though one of their number had been carried off two months before, still continued their usual occupations. But they were very watchful and always kept a sharp look-out, driving the stock inside the yard at night. On the day in question, at dawn, it was noticed that the dogs and cattle betrayed symptoms of uneasiness; for all tame animals dreaded the sight or smell of an Indian as they did that of a wild beast, and by their alarm often warned the settlers and thus saved their lives.

In this case the warning was unheeded. At daybreak the stock were turned loose and four of the men went outside the fort. Two began to clear a patch of turnip-land about a hundred and fifty yards off, leaving their guns against a tree close at hand. The other two started towards the corn-crib, with a horse and bag. After going a quarter of a mile, the path dipped into a hollow, and here they suddenly came on the Indians, advancing stealthily toward the fort. At the first fire one of the men was killed, and the horse, breaking loose, galloped back to the fort. The other man likewise turned and ran towards home, but was confronted by an Indian who leaped into the path directly ahead of him. The two

[1] McAfee MSS. This is the date given in the MS. "Autobiography of Robert McAfee"; the MS. "History of First Settlement on Salt River" says May 6th. I draw my account from these two sources; the discrepancies are trivial.

were so close together that the muzzles of their guns crossed, and both pulled trigger at once ; the Indian's gun missed fire and he fell dead in his tracks. Continuing his flight, the survivor reached the fort in safety.

When the two men in the turnip-patch heard the firing they seized their guns and ran towards the point of attack, but seeing the number of the assailants they turned back to the fort, trying to drive the frightened stock before them. The Indians coming up close, they had to abandon the attempt, although most of the horses and some of the cattle got safely home. One of the men reached the gate ahead of the Indians ; the other was cut off, and took a roundabout route through the woods. He speedily distanced all of his pursuers but one ; several times he turned to shoot the latter, but the Indian always took prompt refuge behind a tree, and the white man then renewed his flight. At last he reach a fenced orchard, on the border of the cleared ground round the fort. Throwing himself over the fence he lay still among the weeds on the other side. In a minute or two the pursuer, running up, cautiously peered over the fence, and was instantly killed ; he proved to be a Shawnee chief, painted, and decked with many silver armlets, rings, and brooches. The fugitive then succeeded in making his way into the fort.

The settlers inside the stockade had sprung to arms the moment the first guns were heard. The men fired on the advancing Indians, while the women and children ran bullets and made ready the rifle-patches. Every one displayed the coolest determina-

tion and courage except one man who hid under a
bed, until found by his wife; whereupon he was
ignominiously dragged out and made to run bullets
with the women.

As the Indians advanced they shot down most of
the cattle and hogs and some of the horses that were
running frantically round the stockade; and they
likewise shot several dogs that had sallied out to
help their masters. They then made a rush on the
fort, but were driven off at once, one of their number
being killed and several badly hurt, while but one
of the defenders was wounded, and he but slightly.
After this they withdrew to cover and began a desultory firing, which lasted for some time.

Suddenly a noise like distant thunder came to the
ears of the men in the fort. It was the beat of
horsehoofs. In a minute or two forty-five horsemen,
headed by McGarry, appeared on the road leading
from Harrodsburg, shouting and brandishing their
rifles as they galloped up. The morning was so
still that the firing had been heard a very long way;
and a band of mounted riflemen had gathered in
hot haste to go to the relief of the beleaguered
stockade.

The Indians, whooping defiance, retired; while
McGarry halted a moment to allow the rescued settlers to bridle their horses—saddles were not thought
of. The pursuit was then begun at full speed. At
the ford of a small creek near by, the rearmost Indians turned and fired at the horsemen, killing one
and wounding another, while a third had his horse
mired down, and was left behind. The main body

was overtaken at the corn-crib, and a running fight
followed; the whites leaving their horses and both
sides taking shelter behind the tree-trunks. Soon
two Indians were killed, and the others scattered in
every direction, while the victors returned in triumph
to the station.

It is worthy of notice that though the Indians
were defeated, and though they were pitted against
first-class rifle shots, they yet had but five   **Slight**
men killed and a very few wounded. They   **Losses of**
rarely suffered a heavy loss in battle with **the Indians.**
the whites, even when beaten in the open or repulsed from a fort. They would not stand heavy
punishment, and in attacking a fort generally relied upon a single headlong rush, made under
cover of darkness or as a surprise; they tried to
unnerve their antagonists by the sudden fury of
their onslaught and the deafening accompaniment
of whoops and yells. If they began to suffer much
loss they gave up at once, and if pursued scattered
in every direction, each man for himself, and owing
to their endurance, woodcraft, and skill in hiding,
usually got off with marvellously little damage. At
the outside a dozen of their men might be killed in
the pursuit by such of the vengeful backwoodsmen
as were exceptionally fleet of foot. The northwestern
tribes at this time appreciated thoroughly that their
marvellous fighting qualities were shown to best advantage in the woods, and neither in the defence nor
in the assault of fortified places. They never cooped
themselves in stockades to receive an attack from
the whites, as was done by the Massachusetts Al-

gonquins in the seventeenth century, and by the
Creeks at the beginning of the nineteenth; and it
was only when behind defensive works from which
they could not retreat that the forest Indians ever
suffered heavily when defeated by the whites. On
the other hand, the defeat of the average white force
was usually followed by a merciless slaughter.
Skilled backwoodsmen scattered out, Indian fashion,
but their less skilful or more panic-struck brethren, and all regulars or ordinary militia, kept together from a kind of blind feeling of safety in com-
panionship, and in consequence their nimble and
ruthless antagonists destroyed them at their ease.

Still, the Indian war parties were often checked,
or scattered; and occasionally one of them received
Indian War some signal discomfiture. Such was the
Parties case with a band that went up the Kan-
Repulsed. awha valley just as Clark was descending the Ohio on his way to the Illinois. Finding
the fort at the mouth of the Kanawha too strong
to be carried, they moved on up the river towards
the Greenbriar settlements, their chiefs shouting
threateningly to the people in the fort, and taunt-
ing them with the impending destruction of their
friends and kindred. But two young men in
the stockade forthwith dressed and painted themselves like Indians, that they might escape notice
even if seen, and speeding through the woods
reached the settlements first and gave warning. The
settlers took refuge on a farm where there was a
block-house with a stockaded yard. The Indians
attacked in a body at daybreak when the door was
opened, thinking to rush into the house; but they

were beaten off, and paid dear for their boldness, for seventeen of them were left dead in the yard, besides the killed and wounded whom they carried away.[1] In the same year a block-house was attacked while the children were playing outside. The Indians in their sudden rush killed one settler, wounded four, and actually got inside the house; yet three were killed or disabled, and they were driven out by the despairing fury of the remaining whites, the women fighting together with the men. Then the savages instantly fled, but they had killed and scalped, or carried off, ten of the children. Be it remembered that these instances are taken at random from among hundreds of others, extending over a series of years longer than the average life of a generation.

The Indians warred with the odds immeasurably in their favor. The Ohio was the boundary between their remaining hunting-grounds and the lands where the whites had settled. In Kentucky alone this frontier was already seventy miles in length.[2] Beyond the river stretched the frowning forest, to the

[1] McKee was the commander at the fort; the block-house was owned by Col. Andrew Donelly; Hanlon and Prior were the names of the two young men. This happened in May, 1778. For the anecdotes of personal prowess in this chapter see De Haas, or else Kercheval, McClung, Doddridge, and the fifty other annalists of those western wars, who repeat many of the same stories. All relate facts of undoubted authenticity and wildly improbable tales, resting solely on tradition, with exactly the same faith. The chronological order of these anecdotes being unimportant, I have grouped them here. It must always be remembered that both the men and the incidents described are interesting chiefly as examples; the old annalists give many hundreds of such anecdotes, and there must have been thousands more that they did not relate.

[2] Virginia State Papers, I., 437. Letter of Col. John Floyd. The Kentuckians, he notices, trust militia more than they do regulars.

Indians a sure shield in battle, a secure haven in disaster, an impenetrable mask from behind which **Nature of** to plan attack. Clark, from his post at **the Indian** the Falls, sent out spies and scouts along **Forays.** the banks of the river, and patrolled its waters with his gun-boat; but it was absolutely impossible to stop all the forays or to tell the point likely to be next struck. A war party starting from the wigwam-towns would move silently down through the woods, cross the Ohio at any point, and stealthily and rapidly traverse the settlements, its presence undiscovered until the deeds of murder and rapine were done, and its track marked by charred cabins and the ghastly, mutilated bodies of men, women, and children.

If themselves assailed, the warriors fought desperately and effectively. They sometimes attacked bodies of troops, but always by ambush or surprise; and they much preferred to pounce on unprepared and unsuspecting surveyors, farmers, or wayfarers, or to creep up to solitary, outlying cabins. They valued the scalps of women and children as highly as those of men. Striking a sudden blow, where there was hardly any possibility of loss to themselves, they instantly moved on to the next settlement, repeating the process again and again. Tireless, watchful, cautious, and rapid, they covered great distances, and their stealth and the mystery of their coming and going added to the terror produced by the horrible nature of their ravages. When pursued they dextrously covered their trail, and started homewards across a hundred leagues of trackless wilderness. The pursuers almost of necessity went slower, for they had to puzzle out the tracks; and after a certain number of days either their food gave out or they found themselves too far from home, and were obliged to return. In most instances the pursuit was vain. Thus a party of twenty savages might make a war-trail some hundreds of miles in length, taking forty or fifty scalps, carrying off a dozen women and children, and throwing a number of settlements, with perhaps a total population of a thousand souls, into a rage of terror and fury, with a loss to themselves of but one or two men killed and wounded.

Throughout the summer of 1781 the settlers were scourged by an unbroken series of raids of this kind. In August McKee, Brant, and other tory and Indian leaders assembled on the Miami an army of perhaps a thousand warriors. They were collected to oppose Clark's intended march to Detroit; for the British leaders were well aware of Clark's intention, and trusted to the savages to frustrate it if he attempted to put it into execution. Brant went off for a scout with a hundred warriors, and destroyed Loughry's party of Westmoreland men, as already related, returning to the main body after having done so. The fickle savages were much elated by this stroke, but instead of being inspired to greater efforts, took the view that the danger of invasion was now over. After much persuasion Brant, McKee, and the captain of the Detroit rangers, Thompson, persuaded them to march towards

A Great War Band Threatens Kentucky.

the Falls. On September 9th they were within thirty miles of their destination, and halted to send out scouts. Two prisoners were captured, from whom it was learned that Clark had abandoned his proposed expedition.[1] Instantly the Indians began to disband, some returning to their homes, and others scattering out to steal horses and burn isolated cabins. Nor could the utmost efforts of their leaders keep them together. They had no wish to fight Clark unless it was absolutely necessary, in order to save their villages and crops from destruction; and they much preferred plundering on their own account. However, a couple of hundred Hurons and Miamis, under Brant and McKee, were kept together, and moved southwards between the Kentucky and Salt rivers, intending "to attack some of the small forts and infest the roads."[2] About the middle of the month they fell in with a party of settlers led by Squire Boon.

Squire Boon had built a fort, some distance from any other, and when rumors of a great Indian inva-

Squire Boon and Floyd Defeated.

sion reached him, he determined to leave it and join the stations on Bear Grass Creek. When he reached Long Run, with his men, women, and children, cattle, and household goods, he stumbled against the two hundred warriors of McKee and Brant. His people were scattered to the four winds, with the loss of many scalps and all their goods and cattle. The victors camped on the ground with the intention of ambush-

[1] Haldimand MSS. Captain A. Thompson to De Peyster, September 26, 1781.

[2] *Do.* Captain A. McKee to De Peyster, September 26, 1781.

ing any party that arrived to bury the dead ; for they were confident some of the settlers would come for this purpose.   Nor were they disappointed ; for next morning Floyd, the county lieutenant, with twenty-five men, made his appearance.   Floyd marched so quickly that he came on the Indians before they were prepared to receive him.   A smart skirmish ensued ; but the whites were hopelessly outnumbered, and were soon beaten and scattered, with a loss of twelve or thirteen men.   Floyd himself, exhausted and with his horse shot, would have been captured had not another man, one Samuel Wells, who was excellently mounted, seen his plight. Wells reined in, leaped off his horse, and making Floyd ride, he ran beside him, and both escaped. The deed was doubly noble, because the men had previously been enemies.[1]   The frontiersmen had made a good defence in spite of the tremendous odds against them, and had slain four of their opponents, three Hurons and a Miami.[2]   Among the former was the head chief, a famous warrior ; his death so discouraged the Indians that they straightway returned home with their scalps and plunder, resist-

[1] Marshall, I., 116.   Floyd had previously written Jefferson (Virginia State Papers, I., 47) that in his county there were but three hundred and fifty-four militia between sixteen and fifty-four years old ; that all people were living in forts, and that forty-seven of the settlers of all ages had been killed, and many wounded, since January ; so his defeat was a serious blow.

[2] Haldimand MSS.   Thompson's letter ; McKee only mentions the three Hurons.   As already explained, the partisan leaders were apt, in enumerating the Indian losses, only to give such as had occurred in their own particular bands.   Marshall makes the fight take place in April ; the Haldimand MSS. show that it was in September.   Marshall is as valuable for early Kentucky history as Haywood for the corresponding periods in Tennessee ; but both one and the other write largely from tradition, and can never be followed when they contradict contemporary reports.

ing McKee's entreaty that they would first attack Boonsborough.

One war party carried off Logan's family; but Logan, following swiftly after, came on the savages so suddenly that he killed several of their number, and rescued all his own people unhurt.[1]

Often French Canadians, and more rarely tories, accompanied these little bands of murderous plun-

Complicity of the British.

derers[2]—besides the companies of Detroit rangers who went with the large war parties,—and they were all armed and urged on by the British at Detroit. One of the official British reports to Lord George Germaine, made on October 23d of this year, deals with the Indian war parties employed against the northwestern frontier. "Many smaller Indian parties have been very successful. . . . It would be endless and difficult to enumerate to your Lordship the parties that are continually employed upon the back settlements. From the Illinois country to the frontiers of New York there is a continual succession . . . the perpetual terror and losses of the inhabitants will I hope operate powerfully in our favor"[3];—so runs the letter. At the same time the British commander in Canada was pointing out to his subordinate at Detroit that the real danger to British rule arose

[1] Bradford MSS.

[2] At this very time a small band that had captured a family in the Kanawha valley were pursued fifty miles, overtaken, several killed and wounded, and the prisoners recaptured, by Col. Andrew Donelly, mentioned in a previous note; it consisted of two French and eight Indians. Virginia State Papers, I., 601.

[3] See full copy of the letter in Mr. Martindale's excellent pamphlet, above quoted.

from the extension of the settlements westwards, and that this the Indians could prevent [1] ; in other words, the savages were expressly directed to make war on non-combatants, for it was impossible to attack a settlement without attacking the women and children therein. In return the frontiersmen speedily grew to regard both British and Indians with the same venomous and indiscriminate anger.

In the writings of the early annalists of these Indian wars are to be found the records of countless deeds of individual valor and cowardice, **Nature of** prowess and suffering, of terrible woe in **the Cease-** time of disaster and defeat, and of the **less Strife.** glutting of ferocious vengeance in the days of triumphant reprisal. They contain tales of the most heroic courage and of the vilest poltroonery ; for the iron times brought out all that was best and all that was basest in the human breast. We read of husbands leaving their wives, and women their children, to the most dreadful of fates, on the chance that they themselves might thereby escape ; and on the other hand, we read again and again of the noblest acts of self-sacrifice, where the man freely gave his life for that of his wife or child, his brother or his friend. Many deeds of unflinching loyalty are

[1] Haldimand MSS. Haldimand to De Peyster, June 24, 1781. Throughout the letters of the British officers at and near Detroit there are constant allusions to scalps being brought in ; but not one word, as far as I have seen, to show that the Indians were ever reproved because many of the scalps were those of women and children. It is only fair to say, however, that there are several instances of the commanders exhorting the Indians to be merciful—which was a waste of breath,—and several other instances where successful efforts were made to stop the use of torture. The British officers were generally personally humane to their prisoners.

recorded, but very, very few where magnanimity was shown to a fallen foe. The women shared the stern qualities of the men; often it happened that, when the house-owner had been shot down, his wife made good the defence of the cabin with rifle or with axe, hewing valiantly at the savages who tried to break through the door, or dig under the puncheon floor, or, perhaps, burst down through the roof or wide chimney. Many hundreds of these tales could be gathered together; one or two are worth giving, not as being unique, but rather as samples of innumerable others of the same kind.

In those days [1] there lived beside the Ohio, in extreme northwestern Virginia, two tall brothers, **Feat of the** famed for their strength, agility, and cour- **Two Poes.** age. They were named Adam and Andrew Poe. In the summer of '81 a party of seven Wyandots or Hurons came into their settlement, burned some cabins, and killed one of the settlers. Immediately eight backwoodsmen started in chase of the marauders; among them were the two Poes.

The Wyandots were the bravest of all the Indian tribes, the most dangerous in battle, and the most merciful in victory, rarely torturing their prisoners; the backwoodsmen respected them for their prowess more than they did any other tribe, and, if captured, esteemed themselves fortunate to fall into Wyandot hands. These seven warriors were the most famous and dreaded of the whole tribe. They included four brothers, one being the chief Bigfoot, who was of

[1] 1781, De Haas; Doddridge, whom the other compilers follow, gives a wrong date (1782), and reverses the parts the two brothers played.

gigantic strength and stature, the champion of all, their most fearless and redoubtable fighter. Yet their very confidence ruined them, for they retreated in a leisurely manner, caring little whether they were overtaken or not, as they had many times worsted the whites, and did not deem them their equals in battle.

The backwoodsmen followed the trail swiftly all day long, and, by the help of the moon, late into the night. Early next morning they again started and found themselves so near the Wyandots that Andrew Poe turned aside and went down to the bed of a neighboring stream, thinking to come up behind the Indians while they were menaced by his comrades in front. Hearing a low murmur, he crept up through the bushes to a jutting rock on the brink of the watercourse, and peering cautiously over, he saw two Indians beneath him. They were sitting under a willow, talking in deep whispers; one was an ordinary warrior, the other, by his gigantic size, was evidently the famous chief himself. Andrew took steady aim at the big chief's breast and pulled trigger. The rifle flashed in the pan; and the two Indians sprang to their feet with a deep grunt of surprise. For a second all three stared at one another. Then Andrew sprang over the rock, striking the big Indian's breast with a shock that bore him to the earth; while at the moment of alighting, he threw his arm round the small Indian's neck, and all three rolled on the ground together.

At this instant they heard sharp firing in the woods above them. The rest of the whites and

Indians had discovered one another at the same time. A furious but momentary fight ensued; three backwoodsmen and four Indians were killed outright, no other white being hurt, while the single remaining red warrior made his escape, though badly wounded. But the three men who were struggling for life and death in the ravine had no time to pay heed to outside matters. For a moment Andrew kept down both his antagonists, who were stunned by the shock; but before he could use his knife the big Indian wrapped him in his arms and held him as if in a vise. This enabled the small Indian to wrest himself loose, when the big chief ordered him to run for his tomahawk, which lay on the sand ten feet away, and to kill the white man as he lay powerless in the chief's arms. Andrew could not break loose, but watching his chance, as the small Indian came up, he kicked him so violently in the chest that he knocked the tomahawk out of his hand and sent him staggering into the water. Thereat the big chief grunted out his contempt, and thundered at the small Indian a few words that Andrew could not understand. The small Indian again approached and after making several feints, struck with the tomahawk, but Andrew dodged and received the blow on his wrist instead of his head; and the wound though deep was not disabling. By a sudden and mighty effort he now shook himself free from the giant, and snatching up a loaded rifle from the sand, shot the small Indian as he rushed on him. But at that moment the larger Indian, rising up, seized him and hurled him to the ground. He was on his feet in a second, and the two grappled furiously, their knives being lost; Andrew's activity and skill as a wrestler and boxer making amends for his lack of strength. Locked in each other's arms they rolled into the water. Here each tried to drown the other, and Andrew catching the chief by the scalp lock held his head under the water until his faint struggles ceased. Thinking his foe dead, he loosed his grip to try to get at his knife, but, as Andrew afterwards said, the Indian had only been "playing possum," and in a second the struggle was renewed. Both combatants rolled into deep water, when they separated and struck out for the shore. The Indian proved the best swimmer, and ran up to the rifle that lay on the sand, whereupon Andrew turned to swim out into the stream, hoping to save his life by diving. At this moment his brother Adam appeared on the bank, and seeing Andrew covered with blood and swimming rapidly away, mistook him for an Indian, and shot him in the shoulder. Immediately afterwards he saw his real antagonist. Both had empty guns, and the contest became one as to who could beat the other in loading, the Indian exclaiming: "Who load first, shoot first!" The chief got his powder down first, but, in hurriedly drawing out his ramrod, it slipped through his fingers and fell in the river. Seeing that it was all over, he instantly faced his foe, pulled open the bosom of his shirt, and the next moment received the ball fair in his breast. Adam, alarmed for his brother, who by this time could barely keep himself afloat, rushed into the river to save him, not heeding Andrew's repeated cries to take the big Indian's scalp. Meanwhile the dying chief, resolute to save the long locks his enemies coveted—always a point of honor among the red men,—painfully rolled himself into the stream. Before he died he reached the deep water, and the swift current bore his body away.

About this time a hunter named McConnell was captured near Lexington by five Indians. At night Other Feats he wriggled out of his bonds and slew four of Personal of his sleeping captors, while the fifth, who Prowess. escaped, was so bewildered that, on reaching the Indian town, he reported that his party had been attacked at night by a number of whites, who had not only killed his companions but the prisoner likewise.

A still more remarkable event had occurred a couple of summers previously. Some keel boats, manned by a hundred men under Lieutenant Rogers, and carrying arms and provisions procured from the Spaniards at New Orleans, were set upon by an Indian war party under Girty and Elliott,[1] while drawn up on a sand beach of the Ohio. The boats were captured and plundered, and most of the men were killed; several escaped, two under very extraordinary circumstances. One had both his arms, the other both his legs, broken. They lay hid till the Indians disappeared, and then accidentally discovered each other. For weeks the two crippled beings lived in the lonely spot where the battle had been fought, unable to leave it, each supplementing what the other could do. The man who could walk kicked wood to him who could not, that he might

[1] Haldimand MSS. De Peyster to Haldimand, November 1, 1779.

make a fire, and making long circuits, chased the game towards him for him to shoot it. At last they were taken off by a passing flat-boat.

The backwoodsmen, wonted to vigorous athletic pastimes, and to fierce brawls among themselves, were generally overmatches for the Indians in hand-to-hand struggles. One such fight, that took place some years before this time, deserves mention. A man of herculean strength and of fierce, bold nature, named Bingaman, lived on the frontier in a lonely log-house. The cabin had but a single room below, in which Bingaman slept, as well as his mother, wife, and child; a hired man slept in the loft. One night eight Indians assailed the house. As they burst in the door Bingaman thrust the women and the child under the bed, his wife being wounded by a shot in the breast. Then having discharged his piece he began to beat about at random with the long heavy rifle. The door swung partially to, and in the darkness nothing could be seen. The numbers of the Indians helped them but little, for Bingaman's tremendous strength enabled him to shake himself free whenever grappled. One after another his foes sank under his crushing blows, killed or crippled; it is said that at last but one was left to flee from the house in terror. The hired man had not dared to come down from the loft, and when Bingaman found his wife wounded he became so enraged that it was with difficulty he could be kept from killing him.[1]

[1] It is curious how faithfully, as well as vividly, Cooper has reproduced these incidents. His pictures of the white frontiersmen are generally true to life; in his most noted Indian characters he is much less fortunate. But his "Indian John" in the "Pioneers" is one of his best portraits; almost equal praise can be given to Susquesus in the "Chainbearers."

Incidents such as these followed one another in quick succession. They deserve notice less for their own sakes than as examples of the way the West was won; for the land was really conquered not so much by the actual shock of battle between bodies of soldiers, as by the continuous westward movement of the armed settlers and the unceasing individual warfare waged between them and their red foes.

For the same reason one or two of the more noted hunters and Indian scouts deserve mention, as types of hundreds of their fellows, who spent their lives and met their deaths in the forest. It was their warfare that really did most to diminish the fighting force of the tribes. They battled exactly as their foes did, making forays, alone or in small parties, for scalps and horses, and in their skirmishes inflicted as much loss as they received; in striking contrast to what occurred in conflicts between the savages and regular troops.

One of the most formidable of these hunters was Lewis Wetzel.[1] Boon, Kenton, and Harrod illus-
The Hunter trate by their lives the nobler, kindlier
Wetzel. traits of the dauntless border-folk; Wetzel, like McGarry, shows the dark side of the picture. He was a good friend to his white neighbors, or at least to such of them as he liked, and as a hunter and fighter there was not in all the land his superior. But he was of brutal and violent temper, and for the Indians he knew no pity and felt no generosity.

[1] The name is variously spelt; in the original German records of the family it appears as Wätzel, or Watzel.

They had killed many of his friends and relations, among others his father; and he hunted them in peace or war like wolves. His admirers denied that he ever showed "unwonted cruelty"[1] to Indian women and children; that he sometimes killed them cannot be gainsaid. Some of his feats were cold-blooded murders, as when he killed an Indian who came in to treat with General Harmar, under pledge of safe conduct; one of his brothers slew in like fashion a chief who came to see Col. Brodhead. But the frontiersmen loved him, for his mere presence was a protection, so great was the terror he inspired among the red men. His hardihood and address were only equalled by his daring and courage. He was literally a man without fear; in his few days of peace his chief amusements were wrestling, foot-racing, and shooting at a mark. He was a dandy, too, after the fashion of the backwoods, especially proud of his mane of long hair, which, when he let it down, hung to his knees. He often hunted alone in the Indian country, a hundred miles beyond the Ohio. As he dared not light a bright fire on these trips, he would, on cold nights, make a small coal-pit, and cower over it, drawing his blanket over his head, when, to use his own words, he soon became as hot as in a "stove room." Once he surprised four Indians sleeping in their camp; falling on them he killed three. Another time, when pursued by the same number of foes, he loaded his rifle as he ran, and killed in succession the three foremost, whereat the other fled. In all, he took over

[1] De Haas, 345.

thirty scalps of warriors, thus killing more Indians than were slain by either one of the two large armies of Braddock and St. Clair during their disastrous campaigns. Wetzel's frame, like his heart, was of steel. But his temper was too sullen and unruly for him ever to submit to command or to bear rule over others. His feats were performed when he was either alone or with two or three associates. An army of such men would have been wholly valueless.

Another man, of a far higher type, was Captain Samuel Brady, already a noted Indian fighter on the **Brady and** Alleghany. For many years after the close **his Scouts.** of the Revolutionary war he was the chief reliance of the frontiersmen of his own neighborhood. He had lost a father and a brother by the Indians; and in return he followed the red men with relentless hatred. But he never killed peaceful Indians nor those who came in under flags of truce. The tale of his wanderings, his captivities, his hairbreadth escapes, and deeds of individual prowess would fill a book. He frequently went on scouts alone, either to procure information or to get scalps. On these trips he was not only often reduced to the last extremity by hunger, fatigue, and exposure, but was in hourly peril of his life from the Indians he was hunting. Once he was captured; but when about to be bound to the stake for burning, he suddenly flung an Indian boy into the fire, and in the confusion burst through the warriors, and actually made his escape, though the whole pack of yelling savages followed at his heels with rifle and tomahawk. He raised a small company of scouts or rangers, and was one of the very few captains able to reduce the unruly frontiersmen to order. In consequence his company on several occasions fairly whipped superior numbers of Indians in the woods; a feat that no regulars could perform, and to which the backwoodsmen themselves were generally unequal, even though an overmatch for their foes singly, because of their disregard of discipline.[1]

So, with foray and reprisal, and fierce private war, with all the border in a flame, the year 1781 came to an end. At its close there were in Kentucky seven hundred and sixty able-bodied militia, fit for an offensive campaign.[2] As this did not include the troops at the Falls, nor the large shifting population, nor the "fort soldiers," the weaker men, graybeards, and boys, who could handle a rifle behind a stockade, it is probable that there were then somewhere between four and five thousand souls in Kentucky.

[1] In the open plain the comparative prowess of these forest Indians, of the backwoodsmen, and of trained regulars was exactly the reverse of what it was in the woods.

[2] Letter of John Todd, October 21, 1781. Virginia State Papers, II., 562. The troops at the Falls were in a very destitute condition, with neither supplies nor money, and their credit worn threadbare, able to get nothing from the surrounding country (*do.*, p. 313). In Clark's absence the colonel let his garrison be insulted by the townspeople, and so brought the soldiers into contempt, while some of the demoralized officers tampered with the public stores. It was said that much dissipation prevailed in the garrison, to which accusation Clark answered sarcastically: "However agreeable such conduct might have been to their sentiments, I believe they seldom had the means in their power, for they were generally in a starving condition" (*do.*, Vol. III., pp. 347 and 359).

CHAPTER V.

AFTER the Moravian Indians were led by their missionary pastors to the banks of the Muskingum **The** they dwelt peacefully and unharmed for sev- **Moravians.** eral years. In Lord Dunmore's war special care was taken by the white leaders that these Quaker Indians should not be harmed ; and their villages of Salem, Gnadenhutten, and Schönbrunn received no damage whatever. During the early years of the Revolutionary struggle they were not molested, but dwelt in peace and comfort in their roomy cabins of squared timbers, cleanly and quiet, industriously till- ing the soil, abstaining from all strong drink, school- ing their children, and keeping the Seventh Day as a day of rest. They sought to observe strict neutral- ity, harming neither the Americans nor the Indians, nor yet the allies of the latter, the British and French at Detroit. They hoped thereby to offend neither side, and to escape unhurt themselves.

But this was wholly impossible. They occupied an utterly untenable position. Their villages lay mid-way between the white settlements southeast of the Ohio, and the towns of the Indians round Sandusky, the bitterest foes of the Americans, and those most completely under British influence. They were on the trail that the war-parties followed whether they struck at Kentucky or at the valleys of the Alleghany and Monongahela. Consequently the Sandusky Indians used the Moravian villages as half-way houses, at which to halt and refresh themselves whether starting on a foray or returning with scalps and plunder.

By the time the war had lasted four or five years both the wild or heathen Indians and the backwoodsmen had become fearfully exasperated **The Wild** with the unlucky Moravians. The Sandusky **Indians** Indians were largely Wyandots, Shawnees, **Hate Them.** and Delawares, the latter being fellow-tribesmen of the Christian Indians; and so they regarded the Moravians as traitors to the cause of their kinsfolk, because they would not take up the hatchet against the whites. As they could not goad them into declaring war, they took malicious pleasure in trying to embroil them against their will, and on returning from raids against the settlements often passed through their towns solely to cast suspicion on them and to draw down the wrath of the backwoodsmen on their heads. The British at Detroit feared lest the Americans might use the Moravian villages as a basis from which to attack the lake posts; they also coveted their men as allies; and so the baser among their officers urged the Sandusky tribes to break up the villages and drive off the missionaries. The other Indian tribes likewise regarded them with angry contempt and hostility; the Iroquois once sent word to the Chippewas and Ottawas that they gave them the Christian Indians " to make broth of."

The Americans became even more exasperated. The war parties that plundered and destroyed their **So Do the** homes, killing their wives, children, and **Americans.** friends with torments too appalling to mention, got shelter and refreshment from the Moravians,[1]—who, indeed, dared not refuse it. The backwoodsmen, roused to a mad frenzy of rage by the awful nature of their wrongs, saw that the Moravians rendered valuable help to their cruel and inveterate foes, and refused to see that the help was given with the utmost reluctance. Moreover, some of the young Christian Indians backslid, and joined their savage brethren, accompanying them on their war parties and ravaging with as much cruelty as any of their number.[2] Soon the frontiersmen began to clamor for the destruction of the Moravian towns; yet for a little while they were restrained by the Continental officers of the few border forts, who always treated these harmless Indians with the utmost kindness.

On either side were foes, who grew less governable day by day, and the fate of the hapless and peaceful **They Blind-** Moravians, if they continued to dwell on the **ly Court** Muskingum, was absolutely inevitable. With **their Fate.** blind fatuity their leaders, the missionaries, refused to see the impending doom; and the poor, simple Indians clung to their homes till destroyed. The American commander at Pittsburg, Col. Gibson,

[1] Heckewelder's "Narrative of the Mission of the United Brethren," Philadelphia, 1820, p. 166.

[2] *Pennsylvania Packet* (Philadelphia, April 16, 1782); Heckewelder, 180; Loskiel's "History of the Mission of the United Brethren" (London, 1794), p. 172.

endeavored to get them to come into the American lines, where he would have the power, as he already had the wish, to protect them; he pointed out that where they were they served in some sort as a shield to the wild Indians, whom he had to spare so as not to harm the Moravians.[1] The Half King of the Wyandots, from the other side, likewise tried to persuade them to abandon their dangerous position, and to come well within the Indian and British lines, saying: " Two mighty and angry gods stand opposite to each other with their mouths wide open, and you are between them, and are in danger of being crushed by one or the other, or by both." [2] But in spite of these warnings, and heedless of the safety that would have followed the adoption of either course, the Moravians followed the advice of their missionaries [3] and continued where they were. They suffered greatly from the wanton cruelty of their red brethren; and their fate remains a monument to the cold-blooded and cowardly brutality of the borderers, a stain on frontier character that the lapse of time cannot wash away; but it is singular that historians have not yet pointed out the obvious truth, that no small share of the blame for their sad end should be put to the credit of the blind folly of their missionary leaders. Their only hope in such a conflict as was then raging, was to be removed from their fatally dangerous position; and this the missionaries would not see. As long at they stayed where they were,

[1] Loskiel, p. 137.

[2] State Department MSS., No. 41, Vol. III., pp. 78, 79; extract from diary of Rev. David Zeisburger.

it was a mere question of chance and time whether they would be destroyed by the Indians or the whites; for their destruction at the hands of either one party or the other was inevitable.

Their fate was not due to the fact that they were Indians; it resulted from their occupying an absolutely false position. This is clearly shown by what happened twenty years previously to a small community of non-resistant Christian whites. They were Dunkards — Quaker-like Germans — who had built a settlement on the Monongahela. As they helped neither side, both distrusted and hated them. The whites harassed them in every way, and the Indians finally fell upon and massacred them.[1] The fates of these two communities, of white Dunkards and red Moravians, were exactly parallel. Each became hateful to both sets of combatants, was persecuted by both, and finally fell a victim to the ferocity of the race to which it did not belong.

The conduct of the backwoodsmen towards these peaceful and harmless Christian Indians was utterly

Evil Conduct of the Backwoodsmen. abhorrent, and will ever be a subject of just reproach and condemnation; and at first sight it seems incredible that the perpetrators of so vile a deed should have gone unpunished and almost unblamed. It is a dark blot on the character of a people that otherwise had many fine and manly qualities to its credit. But the extraordinary conditions of life on the frontier must be kept in mind before passing too severe a judgment. In the turmoil of the harassing and long-

[1] Withers, 59.

continued Indian war, and the consequent loosening of social bonds, it was inevitable that, as regards outside matters, each man should do what seemed right in his own eyes. The bad and the good alike were left free and untrammelled to follow the bent of their desires. The people had all they could do to beat off their savage enemies, and to keep order among themselves. They were able to impose but slight checks on ruffianism that was aimed at outsiders. There were plenty of good and upright men who would not harm any Indians wrongfully, and who treated kindly those who were peaceable. On the other hand, there were many of violent and murderous temper. These knew that their neighbors would actively resent any wrong done to themselves, but knew, also, that, under the existing conditions, they would at the worst do nothing more than openly disapprove of an outrage perpetrated on Indians.

The violence of the bad is easily understood. The indifference displayed towards their actions by the better men of the community, who were certainly greatly in the majority, is harder to explain. It rose from varying causes. In the first place, the long continuance of Indian warfare, and the unspeakable horrors that were its invariable accompaniments had gradually wrought up many even of the best of the backwoodsmen to the point where they barely considered an Indian as a human being. The warrior was not to them a creature of romance. They knew him for what he was—filthy, cruel, lecherous, and faith-

Its Explanation.

less. He sometimes had excellent qualities, but these they seldom had a chance to see. They always met him at his worst. To them he was in peace a lazy, dirty, drunken beggar, whom they despised, and yet whom they feared; for the squalid, contemptible creature might at any moment be transformed into a foe whose like there was not to be found in all the wide world for ferocity, cunning, and blood-thirsty cruelty. The greatest Indians, chiefs like Logan and Cornstalk, who were capable of deeds of the loftiest and most sublime heroism, were also at times cruel monsters or drunken good-for-nothings. Their meaner followers had only such virtues as belong to the human wolf—stealth, craft, tireless endurance, and the courage that prefers to prey on the helpless, but will fight to the death without flinching if cornered.

Moreover, the backwoodsmen were a hard people; a people who still lived in an iron age. They did not **Grimness of the Backwoods Character.** spare themselves, nor those who were dear to them; far less would they spare their real or possible foes. Their lives were often stern and grim; they were wonted to hardship and suffering. In the histories or traditions of the different families there are recorded many tales of how they sacrificed themselves, and, in time of need, sacrificed others. The mother who was a captive among the Indians might lay down her life for her child; but if she could not save it, and to stay with it forbade her own escape, it was possible that she would kiss it good-by and leave it to its certain fate, while she herself, facing death at every step, fled homewards through hundreds of miles of wilderness.[1]   The man who daily imperilled his own life, would, if water was needed in the fort, send his wife and daughter to draw it from the spring round which he knew Indians lurked, trusting that the appearance of the women would make the savages think themselves undiscovered, and that they would therefore defer their attack.[2]   Such people were not likely to spare their red-skinned foes.   Many of their friends, who had never hurt the savages in any way, had perished the victims of wanton aggression.   They themselves had seen innumerable instances of Indian treachery.   They had often known the chiefs of a tribe to profess warm friendship at the very moment that their young men were stealing and murdering.   They grew to think of even the most peaceful Indians as merely sleeping wild beasts, and while their own wrongs were ever vividly before them, they rarely heard of or heeded those done to their foes.   In a community where every strong

[1] See Hale's "Trans-Alleghany Pioneers," the adventures of Mrs. Inglis. She was captured on the head-waters of the Kanawha, at the time of Braddock's defeat.   The other inhabitants of the settlement were also taken prisoners or massacred by the savages, whom they had never wronged in any way.   She was taken to the Big Bone Lick in Kentucky.   On the way her baby was born, but she was not allowed to halt a day on account of this incident.   She left it in the Indian camp, and made her escape in company with "an old Dutch woman."   They lived on berries and nuts for forty days, while they made their way homewards.   Both got in safely, though they separated after the old Dutch woman, in the extremity of hunger, had tried to kill her companion that she might eat her.   When Cornstalk's party perpetrated the massacre of the Clendennins during Pontiac's war (see Stewart's Narrative), Mrs. Clendennin likewise left her baby to its death, and made her escape ; her husband had previously been killed and his bloody scalp tied across her jaws as a gag.

[2] As at the siege of Bryan's Station.

courageous man was a bulwark to the rest, he was sure to be censured lightly for merely killing a member of a loathed and hated race.

Many of the best of the backwoodsmen were Bible-readers, but they were brought up in a creed that made much of the Old Testament, and laid slight stress on pity, ruth, or mercy. They looked at their foes as the Hebrew prophets looked at the enemies of Israel. What were the abominations because of which the Canaanites were destroyed before Joshua, when compared with the abominations of the red savages whose lands they, another chosen people, should in their turn inherit? They believed that the Lord was king for ever and ever, and they believed no less that they were but obeying His commandment as they strove mightily to bring about the day when the heathen should have perished out of the land; for they had read in The Book that he was accursed who did the work of the Lord deceitfully, or kept his sword back from blood. There was many a stern frontier zealot who deemed all the red men, good and bad, corn ripe for the reaping. Such a one rejoiced to see his fellows do to the harmless Moravians as the Danites once did to the people of Laish, who lived quiet and secure, after the manner of the Sidonians, and had no business with any man, and who yet were smitten with the edge of the sword, and their city burnt with fire.

Finally, it must not be forgotten that there were men on the frontier who did do their best to save the peaceful Indians, and that there were also many circumstances connected with the latter that justly laid them open to suspicion. When young backsliding Moravians appeared in the war parties, as cruel and murderous as their associates, the whites were warranted in feeling doubtful as to whether their example might not infect the remainder of their people. War parties, whose members in dreadful derision left women and children impaled by their trail **The Moravians Themselves not Blameless.** to greet the sight of the pursuing husbands and fathers, found food and lodging at the Moravian towns.   No matter how reluctant the aid thus given, the pursuers were right in feeling enraged, and in demanding that the towns should be removed to where they could no longer give comfort to the enemy.   When the missionaries refused to consent to this removal, they thereby became helpers of the hostile Indians ; they wronged the frontiersmen, and they still more grievously wronged their own flocks.

They certainly had ample warning of the temper of the whites.   Col. Brodhead was in command at Fort Pitt until the end of 1781.   At the time that General Sullivan ravaged the country of the Six Nations, he had led a force up the Alleghany and created a diversion by burning one or two Iroquois towns.   In 1781 he led a successful expedition against a town of hostile Delawares on the Muskingum, taking it by surprise and surrounding it so completely that all within were captured.   Sixteen noted warriors and marauders were singled out and put to death.   The remainder fared but little better, for, while marching back to Fort Pitt, the militia fell on them and murdered all the men, leaving only the women and children.   The militia also started to attack the Moravians, and were only prevented by the strenuous exertions of Brodhead. Even this proof of the brutality of their neighbors was wasted on the missionaries.

The first blow the Moravians received was from the wild Indians. In the fall of this same year **Maltreated by the British and Wild Indians.** (1781) their towns were suddenly visited by a horde of armed warriors, horsemen and footmen, from Sandusky and Detroit. Conspicuous among them were the Wyandots, under the Half King; the Delawares, also led by a famous chief, Captain Pipe; and a body of white rangers from Detroit, including British, French, and tories, commanded by the British Captain Elliott, and flying the British flag.[1]   With them came also Shawnees, Chippewas, and Ottawas. All were acting in pursuance of the express orders of the commandant at Detroit.[2] These warriors insisted on the Christian Indians abandoning their villages and accompanying them back to Sandusky and Detroit; and they destroyed many of the houses, and much of the food for the men and the fodder for the horses and cattle. The Moravians begged humbly to be left where they were, but without avail. They were forced away to Lake Erie, the missionaries being taken to Detroit, while the Indians were left on the plains of Sandusky. The wild Indians were very savage against them, but the British commandant would not let them be seriously maltreated,[3] though they were kept in great want and almost starved.

[1] State Department MSS., No. 41, Vol. III., p. 77.
[2] Haldimand MSS. De Peyster to Haldimand, October 5th and 21st, 1781 ; McKee to De Peyster, October 18th.
[3] *Do.*, December 11, 1781.

A few Moravians escaped, and remained in their villages; but these, three or four weeks later, were captured by a small detachment of Ameri- **Also by the** can militia, under Col. David Williamson, **Americans.** who had gone out to make the Moravians either move farther off or else come in under the protection of Fort Pitt. Williamson accordingly took the Indians to the fort, where the Continental commander, Col. John Gibson, at once released them, and sent them back to the villages unharmed.[1] Gibson had all along been a firm friend of the Moravians. He had protected them against the violence of the borderers, and had written repeated and urgent letters to Congress and to his superior officers, asking that some steps might be taken to protect the friendly Christian Indians.[2] In the general weakness and exhaustion, however, nothing was done; and, as neither the State nor Federal governments took any steps to protect them, and as their missionaries refused to learn wisdom, it was evident that the days of the Moravians were numbered. The failure of the government to protect them was perhaps inevitable, but was certainly discreditable.

The very day after Gibson sent the Christian Indians back to their homes, several murders were committed near Pittsburg, and many of the frontiersmen insisted that they were done with the good will or connivance of the Moravians. The settlements had suffered greatly all summer long, and the

[1] Gibson was the old friend of the chief Logan. It is only just to remember that the Continental officers at Fort Pitt treated the Moravians even better than did the British officers at Detroit.

[2] Haldimand MSS. Jan. 22, 1780 (intercepted letters).

people clamored savagely against all the Indians, blaming both Gibson and Williamson for not having killed or kept captive their prisoners. The ruffianly and vicious of course clamored louder than any; the mass of people who are always led by others, chimed in, in a somewhat lower key; and many good men were silent for the reasons given already. In a frontier democracy, military and civil officers are directly dependent upon popular approval, not only for their offices, but for what they are able to accomplish while filling them. They are therefore generally extremely sensitive to either praise or blame. Ambitious men flatter and bow to popular prejudice or opinion, and only those of genuine power and self-reliance dare to withstand it. Williamson was physically a fairly brave officer and not naturally cruel; but he was weak and ambitious, ready to yield to any popular demand, and, if it would advance his own interests, to connive at any act of barbarity.[1] Gibson, however, who was a very different man, paid no heed to the cry raised against him.

With incredible folly the Moravians refused to heed even such rough warnings as they had re- **They Re-** ceived. During the long winter they suf- **fuse to be** fered greatly from cold and hunger, at **Warned** **and Return** Sandusky, and before the spring of 1782 **to their** opened, a hundred and fifty of them re- **Homes.** turned to their deserted villages.

That year the Indian outrages on the frontiers began very early. In February there was some fine

[1] This is the most favorable estimate of his character, based on what Doddridge says (p. 260). He was a very despicable person, but not the natural brute the missionaries painted him.

weather; and while it lasted, several families of settlers were butchered, some under circumstances of
peculiar atrocity. In particular, four Sandusky Indians having taken some prisoners, impaled two of
them, a woman and a child, while on their way to
the Moravian towns, where they rested and ate, prior
to continuing their journey with their remaining
captives. When they left they warned the Moravians
that white men were on their trail.[1] A white man
who had just escaped this same impaling party, also
warned the Moravians that the exasperated borderers
were preparing a party to kill them; and Gibson, from
Fort Pitt, sent a messenger to them, who, however,
arrived too late. But the poor Christian Indians,
usually very timid, now, in the presence of a real
danger, showed a curious apathy; their senses were
numbed and dulled by their misfortunes, and they
quietly awaited their doom.[2]

It was not long deferred. Eighty or ninety frontiersmen, under Williamson, hastily gathered together
to destroy the Moravian towns. It was, of course,
just such an expedition as most attracted the brutal,
the vicious, and the ruffianly; but a few decent men.
to their shame, went along. They started in March,
and on the third day reached the fated villages.
That no circumstance might be wanting to fill the
measure of their infamy, they spoke the Indians fair,
assured them that they meant well, and spent an
hour or two in gathering together those who were
in Salem and Gnadenhutten, putting them all in two
houses at the latter place. Those at the third

[1] Heckewelder, 311.   [2] Loskiel, 176.

town, of Schönbrunn, got warning and made their escape.

As soon as the unsuspecting Indians were gathered in the two houses, the men in one, the women and children in the other, the whites held a council as to what should be done with them. The great majority were for putting them instantly to death. Eighteen men protested, and asked that the lives of the poor creatures should be spared; and then withdrew, calling God to witness that they were innocent of the crime about to be committed. By rights they should have protected the victims at any hazard. One of them took off with him a small Indian boy, whose life was thus spared. With this exception only two lads escaped.

When the murderers told the doomed Moravians their fate, they merely requested a short delay in **They are** which to prepare themselves for death. **Massacred.** They asked one another's pardon for whatever wrongs they might have done, knelt down and prayed, kissed one another farewell, "and began to sing hymns of hope and of praise to the Most High." Then the white butchers entered the houses and put to death the ninety-six men, women, and children that were within their walls. More than a hundred years have passed since this deed of revolting brutality; but even now a just man's blood boils in his veins at the remembrance. It is impossible not to regret that fate failed to send some strong war party of savages across the path of these inhuman cowards, to inflict on them the punishment they so richly deserved. We know that a few of them were afterwards killed by the Indians; it is a matter of keen regret that any escaped.

When the full particulars of the affair were known, all the best leaders of the border, almost all the most famous Indian fighters, joined in denouncing it.[1] Nor is it right that the whole of the frontier folk should bear the blame for the deed. It is a fact, honorable and worthy of mention, that the Kentuckians were never implicated in this or any similar massacre.[2]

But at the time, and in their own neighborhood— the corner of the Upper Ohio valley where Pennsylvania and Virginia touch,—the conduct of the murderers of the Moravians roused no condemnation. The borderers at first felt about it as the English Whigs originally felt about the massacre of Glencoe. For some time the true circumstances of the affair were not widely known among them. They were hot with wrath against all the red-skinned race; and they rejoiced to hear of the death of a number of treacherous Indians who pretended to be peace-

[1] Col. James Smith, then of Kentucky, in 1799 calls it "an act of barbarity equal to any thing I ever knew to be committed by the savages themselves, except the burning of prisoners."

[2] The Germans of up-country North Carolina were guilty of as brutal massacres as the Scotch-Irish backwoodsmen of Pennsylvania. See Adair, 245. There are two or three individual instances of the barbarity of Kentuckians —one being to the credit of McGarry,—but they are singularly few, when the length and the dreadful nature of their Indian wars are taken into account. Throughout their history the Kentucky pioneers had the right on their side in their dealings with the Indians. They were not wanton aggressors; they entered upon vacant hunting-grounds, to which no tribe had a clear title, and to which most even of the doubtful titles had been fairly extinguished. They fought their foes fiercely, with varying fortune, and eventually wrested the land from them; but they very rarely wronged them; and for the numerous deeds of fearful cruelty that were done on Kentucky soil, the Indians were in almost every case to blame.

ful, while harboring and giving aid and comfort to, and occasionally letting their own young men join, bands of avowed murderers. Of course, the large wicked and disorderly element was loud in praise of the deed. The decent people, by their silence, acquiesced.

A terrible day of reckoning was at hand; the retribution fell on but part of the real criminals, and bore most heavily on those who were innocent of any actual complicity in the deed of evil. Nevertheless it is impossible to grieve overmuch for the misfortune that befell men who freely forgave and condoned such treacherous barbarity.

In May a body of four hundred and eighty Pennsylvania and Virginia militia gathered at Mingo Bottom, on the Ohio, with the purpose of marching **Crawford Marches against Sandusky.** against and destroying the towns of the hostile Wyandots and Delawares in the neighborhood of the Sandusky River. The Sandusky Indians were those whose attacks were most severely felt by that portion of the frontier; and for their repeated and merciless ravages they deserved the severest chastisement. The expedition against them was from every point of view just; and it was undertaken to punish them, and without any definite idea of attacking the remnant of the Moravians who were settled among them. On the other hand, the militia included in their ranks most of those who had taken part in the murderous expedition of two months before; this fact, and their general character, made it certain that the peaceable and inoffensive Indians would, if encountered, be slaughtered as pitilessly as their hostile brethren.

How little the militia volunteers disapproved of the Moravian massacre was shown when, as was the custom, they met to choose a leader. There were two competitors for the place, Williamson, who commanded at the massacre, being one; and he was beaten by only five votes. His successful opponent, Colonel William Crawford, was a fairly good officer, a just and upright man, but with no special fitness for such a task as that he had undertaken. Nor were the troops he led of very good stuff[1]; though they included a few veteran Indian fighters.

The party left Mingo Bottom on the 25th of May. After nine days' steady marching through the unbroken forests they came out on the Sandusky plains; billowy stretches of prairie, covered with high coarse grass and dotted with islands of timber. As the men marched across them they roused quanti-

---

[1] A minute and exhaustive account of Crawford's campaign is given by Mr. C. W. Butterfield in his " Expedition against Sandusky." (Cincinnati: Robert Clarke & Co., 1873). Mr. Butterfield shows conclusively that the accepted accounts are wholly inaccurate, being derived from the reports of the Moravian missionaries, whose untruthfulness (especially Heckewelder's) is clearly demonstrated. He shows the apocryphal nature of some of the pretended narratives of the expedition, such as two in " The American Pioneer," etc. He also shows how inaccurate McClung's "sketches" are—for McClung was like a host of other early western annalists, preserving some valuable facts in a good deal of rubbish, and having very little appreciation indeed of the necessity of so much as approximate accuracy. Only a few of these early western historians had the least conception of the value of evidence or of the necessity of sifting it, or of weighing testimony.

On the other hand, Mr. Butterfield is drawn into grave errors by his excessive partisanship of the borderers. He passes lightly over their atrocious outrages, colors favorably many of their acts, and praises the generalship of Crawford and the soldiership of his men; when in reality the campaign was badly conducted from beginning to end, and reflected discredit on most who took part in it; Crawford did poorly, and the bulk of his men acted like unruly cowards.

ties of prairie fowl, and saw many geese and sand-hill cranes, which circled about in the air, making a strange clamor.

Crawford hoped to surprise the Indian towns; but his progress was slow and the militia every now and then fired off their guns. The spies of the savages dogged his march and knew all his movements [1]; and runners were sent to Detroit asking help. This the British commandant at once granted. He sent to the assistance of the threatened tribes a number of lake Indians and a body of rangers and Canadian volunteers, under Captain Caldwell.[2]

On the fourth of June Crawford's troops reached one of the Wyandot towns. It was found to **The** be deserted; and the army marched on **Fight at** to try and find the others. Late in **Sandusky.** the afternoon, in the midst of the plains, near a cranberry marsh, they encountered Caldwell and his Detroit rangers, together with about two hundred Delawares, Wyandots, and lake Indians.[3] The British and Indians united certainly did not much exceed three hundred men; but they were hourly expecting reinforcements, and decided to give battle. They were posted in a grove of trees, from which they were driven by the first charge of the Americans. A hot skirmish ensued, in which, in spite of Crawford's superiority in force, and of the exceptionally favorable nature of the

[1] Heckewelder, 336. Butterfield shows conclusively that there is not the slightest ground to accept Heckewelder's assertion that Crawford's people openly declared that "no Indian was to be spared, friend or foe."

[2] Haldimand MSS. May 14, 1782. De Peyster to Haldimand.

[3] *Do.* Official report of Lt. John Turney of the rangers, June 7, 1782.

country, he failed to gain any marked advantage. His troops, containing so large a leaven of the murderers of the Moravians, certainly showed small fighting capacity when matched against armed men who could defend themselves. After the first few minutes neither side gained or lost ground.

Of the Americans five were killed and nineteen wounded—in all twenty-four. Of their opponents the rangers lost two men killed and three wounded, Caldwell being one of the latter; and the Indians four killed and eight wounded—in all seventeen.[1]

That night Crawford's men slept by their watchfires in the grove, their foes camping round about in the open prairie. Next morning the British and Indians were not inclined to renew the attack; they wished to wait until their numbers were increased. The only chance of the American militia was to crush their enemies before reinforcements arrived, yet they lay supine and idle all day long, save for an occasional harmless skirmish. Crawford's generalship was as poor as the soldiership of his men.

In the afternoon the Indians were joined by one hundred and forty Shawnees. At sight of this accession of strength the disspirited militia gave up all thought of any thing but flight, though they were still equal in numbers to their foes. That night they began a hurried and disorderly retreat. The Shawnees and Delawares

Rout
of the
Whites.

---

[1] *Do.* Probably some of this loss occurred on the following day. I rely on Butterfield for the American loss, as he quotes Irvine's official report, etc. He of course wrote without knowledge of the British reports; and his account of the Indian losses and numbers is all wrong. He fails signally in his effort to prove that the Americans behaved bravely.

attacked them in the darkness, causing some loss and
great confusion, and a few of the troops got into the
marsh.   Many thus became scattered, and next
morning there were only about three hundred men
left together in a body.   Crawford himself was
among the missing, so Williamson took command,
and hastily continued the retreat.   The savages did
not make a very hot pursuit; nevertheless, in the
afternoon of that day a small number of Indians and
Detroit rangers overtook the Americans.   They were
all mounted.   A slight skirmish followed, and the
Americans lost eleven men, but repulsed their pursuers.[1]   After this they suffered little molestation,
and reached Mingo Bottom on the 13th of the
month.[2]

Many of the stragglers came in afterwards.   In all
about seventy either died of their wounds, were
killed outright, or were captured.   Of the latter,
those who were made prisoners by the Wyandots
were tomahawked and their heads stuck on poles;
but if they fell into the hands of the Shawnees or
Delawares they were tortured to death with fiendish
cruelty.   Among them was Crawford himself, who
had become separated from the main body when it
began its disorderly night retreat.   After abandoning his jaded horse he started homewards on foot,
but fell into the hands of a small party of Delawares, together with a companion named Knight.

[1] Who were probably at this point much fewer in number than the Americans ; Butterfield says the reverse, but his account is untrustworthy on these
matters.

[2] As Butterfield shows, Heckewelder's account of Crawford's whole expedition is a piece of sheer romancing.

These two prisoners were taken to one of the Delaware villages. The Indians were fearfully exasperated by the Moravian massacre[1]; and some of the former Moravians, who had rejoined their wild tribesmen, told the prisoners that from that time on not a single captive should escape torture. Nevertheless it is likely that Crawford would have been burned in any event, and that most of the prisoners would have been tortured to death even had the Moravians never been harmed; for such had always been the custom of the Delawares.

The British, who had cared for the remnants of the Moravians, now did their best to stop the cruelties of the Indians,[2] but could accomplish little or nothing. Even the Mingos and Hurons told them that though they would not torture any Americans, they intended thenceforth to put all their prisoners to death.[3]

Crawford was tied to the stake in the presence of a hundred Indians. Among them were Simon Girty, the white renegade, and a few Wyandots. Knight, Crawford's fellow-captive, was a horrified spectator of the awful sufferings which he knew he was destined by his captors ultimately to share. Crawford, stripped naked, and with his hands bound behind him, was fastened to a high stake by a strong rope; the rope was long enough for him to walk once or twice round the stake. The fire, of small hickory poles, was several yards from

Crawford Tortured to Death.

[1] Haldimand MSS. De Peyster to Haldimand, June 23, 1782.
[2] *Do.* Aug. 18, 1782.
[3] *Do.* Dec. 1, 1782.

the post, so as only to roast and scorch him. Powder
was shot into his body, and burning fagots shoved
against him, while red embers were strewn beneath
his feet. For two hours he bore his torments
with manly fortitude, speaking low, and beseeching
the Almighty to have mercy on his soul. Then he
fell down, and his torturers scalped him, and threw
burning coals on his bare skull. Rising, he walked
about the post once or twice again, and then died.
Girty and the Wyandots looked on, laughing at his
agony, but taking no part in the torture. When the
news of his dreadful fate was brought to the settlements, it excited the greatest horror, not only along
the whole frontier, but elsewhere in the country; for
he was widely known, was a valued friend of Washington and was everywhere beloved and respected.

Knight, a small and weak-looking man, was sent
to be burned at the Shawnee towns, under the care
of a burly savage. Making friends with the latter,
he lulled his suspicions, the more easily because the
Indian evidently regarded so small a man with contempt; and then, watching his opportunity, he
knocked his guard down and ran off into the woods,
eventually making his way to the settlements.

Another of the captives, Slover by name, made a
more remarkable escape. Slover's life history had
been curious. When a boy eight years old, living near
the springs of the Kanawha, his family was captured
by Indians, his brother alone escaping. His father
was killed, and his two little sisters died of fatigue
on the road to the Indian villages; his mother was
afterwards ransomed. He lived twelve years with

the savages, at first in the Miami towns, and then with the Shawnees. When twenty years old he went to Fort Pitt, where, by accident, he was made known to some of his relations. They pressed him to rejoin his people, but he had become so wedded to savage life that he at first refused. At last he yielded, however, took up his abode with the men of his own color, and became a good citizen, and a worthy member of the Presbyterian Church. At the outbreak of the Revolution he served fifteen months as a Continental soldier, and when Crawford started against the Sandusky Indians, he went along as a scout.

Slover, when captured, was taken round to various Indian towns, and saw a number of his companions, as well as other white prisoners, tomahawked or tortured to death. He was examined publicly about many matters at several Great Councils—for he spoke two or three different Indian languages fluently. At one of the councils he heard the Indians solemnly resolve to take no more prisoners thereafter, but to kill all Americans, of whatever sex and age ; some of the British agents from Detroit signifying their approval of the resolution.[1]

[1] Slover asserts that it was taken in consequence of a message sent advising it by the commandant at Detroit. This is doubtless untrue ; the commandant at Detroit did what he could to stop such outrages, although many of his more reckless and uncontrollable subordinates very probably pursued an opposite course. The ignorant and violently prejudiced backwoodsmen naturally believed all manner of evil of their British foes ; but it is singular that writers who ought to be well informed should even now continue to accept all their wild assertions as unquestioned facts. The conduct of the British was very bad ; but it is silly to describe it in the terms often used. The year after their escape Slover dictated, and Knight wrote, narratives of their adventures, which were together published in book form at Philadelphia in 1783. They are very interesting.

At last he was condemned to be burned, and was actually tied to the stake. But a heavy shower came on, so wetting the wood that it was determined to **Slover's** reprieve him till the morrow. That night **Escape.** he was bound and put in a wigwam under the care of three warriors. They laughed and chatted with the prisoner, mocking him, and describing to him with relish all the torments that he was to suffer. At last they fell asleep, and, just before daybreak, he managed to slip out of his rope and escape, entirely naked.

Catching a horse, he galloped away sitting on a piece of old rug, and guiding the animal with the halter. He rode steadily and at speed for seventy miles, until his horse dropped dead under him late in the afternoon. Springing off, he continued the race on foot. At last he halted, sick and weary; but, when he had rested an hour or two, he heard afar off the halloo of his pursuers. Struggling to his feet he continued his flight, and ran until after dark. He then threw himself down and snatched a few hours' restless sleep, but, as soon as the moon rose, he renewed his run for life, carefully covering his trail whenever possible. At last he distanced his enemies. For five days he went straight through the woods, naked, bruised, and torn, living on a few berries and a couple of small crawfish he caught in a stream. He could not sleep nor sometimes even lie down at night because of the mosquitoes. On the morning of the sixth day he reached Wheeling, after experiencing such hardship and suffering as none but an iron will and frame could have withstood.

Until near the close of the year 1782 the frontiers suffered heavily. A terrible and deserved retribution fell on the borderers for their crime in failing to punish the dastardly deed of Williamson **Woe** and his associates. The Indians were **on the** roused to savage anger by the murder of **Frontier.** the Moravians, and were greatly encouraged by their easy defeat of Crawford's troops. They harassed the settlements all along the Upper Ohio, the Alleghany and the Monongahela, and far into the interior,[1] burning, ravaging, and murdering, and bringing dire dismay to every lonely clearing, and every palisaded hamlet of rough log-cabins.

[1] Va. State Papers, III., 235.

CHAPTER VI.

THE ADMINISTRATION OF THE CONQUERED FRENCH SETTLEMENTS, 1779–1783.

THE Virginian Government took immediate steps to provide for the civil administration of the country

Illinois Made a County. Clark had conquered. In the fall of 1778 the entire region northwest of the Ohio was constituted the county of Illinois, with John Todd as county-lieutenant or commandant.

Todd was a firm friend and follower of Clark's, and had gone with him on his campaign against Vincennes. It therefore happened that he received his commission while at the latter town, early in the spring of '79. In May he went to Kaskaskia, to organize the county; and Clark, who remained military commandant of the Virginia State troops that were quartered in the district, was glad to turn over the civil government to the charge of his old friend.

Together with his commission, Todd received a long and excellent letter of instructions from Governor Patrick Henry. He was empowered to choose a deputy-commandant, and officers for the militia; but the judges and officers of the court were to be elected by the people themselves. He was given large discretionary power, Henry impressing upon

him with especial earnestness the necessity to "culti-
vate and conciliate the French and Indians."[1] With
this end in view, he was bidden to pay special heed
to the customs of the creoles, to avoid shocking their
prejudices, and to continually consult with their most
intelligent and upright men. He was to coöperate
in every way with Clark and his troops, while at
the same time the militia were to be exclusively
under his own control. The inhabitants were to
have strict justice done them if wronged by the
troops; and Clark was to put down rigorously any
licentiousness on the part of his soldiers. The wife
and children of the former British commandant—
the creole Rocheblave—were to be treated with
particular respect, and not suffered to want for
any thing. He was exhorted to use all his diligence
and ability to accomplish the difficult task set him.
Finally Henry advised him to lose no opportunity of
inculcating in the minds of the French the value of
the liberty the Americans brought them, as con-
trasted with "the slavery to which the Illinois was
destined" by the British.

This last sentence was proved by subsequent
events to be a touch of wholly unconscious but very
grim humor. The French were utterly unsuited
for liberty, as the Americans understood the term,
and to most of them the destruction of British rule
was a misfortune. The bold, self-reliant, and ener-

[1] See Col. John Todd's "Record Book," while County Lieutenant of
Illinois. There is an MS. copy in Col. Durrett's library at Louisville. It
is our best authority for these years in Illinois. The substance of it is given
on pp. 49–68 of Mr. Edward G. Mason's interesting and valuable pamphlet
on " Illinois in the 18th Century " (Chicago, Fergus Printing Co., 1881).

getic spirits among them, who were able to become Americanized, and to adapt themselves to the new conditions, undoubtedly profited immensely by the change. As soon as they adopted American ways, they were received by the Americans on terms of perfect and cordial equality, and they enjoyed a far higher kind of life than could possibly have been theirs formerly, and achieved a much greater measure of success. But most of the creoles were helplessly unable to grapple with the new life. They had been accustomed to the paternal rule of priest and military commandant, and they were quite unable to govern themselves, or to hold their own with the pushing, eager, and often unscrupulous, new-comers. So little able were they to understand precisely what the new form of government was, that when they went down to receive Todd as commandant, it is said that some of them, joining in the cheering, from force of habit cried " Vive le roi."

For the first year of Todd's administration, while Clark still remained in the county as commandant of the State troops, matters went fairly well. Clark kept the Indians completely in check, and when some of them finally broke out, and started on a marauding expedition against Cahokia, he promptly repulsed them, and by a quick march burned their towns on Rock River, and forced them to sue for peace.[1]

Todd appointed a Virginian, Richard Winston, as commandant at Kaskaskia; all his other appointees were Frenchmen. An election was forthwith held for

[1] In the beginning of 1780. Bradford MS.

justices; to the no small astonishment of the creoles, unaccustomed as they were to American methods of self-government. Among those whom they elected as judges and court officers were some of the previously appointed militia captains and lieutenants, who thus held two positions. The judges governed their decisions solely by the old French laws and customs.[1] Todd at once made the court proceed to business. On its recommendation he granted licenses to trade to men of assured loyalty. He also issued a proclamation in reference to new settlers taking up lands. Being a shrewd man, he clearly foresaw the ruin that was sure to arise from the new Virginia land laws as applied to Kentucky, and he feared the inrush of a horde of speculators, who would buy land with no immediate intention of settling thereon. Besides, the land was so fertile in the river bottoms, that he deemed the amount Virginia allotted to each person excessive. So he decreed that each settler should take up his land in the shape of one of the long narrow French farms, that stretched back from the water-front; and that no claim should contain a greater number of acres than did one of these same farms. This proclamation undoubtedly had a very good effect.

He next wrestled steadily, but much less successfully, with the financial question. He attempted to establish a land bank, as it were, setting Financial aside a great tract of land to secure certain Difficulties. issues of Continental money. The scheme failed, and in spite of his public assurance that the Conti-

[1] State Department MSS., No. 48, p. 51.

nental currency would shortly be equal in value to gold and silver, it swiftly sank until it was not worth two cents on the dollar.

This wretched and worthless paper-money, which the Americans brought with them, was a perfect curse to the country. Its rapid depreciation made it almost impossible to pay the troops, or to secure them supplies, and as a consequence they became disorderly and mutinous. Two or three prominent creoles, who were devoted adherents of the American cause, made loans of silver to the Virginian Government, as represented by Clark, thereby helping him materially in the prosecution of his campaign. Chief among these public-spirited patriots were Francis Vigo, and the priest Gibault, both of them already honorably mentioned. Vigo advanced nearly nine thousand dollars in specie,—piastres or Spanish milled dollars,— receiving in return bills on the " Agent of Virginia," which came back protested for want of funds ; and neither he nor his heirs ever got a dollar of what was due them. He did even more. The creoles at first refused to receive any thing but peltries or silver for their goods ; they would have nothing to do with the paper, and to all explanations as to its uses, simply answered "that their commandants never made money." [1] Finally they were persuaded to take it on Vigo's personal guaranty, and his receiving it in his store. Even he, however, could not buoy it up long.

Gibault likewise [2] advanced a large sum of money,

---

[1] Law's "Vincennes," pp. 49, 126. For some inscrutable reason, by the way, the Americans for a long time persisted in speaking of the place as *St.* Vincennes.   [2] See his letter to Governor St. Clair, May 1, 1790.

parted with his titles and beasts, so as to set a good example to his parishioners, and, with the same purpose, furnished goods to the troops at ordinary prices, taking the paper in exchange as if it had been silver. In consequence he lost over fifteen hundred dollars, was forced to sell his only two slaves, and became almost destitute; though in the end he received from the government a tract of land which partially reimbursed him. Being driven to desperate straits, the priest tried a rather doubtful shift. He sold, or pretended to sell, a great natural meadow, known as la prairie du pont, which the people of Cahokia claimed as a common pasture for their cattle. His conduct drew forth a sharp remonstrance from the Cahokians, in the course of which they frankly announced that they believed the priest should confine himself to ecclesiastical matters, and should not meddle with land grants, especially when the land he granted did not belong to him.[1]

It grew steadily more difficult to get the creoles to furnish supplies; Todd had to forbid the exportation of any provisions whatever, and, finally, the soldiers were compelled to levy on all that they needed. Todd paid for these impressed goods, as well as for what the contractors furnished, at the regulation prices—one third in paper-money and two thirds in peltries; and thus the garrisons at Kaskaskia, Cahokia, and Vincennes were supplied with powder, lead, sugar, flour, and, above all, hogsheads of taffia, of which they drank an inordinate quantity.

[1] State Department MSS., No. 48, p. 41.   Petition of J. B. La Croix and A. Girardin.

The justices did not have very much work; in most of the cases that came before them the plaintiff and defendant were both of the same race. One piece of recorded testimony is rather amusing, being to the effect that "Monsieur Smith est un grand vilain coquin."[1]

Yet there are two entries in the proceedings of the creole courts for the summer of 1779, as preserved in Todd's "Record Book," which are of startling significance. To understand them it must be remembered that the creoles were very ignorant and superstitious, and that they one and all, including, apparently, even their priests, firmly believed in witchcraft and sorcery. Some of their negro slaves had been born in Africa, the others had come from the Lower Mississippi or the West Indies; they practised the strange rites of voudooism, and a few were adepts in the art of poisoning. Accordingly the French were always on the look-out lest their slaves should, by spell or poison, take their lives. It must also be kept in mind that the pardoning power of the commandant did not extend to cases of treason or murder —a witchcraft trial being generally one for murder, —and that he was expressly forbidden to interfere with the customs and laws, or go counter to the prejudices, of the inhabitants.

Burning of Negroes Accused of Sorcery.

At this time the creoles were smitten by a sudden epidemic of fear that their negro slaves were trying to bewitch and poison them. Several of the negroes

[1] This and most of the other statements for which no authority is quoted, are based on Todd's MS. "Record Book."

were seized and tried, and in June two were condemned to death. One, named Moreau, was sentenced to be hung outside Cahokia. The other, a
Kaskaskian slave named Manuel, suffered a worse
fate. He was sentenced " to be chained to a post at
the water-side, and there to be burnt alive and his
ashes scattered." [1] These two sentences, and the directions for their immediate execution, reveal a dark
chapter in the early history of Illinois. It seems a
strange thing that, in the United States, three years
after the declaration of independence, men should
have been burnt and hung for witchcraft, in accordance with the laws, and with the decision of the
proper court. The fact that the victim, before being
burned, was forced to make " honorable fine " at the
door of the Catholic church, shows that the priest at
least acquiesced in the decision. The blame justly
resting on the Puritans of seventeenth-century New
England must likewise fall on the Catholic French
of eighteenth-century Illinois.

Early in the spring of 1780 Clark left the country;
he did not again return to take command, for after
visiting the fort on the Mississippi, and spending the
summer in the defence of Kentucky, he went to
Virginia to try to arrange for an expedition against
Detroit. Todd also left about the same time, having
been elected a Kentucky delegate to the Virginia
Legislature. He afterwards made one or two flying
visits to Illinois, but exerted little influence over her

[1] The entries merely record the sentences, with directions that they be
immediately executed. But there seems very little doubt that they were for
witchcraft, or voudouism, probably with poisoning at the bottom—and that
they were actually carried out. See Mason's pamphlet, p. 59.

destiny, leaving the management of affairs entirely in the hands of his deputy, or lieutenant-commandant for the time being. He usually chose for this position either Richard Winston, the Virginian, or else a creole named Thimothé Demunbrunt.

Todd's departure was a blow to the country; but Clark's was a far more serious calamity. By his personal influence he had kept the Indians in check, the **Disorders** creoles contented, and the troops well fed **in the Gov-** and fairly disciplined. As soon as he **ernment.** went, trouble broke out. The officers did not know how to support their authority; they were very improvident, and one or two became implicated in serious scandals. The soldiers soon grew turbulent, and there was constant clashing between the civil and military rulers. Gradually the mass of the creoles became so angered with the Americans that they wished to lay their grievances before the French Minister at Philadelphia; and many of them crossed the Mississippi and settled under the Spanish flag. The courts rapidly lost their power, and the worst people, both Americans and creoles, practised every kind of rascality with impunity. All decent men joined in clamoring for Clark's return; but it was impossible for him to come back. The freshets and the maladministration combined to produce a dearth, almost a famine, in the land. The evils were felt most severely in Vincennes, where Helm, the captain of the post, though a brave and capable man, was utterly unable to procure supplies of any kind. He did not hear of Clark's success against Piqua and Chillicothe until October.

Then he wrote to one of the officers at the Falls, saying that he was " sitting by the fire with a piece of lightwood and two ribs of an old buflloe, which is all the meat we have seen this many days. I congratulate your success against the Shawanohs, but there 's never doubts where that brave Col. Clark commands ; we well know the loss of him in Illinois. . . . Excuse Haste as the Lightwood's Just out and mouth watering for part of the two ribs." [1]

In the fall of 1780 a Frenchman, named la Balme, led an expedition composed purely of creoles against Detroit. He believed that he could win **La Balme's** over the French at that place to his side, and **Expedition.** thus capture the fort as Clark had captured Vincennes. He raised some fifty volunteers round Cahokia and Kaskaskia, perhaps as many more on the Wabash, and marched to the Maumee River. Here he stopped to plunder some British traders; and in November the neighboring Indians fell on his camp, killed him and thirty or forty of his men, and scattered the rest.[2] His march had been so quick and unexpected that it rendered the British very uneasy, and they were much rejoiced at his discomfiture and death.

The following year a new element of confusion was added. In 1779 Spain declared war on Great Britain. The Spanish commandant at New Orleans was Don Bernard de Galvez, one of the very few strikingly able men Spain has sent to the western hemisphere during the past two centuries. He was bold, resolute, and ambitious; there is reason to

---

[1] Calendar of Va. State Papers, I., pp. 380, 382, 383, Oct. 24–29, 1780.
[2] Haldimand MSS. De Peyster to Haldimand, Nov. 16, 1780.

believe that at one time he meditated a separation
from Spain, the establishment of a Spanish-American
empire, and the founding of a new imperial house.
However this may be, he threw himself heart and
soul into the war against Britain; and attacked
British West Florida with a fiery energy worthy
of Wolfe or Montcalm. He favored the Americans;
but it was patent to all that he favored them only
the better to harass the British.[1]

Besides the creoles and the British garrisons, there
were quite a number of American settlers in West
Florida. In the immediate presence of Spanish and
Indian foes, these, for the most part, remained royalists. In 1778 a party of armed Americans, coming
down the Ohio and Mississippi, tried to persuade
them to turn whig, but, becoming embroiled with
them, the militant missionaries were scattered and
driven off. Afterwards the royalists fought among
themselves; but this was a mere faction quarrel,
and was soon healed. Towards the end of 1779,
Galvez, with an army of Spanish and French creole
troops, attacked the forts along the Mississippi—
Manchac, Baton Rouge, Natchez, and one or two
smaller places,—speedily carrying them and capturing their garrisons of British regulars and royalist
militia. During the next eighteen months he laid
siege to and took Mobile and Pensacola. While he
was away on his expedition against the latter place,
the royalist Americans round Natchez rose and
retook the fort from the Spaniards; but at the approach of Galvez they fled in terror, marching over-

---

[1] State Department MSS., No. 50, p. 109.

land towards Georgia, then in the hands of the tories. On the way they suffered great loss and damage from the Creeks and Choctaws.

The Spanish commander at St. Louis was inspired by the news of these brilliant victories to try if he, **A Spanish** too, could not gain a small wreath at the **Attempt on** expense of Spain's enemies. Clark had **St. Joseph.** already become thoroughly convinced of the duplicity of the Spaniards on the upper Mississippi; he believed that they were anxious to have the British retake Illinois, so that they, in their turn, might conquer and keep it.[1] They never had the chance to execute this plan; but, on January 2, 1781, a Spanish captain, Don Eugénio Pierro, led a hundred and twenty men, chiefly Indians and creoles, against the little French village, or fur post, of St. Joseph, where they burned the houses of one or two British traders, claimed the country round the Illinois River as conquered for the Spanish king, and forthwith returned to St. Louis, not daring to leave a garrison of any sort behind them, and being harassed on their retreat by the Indians. On the strength of this exploit Spain afterwards claimed a large stretch of country to the east of the Mississippi. In reality it was a mere plundering foray. The British at once retook possession of the place, and, indeed, were for some time ignorant whether the raiders had been Americans or Spaniards.[2] Soon after the recapture, the Detroit authorities sent a scouting party

[1] Clark to Todd, March, 1780. Va. State Papers, I., 338.
[2] Haldimand MSS. Haldimand to De Peyster, April 10, 1781. Report of Council at St. Joseph, March 11, 1781.

to dislodge some Illinois people who had attempted to make a settlement at Chicago.[1]

At the end of the year 1781 the unpaid troops in Vincennes were on the verge of mutiny, and it was impossible longer even to feed them, for the inhabitants themselves were almost starving. The garrison was therefore withdrawn; and immediately the Wabash Indians joined those of the Miami, the Sandusky, and the Lakes in their raids on the settlements.[2] By this time, however, Cornwallis had surrendered at York-town, and the British were even more exhausted than the Americans. Some of the French partisans of the British at Detroit, such as Rocheblave and Lamothe, who had been captured by Clark, were eager for revenge, and desired to be allowed to try and retake Vincennes and the Illinois; they saw that the Americans must either be exterminated or else the land abandoned to them.[3] But the British commandant was in no condition to comply with their request, or to begin offensive operations. Clark had not only conquered the land, but he had held it firmly while he dwelt therein; and even when his hand was no longer felt, the order he had established took some little time before crumbling. Meanwhile, his presence at the Falls, his raids into the Indian country, and his preparations for an onslaught on Detroit kept the British authorities at the latter place fully occupied, and prevented their making

[1] *Do.* Haldimand to De Peyster, May 19, 1782. This is the first record of an effort to make a permanent settlement at Chicago.

[2] Va. State Papers, III., 502.

[3] Haldimand MSS. Letter of Rocheblave, Oct. 7, 1781; of Lamothe, April 24, 1782.

any attempt to recover what they had lost. By the beginning of 1782 the active operations of the Revolutionary war were at an end, and the worn-out British had abandoned all thought of taking the offensive anywhere, though the Indian hostilities continued with unabated vigor. Thus the grasp with which the Americans held the conquered country was not relaxed until all danger that it would be taken from them had ceased.

In 1782 the whole Illinois region lapsed into anarchy and confusion. It was perhaps worst at Vincennes, where the departure of the troops had left the French free to do as they wished. Accustomed for generations to a master, they could do nothing with their new-found liberty beyond making it a curse to themselves and their neighbors. They had been provided with their own civil government in the shape of their elective court, but the judges had literally no idea of their proper functions as a governing body to administer justice. At first they did nothing whatever beyond meet and adjourn. Finally it occurred to them that perhaps their official position could be turned to their own advantage. Their townsmen were much too poor to be plundered; but there were vast tracts of fertile wild land on every side, to which, as far as they knew, there was no title, and which speculators assured them would ultimately be of great value. Vaguely remembering Todd's opinion, that he had power to interfere under certain conditions with the settlement of the lands, and concluding that he had delegated this power, as well as others, to themselves, the justices of the court proceeded to make immense grants of territory, reciting that they did so under "*les pouvoirs donnés a Mons'rs Les Magistrats de la cour de Vincennes par le Snr. Jean Todd, colonel et Grand Judge civil pour les États Unis*"; Todd's title having suffered a change and exaltation in their memories. They granted one another about fifteen thousand square miles of land round the Wabash; each member of the court in turn absenting himself for the day on which his associates granted him his share.

This vast mass of virgin soil they sold to speculators at nominal prices, sometimes receiving a horse or a gun for a thousand acres. The speculators of course knew that their titles were worthless, and made haste to dispose of different lots at very low prices to intending settlers. These small buyers were those who ultimately suffered by the transaction, as they found they had paid for worthless claims. The speculators reaped the richest harvest; and it is hard to decide whether to be amused or annoyed at the childish and transparent rascality of the French creoles.[1]

In the Illinois country proper the troops, the American settlers, speculators, and civil officials, and **Lawlessness in the Illinois.** the creole inhabitants all quarrelled together indiscriminately. The more lawless new-comers stole horses from the quieter creoles; the worst among the French, the idle coureurs-des-bois, voyageurs, and trappers plun-

[1] State Department MSS., Nos. 30 and 48. Laws " Vincennes."

dered and sometimes killed the peaceable citizens
of either nationality. The soldiers became little
better than an unruly mob; some deserted, or
else in company with other ruffians, both French
and American, indulged in furious and sometimes
murderous orgies, to the terror of the creoles who
had property. The civil authorities, growing day
by day weaker, were finally shorn of all power
by the military. This, however, was in nowise a
quarrel between the French and the Americans. As
already explained, in Todd's absence the position of
deputy was sometimes filled by a creole and sometimes by an American. He had been particular to
caution them in writing to keep up a good under-
standing with the officers and troops, adding, as a
final warning: " If this is not the case you will be
unhappy." Unfortunately for one of the deputies,
Richard Winston, he failed to keep up the good un-
derstanding, and, as Todd had laconically foretold,
he in consequence speedily became very "unhappy."
We have only his own account of the matter. According to this, in April, 1782, he was taken out of
his house " in despite of the civil authority, disregarding the laws and on the malitious alugation
of Jno. Williams and Michel Pevante." Thus a
Frenchman and an American joined in the accusation, for some of the French supported the civil,
others the military, authorities. The soldiers had
the upper hand, however, and Winston records that
he was forthwith "confined by tyrannick military
force." From that time the authority of the laws
was at an end, and as the officers of the troops

had but little control, every man did what pleased him best.

In January, 1781, the Virginia Legislature passed an act ceding to Congress, for the benefit of the United States, all of Virginia's claim to the territory northwest of the Ohio; but the cession was not consummated until after the close of the war with Great Britain, and the only immediate effect of the act was to still further derange affairs in Illinois. The whole subject of the land cessions of the various States, by which the northwest territory became Federal property, and the heart of the Union, can best be considered in treating of post-revolutionary times.

The French creoles had been plunged in chaos. In their deep distress they sent to the powers that the chances of war had set above them petition after petition, reciting their wrongs and praying that they might be righted. There is one striking difference between these petitions and the similar requests and complaints made from time to time by the different groups of American settlers west of the Alleghanies. Both alike set forth the evils from which the petitioners suffered, and the necessity of governmental remedy. But whereas the Americans invariably asked that they be allowed to govern themselves, being delighted to undertake the betterment of their condition on their own account, the French, on the contrary, habituated through generations to paternal rule, were more inclined to request that somebody fitted for the task should be sent to govern them. They humbly asked Congress either to " immediately establish some form of government among them, and appoint officers to execute the same," or else "to nominate commissioners to repair to the Illinois and inquire into the situation." [1]

One of the petitions is pathetic in its showing of the bewilderment into which the poor creoles were thrown as to who their governors really were. It requests "their Sovereign Lords," [2] whether of the Congress of the United States or of the Province of Virginia, whichever might be the owner of the country, to nominate "a lieutenant or a governor, whomever it may please our Lords to send us." [3]   The letter goes on to ask that this governor may speak French, so that he may preside over the court; and it earnestly beseeches that the laws may be enforced and crime and wrong-doing put down with a strong hand.

The conquest of the Illinois Territory was fraught with the deepest and most far-reaching benefits to all the American people; it likewise benefited, in at least an equal degree, the boldest and most energetic among the French inhabitants, those who could hold their own among freemen, who could swim in troubled waters; but it may well be doubted whether to the mass of the ignorant and simple creoles it was not a curse rather than a blessing.

[1] State Department MSS., No. 30, p. 453.   Memorial of François Carbonneaux, agent for the inhabitants of Illinois.

[2] "Nos Souverains Seigneurs."   The letter is ill-written and worse spelt, in an extraordinary French patois.   State Department MSS., No. 30, page 459.   It is dated December 3, 1782.   Many of the surnames attached are marked with a cross ; others are signed.   Two are given respectively as "Bienvenus fils" and "Blouin fils."

[3] State Department MSS., No. 30, p. 459, "de nomer un lieutenant ou un gouverneur tel qu'il plaira a nos Seigneurs de nous l'envoyer."

CHAPTER VII.

KENTUCKY UNTIL THE END OF THE REVOLU-TION, 1782-1783.

SEVENTEEN hundred and eighty-two proved to be Kentucky's year of blood. The British at Detroit had strained every nerve to drag into the war the entire Indian population of the northwest. They had finally succeeded in arousing even the most distant tribes—not to speak of the twelve thousand savages immediately tributary to Detroit.[1] So lavish had been the expenditure of money and presents to secure the good-will of the savages and enlist their active services against the Americans, that it had caused serious complaint at headquarters.[2]

Early in the spring the Indians renewed their forays; horses were stolen, cabins burned, and Renewal of women and children carried off captive. the Indian The people were confined closely to their Forays. stockaded forts, from which small bands of riflemen sallied to patrol the country. From time to time these encountered marauding parties, and in the fights that followed sometimes the whites, sometimes the reds, were victorious.

One of these conflicts attracted wide attention on the border because of the obstinacy with which it

[1] Haldimand MSS. Census for 1782, 11,402.
[2] *Do.* Haldimand to De Peyster, April 10, October 6, 1781.

was waged and the bloodshed that accompanied it. In March a party of twenty-five Wyandots came into the settlements, passed Boonsborough, and killed and scalped a girl within sight of Estill's Station. The men from the latter, also to the number of twenty-five, hastily gathered under Captain Estill, and after two days' hot pursuit overtook the Wyandots. A fair stand-up fight followed, the better marksmanship of the whites being offset, as so often before, by the superiority their foes showed in sheltering themselves. At last victory declared for the Indians. Estill had despatched a lieutenant and seven men to get round the Wyandots and assail them in the rear; but either the lieutenant's heart or his judgment failed him, he took too long, and meanwhile the Wyandots closed in on the others, killing nine, including Estill, and wounding four, who, with their unhurt comrades, escaped. It is said that the Wyandots themselves suffered heavily.[1]

These various ravages and skirmishes were but the prelude to a far more serious attack. In July the British captains Caldwell and McKee came down from Detroit with a party of rangers, and gathered together a great army of over a thousand Indians [2]—

[1] Of course not as much as their foes. The backwoodsmen (like the regular officers of both the British and American armies in similar cases, as at Grant's and St. Clair's defeats) were fond of consoling themselves for their defeats by snatching at any wild tale of the losses of the victors. In the present instance it is even possible that the loss of the Wyandots was very light instead of very heavy.

[2] Haldimand MSS. Letter from Capt. Caldwell, August 26, 1782; and letter of Captain McKee, August 28, 1782. These two letters are very important, as they give for the first time the British and Indian accounts of the battle of the Blue Licks; I print them in the Appendix.

the largest body of either red men or white that
was ever mustered west of the Alleghanies during
the Revolution. They meant to strike at Wheeling; but while on their march thither were suddenly alarmed by the rumor that Clark intended
to attack the Shawnee towns.[1] They at once
countermarched, but on reaching the threatened
towns found that the alarm had been groundless.
Most of the savages, with characteristic fickleness of
temper, then declined to go farther; but a body of
somewhat over three hundred Hurons and lake
Indians remained. With these, and their Detroit
rangers, Caldwell and McKee crossed the Ohio and
marched into Kentucky, to attack the small forts of
Fayette County.

Fayette lay between the Kentucky and the Ohio
rivers, and was then the least populous and most
exposed of the three counties into which the growing young commonwealth was divided. In 1782 it
contained but five of the small stockaded towns in
which all the early settlers were obliged to gather.
The best defended and most central was Lexington,
round which were grouped the other four—Bryan's
(which was the largest), McGee's, McConnell's, and
Boon's. Boon's Station, sometimes called Boon's
new station, where the tranquil, resolute old pioneer
at that time dwelt, must not be confounded with his
former fort of Boonsborough, from which it was
several miles distant, north of the Kentucky. Since

---

[1] This rumor was caused by Clark's gunboat, which, as will be hereafter
mentioned, had been sent up to the mouth of the Licking; some Shawnees
saw it, and thought Clark was preparing for an inroad.

the destruction of Martin's and Ruddle's stations on the Licking, Bryan's on the south bank of the Elkhorn was left as the northernmost outpost of the settlers. Its stout, loopholed palisades enclosed some forty cabins, there were strong block-houses at the corners, and it was garrisoned by fifty good riflemen.

These five stations were held by backwoodsmen of the usual Kentucky stamp, from the up-country of Pennsylvania, Virginia, and North Carolina. Generations of frontier life had made them with their fellows the most distinctive and typical Americans on the continent, utterly different from their old-world kinsfolk. Yet they still showed strong traces of the covenanting spirit, which they drew from the Irish-Presbyterian, the master strain in their mixed blood. For years they had not seen the inside of a church; nevertheless, mingled with men who were loose of tongue and life, there still remained many Sabbath-keepers and Bible-readers, who studied their catechisms on Sundays, and disliked almost equally profane language and debauchery.[1]

An incident that occurred at this time illustrates well their feelings. In June a fourth of the active militia of the county was ordered on duty, Patterson and Reynolds. to scout and patrol the country. Accordingly forty men turned out under Captain Robert Patterson. They were given ammunition, as well as two pack-horses, by the Commissary Department. Every man was entitled to pay for the time he was out. Whether he would ever get it was problematical; at the best it was certain to be given

[1] McAfee MSS.

him in worthless paper-money. Their hunters kept them supplied with game, and each man carried a small quantity of parched corn.

The company was ordered to the mouth of the Kentucky to meet the armed row-boat, sent by Clark from the Falls. On the way Patterson was much annoyed by a "very profane, swearing man" from Bryan's Station, named Aaron Reynolds. Reynolds was a good-hearted, active young fellow, with a biting tongue, not only given to many oaths, but likewise skilled in the rough, coarse banter so popular with the backwoodsmen. After having borne with him four days Patterson made up his mind that he would have to reprove him, and, if no amendment took place, send him home. He waited until, at a halt, Reynolds got a crowd round him, and began to entertain them "with oaths and wicked expressions," whereupon he promptly stepped in "and observed to him that he was a very wicked and profane man," and that both the company as well as he, the Captain, would thank him to desist. On the next day, however, Reynolds began to swear again; this time Patterson not only reproved him severely, but also tried the effect of judicious gentleness, promising to give him a quart of spirits on reaching the boat if he immediately "quit his profanity and swearing." Four days afterwards they reached the boat, and Aaron Reynolds demanded the quart of spirits. Patterson suggested a doubt as to whether he had kept his promise, whereupon he appealed to the company, then on parade, and they pronounced in his favor, saying that they had not heard him swear since he was reproved. Patterson, who himself records the incident, concludes with the remark: "The spirits were drank."[1]   Evidently the company, who had so impartially acted as judges between their fellow-soldier and their superior officer, viewed with the same equanimity the zeal of the latter and the mixed system of command, entreaty, and reward by which he carried his point. As will be seen, the event had a striking sequel at the battle of the Blue Licks.

Throughout June and July the gunboat patrolled the Ohio, going up to the Licking. Parties of back-woods riflemen, embodied as militia, likewise patrolled the woods, always keeping their scouts and spies well spread out, and exercising the greatest care to avoid being surprised. They greatly hampered the Indian war bands, but now and then the latter slipped by and fell on the people they protected. Early in August such a band committed some ravages south of the Kentucky, beating back with loss a few militia who followed it. Some of the Fayette men were about setting forth to try and cut off its retreat, when the sudden and unlooked-for approach of Caldwell and McKee's great war party obliged them to bend all their energies to their own defence.

The blow fell on Bryan's Station. The rangers and warriors moved down through the forest with

[1] Patterson's paper, given by Col. John Mason Brown, in his excellent pamphlet on the "Battle of the Blue Licks" (Franklin, Ky., 1882). I cannot forbear again commenting on the really admirable historic work now being done by Messrs. Brown, Durrett, Speed, and the other members of the Louisville "Filson Club."

the utmost speed and stealth, hoping to take this, the northernmost of the stockades, by surprise. If they had succeeded, Lexington and the three smaller stations north of the Kentucky would probably likewise have fallen.

The attack was made early on the morning of the 16th of August. Some of the settlers were in the corn-fields, and the rest inside the palisade of standing logs; they were preparing to follow the band of marauders who had gone south of the Kentucky. A few outlying Indian spies were discovered, owing to their eagerness; and the whites being put on their guard, the attempt to carry the fort by the first rush was, of course, foiled. Like so many other stations —but unlike Lexington,—Bryan's had no spring within its walls; and as soon as there was reason to dread an attack, it became a matter of vital importance to lay in a supply of water. It was feared that to send the men to the spring would arouse suspicion in the minds of the hiding savages; and, accordingly, the women went down with their pails and buckets as usual. The younger girls showed some nervousness, but the old housewives marshalled them as coolly as possible, talking and laughing together, and by their unconcern completely deceived the few Indians who were lurking near by —for the main body had not yet come up.[1] This advance guard of the savages feared that, if they attacked the women, all chance of surprising the fort

The Attack on Bryan's Station.

[1] Caldwell's letter says that a small party of Indians was sent ahead first; the watering incident apparently took place immediately on this small party being discovered.

would be lost; and so the water-carriers were suffered to go back unharmed.[1] Hardly were they
within the fort, however, when some of the Indians
found that they had been discovered, and the attack
began so quickly that one or two of the men who
had lingered in the corn-fields were killed, or else
were cut off and fled to Lexington; while, at the
same time, swift-footed runners were sent out to
carry the alarm to the different stockades, and summon their riflemen to the rescue.

At first but a few Indians appeared, on the side
of the Lexington road; they whooped and danced
defiance to the fort, evidently inviting an attack.
Their purpose was to lure the defenders into sallying

[1] This account rests on tradition; it is recorded by McClung, a most untrustworthy writer; his account of the battle of the Blue Licks is wrong from
beginning to end.   But a number of gentlemen in Kentucky have informed
me that old pioneers whom they knew in their youth had told them that they
had themselves seen the incident, and that, as written down, it was substantially true.   So with Reynold's speech to Girty.   Of course, his exact words,
as given by McClung, are incorrect; but Mr. L. C. Draper informs me
that, in his youth, he knew several old men who had been in Bryan's Station,
and had themselves heard the speech.   If if were not for this I should reject
it, for the British accounts do not even mention that Girty was along, and do
not hint at the incident.   It was probably an unauthorized ruse of Girty's.
The account of the decoy party of Indians is partially confirmed by the
British letters.   Both Marshall and McClung get this siege and battle very
much twisted in their narratives; they make so many mistakes that it is difficult to know what portion of their accounts to accept.   Nevertheless it would
be a great mistake to neglect all, even of McClung's statements.   Thus Boon
and Levi Todd in their reports make no mention of McGarry's conduct; and
it might be supposed to be a traditional myth, but McClung's account is unexpectedly corroborated by Arthur Campbell's letter, hereafter to be quoted,
which was written at the time.

Marshall is the authority for Netherland's feat at the ford.   Boon's description in the Filson narrative differs on several points from his earlier
official letter, one or two grave errors being made; it is one of the incidents
which shows how cautiously the Filson sketch must be used, though it is
usually accepted as unquestionable authority.

out after them, when their main body was to rush
at the stockade from the other side. But they did
not succeed in deceiving the veteran Indian fighters
who manned the heavy gates of the fort, stood behind
the loopholed walls, or scanned the country round
about from the high block-houses at the corners. A
dozen active young men were sent out on the Lexington road to carry on a mock skirmish with the
decoy party, while the rest of the defenders gathered behind the wall on the opposite side. As
soon as a noisy but harmless skirmish had been
begun by the sallying party, the main body of warriors burst out of the woods and rushed towards
the western gate. A single volley from the loopholes drove them back, while the sallying party
returned at a run and entered the Lexington gate
unharmed, laughing at the success of their counter-
stratagem.

The Indians surrounded the fort, each crawling
up as close as he could find shelter behind some
stump, tree, or fence. An irregular fire began, the
whites, who were better covered, having slightly
the advantage, but neither side suffering much.
This lasted for several hours, until early in the afternoon a party from Lexington suddenly appeared and
tried to force its way into the fort.

The runners who slipped out of the fort at the
first alarm went straight to Lexington. There they
found that the men had just started out to cut
off the retreat of the marauding savages who were
ravaging south of the Kentucky. Following their
trail they speedily overtook the troops, and told of

the attack on Bryan's. Instantly forty men under Major Levi Todd countermarched to the rescue. Being ignorant of the strength of the Indians they did not wait for the others, but pushed boldly forward, seventeen being mounted and the others on foot.[1]

The road from Lexington to Bryan's for the last few hundred yards led beside a field of growing corn taller than a man. Some of the Indians were lying in this field when they were surprised by the sudden appearance of the rescuers, and promptly fired on them. Levi Todd and the horsemen, who were marching in advance, struck spurs into their steeds, and galloping hard through the dust and smoke reached the fort in safety. The footmen were quickly forced to retreat towards Lexington; but the Indians were too surprised by the unlooked-for approach to follow, and they escaped with the loss of one man killed and three wounded.[1]

That night the Indians tried to burn the fort, shooting flaming arrows onto the roofs of the cabins and rushing up to the wooden wall with lighted torches. But they were beaten off at each attempt. When day broke they realized that it was hopeless to make any further effort, though they still kept up a desultory fire on the fort's defenders; they had killed most of the cattle and pigs, and some of the horses, and had driven away the rest.

Girty, who was among the assailants, as a last shift, tried to get the garrison to surrender, assuring them

[1] Va. State Papers, III., p. 300. McClung's and Collins' accounts of this incident are pure romance. [2] *Do.*

that the Indians were hourly expecting reinforcements, including the artillery brought against Ruddle's and Martin's stations two years previously;
and that if forced to batter down the walls no
quarter would be given to any one. Among the
fort's defenders was young Aaron Reynolds, the
man whose profanity had formerly roused Captain
Patterson's ire; and he now undertook to be spokes-
man for the rest. Springing up into sight he answered Girty in the tone of rough banter so dear to
the backwoodsmen, telling the renegade that he knew
him well, and despised him, that the men in the fort
feared neither cannon nor reinforcements, and if need
be, could drive Girty's tawny followers back from
the walls with switches; and he ended by assuring
him that the whites, too, were expecting help, for
the country was roused, and if the renegade and his
followers dared to linger where they were for
another twenty-four hours, their scalps would surely
be sun-dried on the roofs of the cabins.

The Indians knew well that the riflemen were
mustering at all the neighboring forts; and, as soon
as their effort to treat failed, they withdrew during
the forenoon of the 17th.[1] They were angry and

---

[1] There are four contemporary official reports of this battle : two American, those of Boon and Levi Todd ; and two British, those of McKee
and Caldwell. All four agree that the fort was attacked on one day, the
siege abandoned on the next, pursuit made on the third, and the battle
fought on the fourth. Boon and Todd make the siege begin on August 16th,
and the battle take place on the 19th ; Caldwell makes the dates the 15th
and 18th ; McKee makes them the 18th and 21st. I therefore take Boon's
and Todd's dates.

McClung and Marshall make the siege last three or four days instead of
less than two.

All the accounts of the battle of the Blue Licks, so far, have been very

sullen at their discomfiture. Five of their number had been killed and several wounded. Of the fort's defenders four had been killed and three wounded. Among the children within its walls during the siege there was one, the youngest, a Kentucky-born baby, named Richard Johnson; over thirty years later he led the Kentucky mounted riflemen at the victory of the Thames, when they killed not only the great Indian chief Tecumseh, but also, it is said, the implacable renegade Simon Girty himself, then in extreme old age.

All this time the runners sent out from Bryan's had been speeding through the woods, summoning help from each of the little walled towns. The Fayette troops quickly gathered. As soon as Boon heard the news he marched at the head of the men of his station, among them his youngest son Israel, destined shortly to be slain before his eyes. The men from Lexington, McConnell's, and McGee's, rallied under John Todd, who was County Lieutenant, and, by virtue of his commission in the Virginia line, the ranking officer of Kentucky, second only to Clark. Troops also came from south of the Kentucky River; Lieutenant-Colonel Trigg and Majors McGarry and Harlan led the men from Harrodsburg, who were soonest ready to march, and likewise brought the news that Logan,

Battle of the Blue Licks.

inaccurate, because the British reports have never been even known to exist, and the reports of the American commanders, printed in the Virginia State papers, have but recently seen the light. Mr. Whitsitt, in his recent excellent "Life of Judge Wallace," uses the latter, but makes the great mistake of incorporating into his narrative some of the most glaring errors of McClung and Marshall.

their County Lieutenant, was raising the whole force of Lincoln in hot haste, and would follow in a couple of days.

These bands of rescuers reached Bryan's Station on the afternoon of the day the Indians had left. The men thus gathered were the very pick of the Kentucky pioneers; sinewy veterans of border strife, skilled hunters and woodsmen, long wonted to every kind of hardship and danger. They were men of the most dauntless courage, but unruly and impatient of all control. Only a few of the cooler heads were willing to look before they leaped; and even their chosen and trusted leaders were forced to advise and exhort rather than to command them. All were eager for battle and vengeance, and were excited and elated by the repulse that had just been inflicted on the savages; and they feared to wait for Logan lest the foe should escape. Next morning they rode out in pursuit, one hundred and eighty-two strong, all on horseback, and all carrying long rifles. There was but one sword among them, which Todd had borrowed from Boon—a rough weapon, with short steel blade and buckhorn hilt. As with most frontier levies, the officers were in large proportion; for, owing to the system of armed settlement and half-military organization, each wooden fort, each little group of hunters or hard-fighting backwoods farmers, was forced to have its own captain, lieutenant, ensign, and sergeant.[1]

[1] For the American side of the battle of Blue Licks I take the contemporary reports of Boon, Levi Todd, and Logan, Va. State Papers, Vol III., pp. 276, 280, 300, 333. Boon and Todd both are explicit that there were one hundred and eighty-two riflemen, all on horseback, and substantially agree as to the loss of the frontiersmen. Later reports underestimate both the

The Indians, in their unhurried retreat, followed the great buffalo trace that led to the Blue Licks, a broad road, beaten out through the forest by the passing and repassing of the mighty herds through countless generations. They camped on the farther side of the river ; some of the savages had left, but there were still nearly three hundred men in all— Hurons and lake Indians, with the small party of rangers.[1]

The backwoods horsemen rode swiftly on the trail of their foes, and before evening came to where they had camped the night before. A careful examina· tion of the camp-fires convinced the leaders that they

numbers and loss of the whites. Boon's Narrative, written two years after the event, from memory, conflicts in one or two particulars with his earlier report. Patterson, writing long afterwards, and from memory, falls into gross errors, both as to the number of troops and as to some of them being on foot ; his account must be relied on chiefly for his own adventures. Most of the historians of Kentucky give the affair very incorrectly. Butler follows Marshall ; but from the Clark papers he got the right number of men engaged. Marshall gives a few valuable facts ; but he is all wrong on certain important points. For instance, he says Todd hurried into action for fear Logan would supersede him in the command ; but in reality Todd ranked Logan. McClung's ornate narrative, that usually followed, hangs on the very slenderest thread of truth ; it is mainly sheer fiction. Prolix, tedious Collins follows the plan he usually does when his rancorous prejudices do not influence him, and presents half a dozen utterly inconsistent accounts, with no effort whatever to reconcile them. He was an industrious collector of information, and gathered an enormous quantity, some of it very useful ; he recorded with the like complacency authentic incidents of the highest importance and palpable fabrications or irrelevant trivialities ; and it never entered his head to sift evidence or to exercise a little critical power and judgment.

[1] Caldwell says that he had at first " three hundred Indians and Rangers," but that before the battle "nigh 100 Indians left." McKee says that there were at first " upwards of three hundred Hurons and Lake Indians," besides the rangers and a very few Mingos, Delawares, and Shawnees. Later he says of the battle : " We were not much superior to them in numbers, they being about two hundred."

Levi Todd put the number of the Indians at three hundred, which was pretty near the truth ; Boon thought it four hundred ; later writers exaggerate wildly, putting it even at one thousand.

were heavily outnumbered; nevertheless they continued the pursuit, and overtook the savages early
the following morning, the 19th of August.

As they reached the Blue Licks, they saw a few
Indians retreating up a rocky ridge that led from the
north bank of the river. The backwoodsmen halted
on the south bank, and a short council was held.
All turned naturally to Boon, the most experienced
Indian fighter present, in whose cool courage and
tranquil self-possession all confided. The wary old
pioneer strongly urged that no attack be made at the
moment, but that they should await the troops coming up under Logan. The Indians were certainly
much superior in numbers to the whites; they were
aware that they were being followed by a small force,
and from the confident, leisurely way in which they
had managed their retreat, were undoubtedly anxious
to be overtaken and attacked. The hurried pursuit
had been quite proper in the first place, for if the
Indians had fled rapidly they would surely have
broken up into different bands, which could have
been attacked on even terms, while delay would have
permitted them to go off unscathed. But, as it was,
the attack would be very dangerous; while the delay
of waiting for Logan would be a small matter, for the
Indians could still be overtaken after he had arrived.

Well would it have been for the frontiersmen had
they followed Boon's advice.[1] Todd and Trigg both

[1] Va. State Papers, III., 337. Col. Campbell's letter of Oct. 3, 1782.
The letter is interesting as showing by contemporary authority that Boon's
advice and McGarry's misbehavior are not mere matters of tradition. It is
possible that there was some jealousy between the troops from Lincoln and
those from Fayette; the latter had suffered much from the Indians, and
were less rash in consequence; while many of the Lincoln men were hot for
instant battle.

agreed with him, and so did many of the cooler riflemen—among others a man named Netherland, whose
caution caused the young hotheads to jeer at him as
a coward.   But the decision was not suffered to rest
with the three colonels who nominally commanded.
Doubtless the council was hasty and tumultuous, being
held by the officers in the open, closely pressed upon
and surrounded by a throng of eager, unruly soldiers,
who did not hesitate to offer advice or express dis-
satisfaction.   Many of the more headlong and impatient among the bold spirits looking on desired
instant action; and these found a sudden leader in
Major Hugh McGarry.   He was a man utterly
unsuited to command of any kind; and his retention
in office after repeated acts of violence and insubor-
dination shows the inherent weakness of the frontier
militia system.   He not only chafed at control, but
he absolutely refused to submit to it; and his courage
was of a kind better fitted to lead him into a fight
than to make him bear himself well after it was
begun.   He wished no delay, and was greatly angered
at the decision of the council; nor did he hesitate to
at once appeal therefrom.   Turning to the crowd of
backwoodsmen he suddenly raised the thrilling war-
cry, and spurred his horse into the stream, waving
his hat over his head and calling on all who were
not cowards to follow him.   The effect was electrical.
In an instant all the hunter-soldiers plunged in after
him with a shout, and splashed across the ford of
the shallow river in huddled confusion.

Boon and Todd had nothing to do but follow.   On
the other side they got the men into order, and led
them on, the only thing that was possible under the

circumstances. These two leaders acted excellently throughout; and they now did their best to bring the men with honor through the disaster into which they had been plunged by their own headstrong folly.

As the Indians were immediately ahead, the array of battle was at once formed. The troops spread out into a single line. The right was led by Trigg, the centre by Colonel-Commandant Todd in person, with McGarry under him, and an advance guard of twenty-five men under Harlan in front; while the left was under Boon. The ground was equally favorable to both parties, the timber being open and good.[1] But the Indians had the advantage in numbers, and were able to outflank the whites.

In a minute the spies brought word that the enemy were close in front.[2] The Kentuckians galloped up at speed to within sixty yards of their foes, leaped from their horses, and instantly gave and received a heavy fire.[3] Boon was the first to open the combat; and under his command the left wing pushed the Indians opposite them back for a hundred yards. The old hunter of course led in person; his men stoutly backed him up, and their resolute bearing and skilful marksmanship gave to the whites in this part of the line a momentary victory.

[1] Levi Todd's letter, Aug. 26, 1782.

[2] It is absolutely erroneous to paint the battle as in any way a surprise. Boon says : "We discovered the enemy lying in wait for us ; on this discovery we formed our columns into a single line, and marched up in their front." There was no ambush, except that of course the Indians, as usual, sheltered themselves behind trees or in the long grass. From what Boon and Levi Todd say, it is evident that the firing began on both sides at the same time. Caldwell says the Indians fired one gun whereupon the Kentuckians fired a volley.   [3] Levi Todd's letter.

But on the right of the Kentucky advance, affairs went badly from the start. The Indians were thrown out so as to completely surround Triggs' wing. Almost as soon as the firing became heavy in front, crowds of painted warriors rose from some hollows of long grass that lay on Trigg's right and poured in a close and deadly volley. Rushing forward, they took his men in rear and flank, and rolled them up on the centre, killing Trigg himself. Harlan's advance guard was cut down almost to a man, their commander being among the slain. The centre was then assailed from both sides by overwhelming numbers. Todd did all he could by voice and example to keep his men firm, and cover Boon's successful advance, but in vain. Riding to and fro on his white horse, he was shot through the body, and mortally wounded. He leaped on his horse again, but his strength failed him; the blood gushed from his mouth; he leaned forward, and fell heavily from the saddle. Some say that his horse carried him to the river, and that he fell into its current. With his death the centre gave way; and of course Boon and the men of the left wing, thrust in advance, were surrounded on three sides. A wild rout followed, every one pushing in headlong haste for the ford. " He that could remount a horse was well off; he that could not, had no time for delay," wrote Levi Todd. The actual fighting had only occupied five minutes.[1]

In a mad and panic race the Kentuckians reached the ford, which was fortunately but a few hundred

[1] Levi Todd's letter.

yards from the battle-field, the Indians being mixed in with them. Among the first to cross was Netherland, whose cautious advice had been laughed at before the battle. No sooner had he reached the south bank, than he reined up his horse and leaped off, calling on his comrades to stop and cover the flight of the others; and most of them obeyed him. The ford was choked with a struggling mass of horsemen and footmen, fleeing whites and following Indians. Netherland and his companions opened a brisk fire upon the latter, forcing them to withdraw for a moment and let the remainder of the fugitives cross in safety. Then the flight began again. The check that had been given the Indians allowed the whites time to recover heart and breath. Retreating in groups or singly through the forest, with their weapons reloaded, their speed of foot and woodcraft enabled such as had crossed the river to escape without further serious loss.

Boon was among the last to leave the field. His son Israel was slain, and he himself was cut off from the river; but turning abruptly to one side, he broke through the ranks of the pursuers, outran them, swam the river, and returned unharmed to Bryan's Station.

Among the men in the battle were Capt. Robert Patterson and young Aaron Reynolds. When the retreat began Patterson could not get a horse. He was suffering from some old and unhealed wounds received in a former Indian fight, and he speedily became exhausted. As he was on the point of sinking, Reynolds suddenly rode up beside him, jumped off his horse, and without asking Patterson whether he would accept, bade him mount the horse and flee. Patterson did so, and was the last man over the ford. He escaped unhurt, though the Indians were running alongside and firing at him. Meanwhile Reynolds, who possessed extraordinary activity, reached the river in safety and swam across. He then sat down to take off his buckskin trowsers, which, being soaked through, hampered him much; and two Indians suddenly pounced on and captured him. He was disarmed and left in charge of one. Watching his chance, he knocked the savage down, and running off into the woods escaped with safety. When Patterson thanked him for saving his life, and asked him why he had done it, he answered, that ever since Patterson had reproved him for swearing, he had felt a strong and continued attachment for him. The effect of the reproof, combined with his narrow escape, changed him completely, and he became a devout member of the Baptist Church. Patterson, to show the gratitude he felt, gave him a horse and saddle, and a hundred acres of prime land, the first he had ever owned.

The loss of the defeated Kentuckians had been very great. Seventy were killed outright, including Colonel Todd and Lieutenant-Colonel Trigg, the first and third in command. Seven were captured, and twelve of those who escaped were badly wounded.[1] The victors lost one of the Detroit rangers (a Frenchman), and six Indians killed and ten Indians wound-

---

[1] Those are the figures of Boon's official report, and must be nearly accurate. The later accounts give all sorts of numbers.

ed.[1] Almost their whole loss was caused by the successful advance of Boon's troops, save what was due to Netherland when he rallied the flying backwoodsmen at the ford.

Of the seven white captives four were put to death with torture; three eventually rejoined their people. One of them owed his being spared to a singular and amusing feat of strength and daring. When forced to run the gauntlet he, by his activity, actually succeeded in reaching the council-house unharmed; when almost to it, he turned, seized a powerful Indian and hurled him violently to the ground, and then, thrusting his head between the legs of another pursuer, he tossed him clean over his back, after which he sprang on a log, leaped up and knocked his heels together, crowed in the fashion of backwoods victors, and rallied the Indians as a pack of cowards. One of the old chiefs immediately adopted him into the tribe as his son.

All the little forted villages north of the Kentucky, and those lying near its southern bank, were plunged into woe and mourning by the defeat.[2] In

---

[1] Caldwell's letter. But there are some slight discrepancies between the letters of McKee and Caldwell. Caldwell makes the loss at Bryan's Station and the Blue Licks together twelve killed and twelve wounded ; McKee says eleven killed and fourteen wounded. Both exaggerate the American loss, but not as much as the Americans exaggerated that of the Indians, Boon in his narrative giving the wildest of all the estimates.

[2] Arthur Campbell, in the letter already quoted, comments with intense bitterness on the defeat, which, he says, was due largely to McGarry's " vain and seditious expressions." He adds that Todd and Trigg had capacity but no experience, and Boon experience but no capacity, while Logan was "a dull and narrow body," and Clark " a sot, if nothing worse." Campbell was a Holston Virginian, an able but very jealous man, who disliked the Kentucky leaders, and indeed had no love for Kentucky itself ; he had strenuously opposed its first erection as a separate county.

every stockade, in almost every cabin, there was weeping for husband or father, son, brother, or lover. The best and bravest blood in the land had been shed like water. There was no one who had not lost some close and dear friend, and the heads of all the people were bowed and their hearts sore stricken.

The bodies of the dead lay where they had fallen, on the hill-slope, and in the shallow river; torn by wolf, vulture, and raven, or eaten by fishes. In a day or two Logan came up with four hundred men from south of the Kentucky, tall Simon Kenton marching at the head of the troops, as captain of a company.[1] They buried the bodies of the slain on the battle-field, in long trenches, and heaped over them stones and logs. Meanwhile the victorious Indians, glutted with vengeance, recrossed the Ohio and vanished into the northern forests.

The Indian ravages continued throughout the early fall months; all the outlying cabins were destroyed, the settlers were harried from the clearings, and a station on Salt River was taken by surprise, thirty-seven people being captured. Stunned by the crushing disaster at the Blue Licks, and utterly disheartened and cast down by the continued ravages, many of the settlers threatened to leave the country. The county officers sent long petitions to the Virginia Legislature, complaining that the troops posted at the Falls were of no assistance in checking the raids of the Indians, and asserting that the operations carried on by order of the Executive for the past eighteen months had been a detriment rather

[1] McBride's '' Pioneer Biography,'' I., 210.

than a help. The utmost confusion and discouragement prevailed everywhere.[1]

At last the news of repeated disaster roused Clark
into his old-time energy. He sent out runners through
the settlements, summoning all the able-bodied men
to make ready for a blow at the Indians. The pioneers
turned with eager relief towards the man who had

---

[1] Va. State Papers, III., pp. 301, 331. Letter of William Christian, September 28th. Petition of Boon, Todd, Netherland, etc., September 11th
In Morehead's "address" is a letter from Nathaniel Hart. He was himself
as a boy, witness of what he describes. His father, who had been Henderson's partner and bore the same name as himself, was from North Carolina.
He founded in Kentucky a station known as White Oak Springs ; and was
slain by the savages during this year. The letter runs : "It is impossible
at this day to make a just impression of the sufferings of the pioneers about
the period spoken of. The White Oak Springs fort in 1782, with perhaps
one hundred souls in it was reduced in August to three fighting white men—
and I can say with truth that for two or three weeks my mother's family
never unclothed themselves to sleep, nor were all of them within that time at
their meals together, nor was any household business attempted. Food was
prepared and placed where those who chose could eat. It was the period
when Bryant's station was beseiged, and for many days before and after that
gloomy event we were in constant expectation of being made prisoners. We
made application to Col. Logan for a guard and obtained one, but not until
the danger was measureably over. It then consisted of two men only. Col.
Logan did every thing in his power, as County Lieutenant, to sustain the
different forts—but it was not a very easy matter to order a married man from
a fort where his family was to defend some other when his own was in
imminent danger.

"I went with my mother in January, 1783, to Logan's station to prove my
father's will. He had fallen in the preceding July. Twenty armed men
were of the party. Twenty-three widows were in attendance upon the court
to obtain letters of administration on the estates of their husbands who had
been killed during the past year."

The letter also mentions that most of the original settlers of the fort were
from Pennsylvania, "orderly respectable people and the men good soldiers.
But they were unaccustomed to Indian warfare, and the consequence was
that of some ten or twelve men all were killed but two or three." This incident illustrates the folly of the hope, at one time entertained, that the
Continental troops, by settling in the west on lands granted them, would prove
a good barrier against the Indians ; the best Continentals in Washington's
army would have been almost as helpless as British grenadiers in the woods.

so often led them to success. They answered his call with quick enthusiasm; beeves, pack-horses, and supplies were offered in abundance, and every man who could shoot and ride marched to the appointed meeting-places. The men from the eastern stations gathered at Bryan's, under Logan; those from the western, at the Falls, under Floyd. The two divisions met at the mouth of the Licking, where Clark took supreme command. On the 4th of November, he left the banks of the Ohio and struck off northward through the forest, at the head of one thousand and fifty mounted riflemen. On the 10th he attacked the Miami towns. His approach was discovered just in time to prevent a surprise. The Indians hurriedly fled to the woods, those first discovered raising the alarm-cry, which could be heard an incredible distance, and thus warning their fellows. In consequence no fight followed, though there was sharp skirmishing between the advance guard and the hindermost Indians. Ten scalps were taken and seven prisoners, besides two whites being recaptured. Of Clark's men, one was killed and one wounded. The flight of the Indians was too hasty to permit them to save any of their belongings. All the cabins were burned, together with an immense quantity of corn and provisions—a severe loss at the opening of winter. McKee, the Detroit partisan, attempted to come to the rescue with what Indians he could gather, but was met and his force promptly scattered.[1]   Logan led a

Clark's Counter-Stroke.

[1] Haldimand MSS. Letter of Alex. McKee, November 15, 1782. He makes no attempt to hide the severity of the blow; his letter shows a curious contrast in tone to the one he wrote after the Blue Licks. He states that the victory has opened the road to Detroit to the Americans.

detachment to the head of the Miami, and burned the stores of the British traders. The loss to the savages at the beginning of cold weather was very great; they were utterly cast down and panic-stricken at such a proof of the power of the whites, coming as it did so soon after the battle of the Blue Licks. The expedition returned in triumph, and the Kentuckians completely regained their self-confidence; and though for ten years longer Kentucky suffered from the inroads of small parties of savages, it was never again threatened by a serious invasion.[1]

At the beginning of 1783, when the news of peace was spread abroad, immigration began to **Wonderful** flow to Kentucky down the Ohio, and **Growth of** over the Wilderness road, in a flood of **Kentucky.** which the volume dwarfed all former streams into rivulets. Indian hostilities continued at intervals throughout this year,[2] but they were not of a serious nature. Most of the tribes concluded at least a nominal peace, and liberated over two hundred white prisoners, though they retained nearly as many more.[3] Nevertheless in the spring one man of note fell victim to the savages, for John Floyd was waylaid and slain as he was riding out with his brother. Thus within the space of eight months, two of the three county lieutenants had been killed, in battle or ambush.

The inrush of new settlers was enormous,[4] and Kentucky fairly entered on its second stage of

[1] Va. State Papers, p. 381. Clark's letter of November 27, 1782.
[2] *Do.*, p. 522. Letter of Benjamin Logan, August 11, 1783.
[3] *Pennsylvania Packet*, No. 1,079, August 12, 1783.
[4] McAfee MSS.

growth. The days of the first game hunters and Indian fighters were over. By this year the herds of the buffalo, of which the flesh and hides had been so important to the earlier pioners, were nearly exterminated; though bands still lingered in the remote recesses of the mountains, and they were plentiful in Illinois. The land claims began to clash, and interminable litigation followed. This rendered very important the improvement in the judiciary system which was begun in March by the erection of the three counties into the "District of Kentucky," with a court of common law and chancery jurisdiction coextensive with its limits. The name of Kentucky, which had been dropped when the original county was divided into three, was thus permanently revived. The first court sat at Harrodsburg, but as there was no building where it could properly be held, it adjourned to the Dutch Reformed Meeting-house six miles off. The first grand jury empanelled presented nine persons for selling liquor without license, eight for adultery and fornication, and the clerk of Lincoln County for not keeping a table of fees; besides several for smaller offences.[1] A log court-house and a log jail were immediately built.

Manufactories of salt were started at the licks, where it was sold at from three to five silver dollars a bushel.[2] This was not only used by the settlers for themselves, but for their stock, which ranged freely in the woods; to provide for the latter a tree was chopped down and the salt placed in notches or small troughs cut in the trunk, making it what

---

[1] Marshall, I., 159.   [2] McAfee MSS.

was called a lick-log.   Large grist-mills were erected
at some of the stations; wheat crops were raised;
and small distilleries were built. The gigantic system
of river commerce of the Mississippi had been begun
the preceding year by one Jacob Yoder, who loaded
a flat-boat at the Old Redstone Fort, on the Monongahela, and drifted down to New Orleans, where he
sold his goods, and returned to the Falls of the Ohio
by a roundabout course leading through Havana,
Philadelphia, and Pittsburg. Several regular schools
were started. There were already meeting-houses of
the Baptist and Dutch Reformed congregations, the
preachers spending the week-days in clearing and
tilling the fields, splitting rails, and raising hogs; in
1783 a permanent Presbyterian minister arrived, and
a log church was speedily built for him. The sport-
loving Kentuckians this year laid out a race track
at Shallowford Station. It was a straight quarter of a
mile course, within two hundred yards of the stockade; at its farther end was a canebrake, wherein an
Indian once lay hid and shot a rider, who was pulling
up his horse at the close of a race. There was still
but one ferry, that over the Kentucky River at
Boonsborough; the price of ferriage was three
shillings for either man or horse. The surveying
was still chiefly done by hunters, and much of it was
in consequence very loose indeed.[1]

The first retail store Kentucky had seen since Henderson's, at Boonsborough, was closed in 1775, was
established this year at the Falls; the goods were
brought in wagons from Philadelphia to Pittsburg,

[1] McAfee MSS.   Marshall, Collins, Brown's pamphlets.

and thence down the Ohio in flat-boats. The game had been all killed off in the immediate neighborhood of the town at the Falls, and Clark undertook to supply the inhabitants with meat, as a commercial speculation. Accordingly he made a contract with John Saunders, the hunter who had guided him on his march to the Illinois towns; the latter had presumably forgiven his chief for having threatened him with death when he lost the way. Clark was to furnish Saunders with three men, a packhorse, salt, and ammunition; while Saunders agreed to do his best and be " assiduously industrious " in hunting. Buffalo beef, bear's meat, deer hams, and bear oil were the commodities most sought after. The meat was to be properly cured and salted in camp, and sent from time to time to the Falls, where Clark was to dispose of it in market, a third of the price going to Saunders. The hunting season was to last from November 1st to January 15th.[1]

Thus the settlers could no longer always kill their own game; and there were churches, schools, mills, stores, race tracks, and markets in Kentucky.

[1] Original agreement in Durrett MSS.; bound volume of "Papers Relating to G. R. Clark." This particular agreement is for 1784; but apparently he entered into several such in different years.

CHAPTER VIII.

THE HOLSTON SETTLEMENTS, 1777-1779.

THE history of Kentucky and the Northwest has now been traced from the date of the Cherokee war to the close of the Revolution. Those portions of the southwestern lands that were afterwards made into the State of Tennessee, had meanwhile developed with almost equal rapidity. Both Kentucky and Tennessee grew into existence and power at the same time, and were originally settled and built up by precisely the same class of American backwoodsmen. But there were one or two points of difference in their methods of growth. Kentucky sprang up afar off in the wilderness, and as a separate entity from the beginning. The present State has grown steadily from a single centre, which was the part first settled ; and the popular name of the commonwealth has always been Kentucky. Tennessee, on the other hand, did not assume her present name until a quarter of a century after the first exploration and settlement had begun ; and the State grew from two entirely distinct centres. The first settlements, known as the Watauga, or afterwards more generally as the Holston, settlements, grew up while keeping close touch with the Virginians, who

Organization of the Holston Settlements.

lived round the Tennessee head-waters, and also in direct communication with North Carolina, to which State they belonged. It was not until 1779 that a portion of these Holston people moved to the bend of the Cumberland River and started a new community, exactly as Kentucky had been started before. At first this new community, known as the Cumberland settlement, was connected by only the loosest tie with the Holston settlements. The people of the two places were not grouped together; they did not even have a common name. The three clusters of Holston, Cumberland, and Kentucky settlements developed independently of one another, and though their founders were in each case of the same kind, they were at first only knit one to another by a lax bond of comradeship.

In 1776 the Watauga pioneers probably numbered some six hundred souls in all. Having at last found out the State in which they lived, they petitioned North Carolina to be annexed thereto as a district or county. The older settlements had evidently been jealous of them, for they found it necessary to deny that they were, as had been asserted, "a lawless mob"; it may be remarked that the Transylvanian colonists had been obliged to come out with a similar statement. In their petition they christened their country " Washington District," in honor of the great chief whose name already stood first in the hearts of all Americans. The document was written by Sevier. It set forth the history of the settlers, their land purchases from the Indians, their successful effort at self-government, their mili-

tary organization, with Robertson as captain, and
finally their devotion to the Revolutionary cause;
and recited their lack of proper authority to deal
promptly with felons, murderers, and the like, who
came in from the neighboring States, as the reason
why they wished to become a self-governing portion
of North Carolina.[1] The legislature of the State
granted the prayer of the petitioners, Washington
District was annexed, and four representatives therefrom, one of them Sevier, took their seats that fall in
the Provincial Congress at Halifax. But no change
whatever was made in the government of the Watauga people until 1777. In the spring of that year
laws were passed providing for the establishment of
courts of pleas and quarter sessions in the district,
as well as for the appointment of justices of the
peace, sheriffs, and militia officers; and in the fall
the district was made a county, under the same
name. The boundaries of Washington County were
the same as those of the present State of Tennessee,
and seem to have been outlined by Sevier, the only
man who at that time had a clear idea as to what
should be the logical and definite limits of the future
State.

The nominal change of government worked little
real alteration in the way the Holston people man-
Upholding aged their affairs. The members of the old
the Law. committee became the justices of the new
court, and, with a slight difference in forms, proceeded
against all offenders with their former vigor. Being

[1] The petition, drawn up in the summer of '76, was signed by 112 men.
It is given in full by Ramsey, p. 138. See also Phelan, p. 40.

eminently practical men, and not learned in legal tech-
nicalities, their decisions seem to have been governed
mainly by their own ideas of justice, which, though
genuine, were rough.   As the war progressed and the
southern States fell into the hands of the British, the
disorderly men who had streamed across the mountains became openly defiant towards the law.   The
tories gathered in bands, and every man who was
impatient of legal restraint, every murderer, horse-
thief, and highway robber in the community flocked
to join them.   The militia who hunted them down
soon ceased to discriminate between tories and other
criminals, and the courts rendered decisions to the
same effect.   The caption of one indictment that has
been preserved reads against the defendant "in
toryism."   He was condemned to imprisonment
during the war, half his goods was confiscated to
the use of the State, and the other half was turned
over for the support of his family.   In another case
the court granted a still more remarkable order,
upon the motion of the State attorney, which set
forth that fifteen hundred pounds, due to a certain
H., should be retained in the hands of the debtor,
because "there is sufficient reason to believe that
the said H's estate will be confiscated to the use of
the State for his misdemeanours."

There is something refreshing in the solemnity
with which these decisions are recorded, and the evident lack of perception on the part of the judges
that their records would, to their grandchildren, have
a distinctly humorous side.   To tories, and evil-doers
generally, the humor was doubtless very grim; but,

as a matter of fact, the decisions, though certainly of unusual character, were needful and just. The friends of order had to do their work with rough weapons, and they used them most efficiently. Under the stress of so dire an emergency as that they confronted they were quite right in attending only to the spirit of law and justice, and refusing to be hampered by the letter. They would have discredited their own energy and hard common-sense had they acted otherwise, and, moreover, would have inevitably failed to accomplish their purpose.

In the summer of '78, when Indian hostilities almost entirely ceased, most of the militia were disbanded, and, in consequence, the parties of tories and horse-thieves sprang into renewed strength, and threatened to overawe the courts and government officers. Immediately the leaders among the whigs, the friends of order and liberty, gathered together and organized a vigilance committee. The committee raised two companies of mounted riflemen, who were to patrol the country and put to death all suspicious characters who resisted them or who refused to give security to appear before the committee in December. The proceedings of the committee were thus perfectly open ; the members had no idea of acting secretly or against order. It was merely that in a time of general confusion they consolidated themselves into a body which was a most effective, though irregular, supporter of the cause of law. The mounted riflemen scoured the country and broke up the gangs of evil-doers, hanging six or seven of the leaders, while a number of the less prominent were brought before the committee, who fined some and condemned others to be whipped or branded. All of doubtful loyalty were compelled to take the test oath.[1]

Such drastic measures soon brought about peace; but it was broken again and again by similar risings and disturbances. By degrees most of the worst characters fled to the Cherokees, or joined the British as their forces approached the up-country. Until the battle of Kings Mountain, the pioneers had to watch the tories as closely as they did the Indians; there was a constant succession of murders, thefts, and savage retaliations. Once a number of tories attempted to surprise and murder Sevier in his own house; but the plot was revealed by the wife of the leader, to whom Sevier's wife had shown great kindness in her time of trouble. In consequence the tories were themselves surprised and their ringleaders slain. Every man in the country was obliged to bear arms the whole time, not only because of the Indian warfare, but also on account of the inveterate hatred and constant collisions between the whigs and the loyalists. Many dark deeds were done, and though the tories, with whom the criminal classes were in close alliance, were generally the first and chief offenders, yet the patriots cannot be held guiltless of murderous and ferocious

[1] Haywood, p. 58. As Haywood's narrative is based largely on what the pioneers in their old age told him, his dates, and especially his accounts of the numbers and losses of the Indians in their battles, are often very inaccurate. In this very chapter he gives, with gross inaccuracy of detail, an account of one of Sevier's campaigns as taking place in 1779, whereas it really occurred after his return from King's Mountain. There is therefore need to be cautious in using him.

reprisals. They often completely failed to distinguish between the offenders against civil order, and
those whose only crime was an honest, if mistaken,
devotion to the cause of the king.

Early in '78 a land office was opened in the
Holston settlements, and the settlers were re-
Land quired to make entries according to the
Laws. North Carolina land laws. Hitherto they
had lived on their clearings undisturbed, resting
their title upon purchase from the Indians and
upon their own mutual agreements. The old settlers were given the prior right to the locations,
and until the beginning of '79 in which to pay
for them. Each head of a family was allowed
to take up six hundred and forty acres for himself,
one hundred for his wife, and one hundred for
each of his children, at the price of forty shillings
per hundred acres, while any additional amount cost
at the rate of one hundred shillings, instead of forty.
All of the men of the Holston settlements were at
the time in the service of the State as militia, in the
campaign against the Indians; and when the land
office was opened, the money that was due them
sufficed to pay for their claims. They thus had no
difficulty in keeping possession of their lands, much
to the disappointment of the land speculators, many
of whom had come out at the opening of the office.
Afterwards large tracts were given as bounty, or in
lieu of pay, to the Revolutionary soldiers. All the
struggling colonies used their wild land as a sort of
military chest; it was often the only security of
value in their possession.

The same year that the land office was opened, it was enacted that the bridle path across the mountains should be chopped out and made into a rough wagon road.[1] The following spring the successful expedition against the Chicamaugas temporarily put a stop to Indian troubles. The growing security, the opening of the land office, and the increase of knowledge concerning the country, produced a great inflow of settlers in 1779, and from that time onward the volume of immigration steadily increased.

Many of these new-comers were " poor whites," or crackers ; lank, sallow, ragged creatures, living in poverty, ignorance, and dirt, who regarded all strangers with suspicion as " outlandish folks."[2] With every chance to rise, these people remained mere squalid cumberers of the earth's surface, a rank, up-country growth, containing within itself the seeds of vicious, idle pauperism, and semicriminality. They clustered in little groups, scattered throughout the backwoods settlements, in strong contrast to the vigorous and manly people around them.

Character and Life of the Settlers.

By far the largest number of the new-comers were of the true, hardy backwoods stock, fitted to grapple with the wilderness and to hew out of it a prosperous commonwealth. The leading settlers began, by thrift and industry, to acquire what in the backwoods passed for wealth. Their horses, cattle, and hogs throve and multiplied. The stumps were grubbed out of the clearings, and different kinds of

---

[1] However this was not actually done until some years later.

[2] Smythe's Tours, I., 103, describes the up-country crackers of North Carolina and Virginia.

grains and roots were planted. Wings were added
to the houses, and sometimes they were roofed with
shingles. The little town of Jonesboro, the first that
was not a mere stockaded fort, was laid off midway
between the Watauga and the Nolichucky.

As soon as the region grew at all well settled,
clergymen began to come in. Here, as elsewhere,
most of the frontiersmen who had any religion at all
professed the faith of the Scotch-Irish; and the first
regular church in this cradle-spot of Tennessee was a
Presbyterian log meeting-house, built near Jonesboro
in 1777, and christened Salem Church. Its pastor
was a pioneer preacher, who worked with fiery and
successful energy to spread learning and religion
among the early settlers of the southwest. His name
was Samuel Doak. He came from New Jersey, and
had been educated in Princeton. Possessed of the
vigorous energy that marks the true pioneer spirit,
he determined to cast in his lot with the frontier
folk. He walked through Maryland and Virginia,
driving before him an old "flea-bitten grey" horse,
loaded with a sackful of books; crossed the Alleghanies, and came down along blazed trails to the
Holston settlements. The hardy people among
whom he took up his abode were able to appreciate
his learning and religion as much as they admired
his adventurous and indomitable temper; and the
stern, hard, God-fearing man became a most powerful influence for good throughout the whole formative period of the southwest.[1]

[1] See "East Tennessee a Hundred Years Ago," by the Hon. John Alli-
son, Nashville, 1887, p. 8.

Not only did he found a church, but near it he built a log high-school, which soon became Washington College, the first institution of the kind west of the Alleghanies. Other churches, and many other schools, were soon built. Any young man or woman who could read, write, and cipher felt competent to teach an ordinary school; higher education, as elsewhere at this time in the west, was in the hands of the clergy.

As elsewhere, the settlers were predominantly of Calvinistic stock; for of all the then prominent faiths Calvinism was nearest to their feelings and ways of thought. Of the great recognized creeds it was the most republican in its tendencies, and so the best suited to the backwoodsmen. They disliked Anglicanism as much as they abhorred and despised Romanism—theoretically at least, for practically then as now frontiersmen were liberal to one another's religious opinions, and the staunch friend and good hunter might follow whatever creed he wished, provided he did not intrude it on others. But backwoods Calvinism differed widely from the creed as first taught. It was professed by thorough-going Americans, essentially free and liberty-loving, who would not for a moment have tolerated a theocracy in their midst. Their social, religious, and political systems were such as naturally flourished in a country remarkable for its temper of rough and self-asserting equality. Nevertheless the old Calvinistic spirit left a peculiar stamp on this wild border democracy. More than any thing else, it gave the backwoodsmen their code of right and wrong. Though they were a hard, narrow, dogged people, yet they intensely believed in their own standards and ideals. Often warped and twisted, mentally and morally, by the strain of their existence, they at least always retained the fundamental virtues of hardihood and manliness

Presbyterianism was not, however, destined even here to remain the leading frontier creed. Other sects still more democratic, still more in keeping with backwoods life and thought, largely supplanted it. Methodism did not become a power until after the close of the Revolution; but the Baptists followed close on the heels of the Presbyterians. They, too, soon built log meeting-houses here and there, while their preachers cleared the forest and hunted elk and buffalo like the other pioneer settlers.[1]

To all the churches the preacher and congregation alike went armed, the latter leaning their rifles in their pews or near their seats, while the pastor let his stand beside the pulpit. On week-days the clergymen usually worked in the fields in company with the rest of the settlers; all with their rifles close at hand and a guard stationed. In more than one instance when such a party was attacked by Indians the servant of the Lord showed himself as skilled in the use of carnal weapons as were any of his warlike parishioners.

The leaders of the frontiersmen were drawn from among several families, which, having taken firm root, were growing into the position of backwoods gentry. Of course the use of this term does not imply any sharp social distinctions in backwoods life,

[1] Ramsey, 144.

for there were none such. The poorest and richest met on terms of perfect equality, slept in one another's houses, and dined at one another's tables. But certain families, by dint of their thrift, the ability they showed in civil affairs, or the prowess of some of their members in time of war, had risen to acknowledged headship.

The part of Washington County northwest of the Holston was cut off and made into the county of Sullivan by the North Carolina Legislature in 1779. In this part the Shelbys were the leading family; and Isaac Shelby was made county lieutenant. It had been the debatable ground between Virginia and North Carolina, the inhabitants not knowing to which province they belonged, and sometimes serving the two governments alternately. When the line was finally drawn, old Evan Shelby's estate was found to lie on both sides of it; and as he derived his title from Virginia, he continued to consider himself a Virginian, and held office as such.[1]

In Washington County Sevier was treated as practically commander of the militia some time before he received his commission as county lieutenant. He was rapidly becoming the leader of the whole district. He lived in a great, rambling one-story log house on the Nolichucky, a rude, irregular building with broad verandas and great stone fire-places. The rooms were in two groups, which were connected by a covered porch—a " dog alley," as old settlers still call it, because the dogs are apt to sleep there at night. Here he kept open house to all comers,

[1] Campbell MSS.   Notes by Gov. David Campbell.

for he was lavishly hospitable, and every one was
welcome to bed and board, to apple-jack and cider,
hominy and corn-bread, beef, venison, bear meat, and
wild fowl.   When there was a wedding or a merry-
making of any kind he feasted the neighborhood,
barbecuing oxen—that is, roasting them whole on
great spits,—and spreading board tables out under
the trees.   He was ever on the alert to lead his
mounted riflemen against the small parties of marauding Indians that came into the country.   He soon
became the best commander against Indians that
there was on this part of the border, moving with a
rapidity that enabled him again and again to overtake and scatter their roving parties, recovering the
plunder and captives, and now and then taking a
scalp or two himself.   His skill and daring, together
with his unfailing courtesy, ready tact, and hospitality, gained him unbounded influence with the
frontiersmen, among whom he was universally known
as " Nolichucky Jack." [1]

The Virginian settlements on the Holston, adjoining those of North Carolina, were in 1777 likewise
made into a county of Washington.   The people
were exactly the same in character as those across
the line ; and for some years the fates of all these
districts were bound up together.   Their inhabitants
were still of the usual backwoods type, living by tilling their clearings and hunting ; the elk and buffalo
had become very scarce, but there were plenty of deer
and bear, and in winter countless wild swans settled

---

[1] MSS. " Notes of Conversations with Old Pioneers," by Ramsey, in
Tenn. Hist. Soc. Campbell MSS.

down on the small lakes and ponds. The boys followed these eagerly; one of them, when an old man, used to relate how his mother gave him a pint of cream for every swan he shot, with the result that he got the pint almost every day.[1]

The leading family among these Holston Virginians was that of the Campbells, who lived near Abingdon. They were frontier farmers, who chopped down the forest and tilled the soil with their own hands. They used the axe and guided the plow as skilfully as they handled their rifles; they were also mighty hunters, and accustomed from boyhood to Indian warfare. The children received the best schooling the back country could afford, for they were a book-loving race, fond of reading and study as well as of out-door sports. The two chief members were cousins, Arthur and William. Arthur was captured by the northern Indians when sixteen, and was kept a prisoner among them several years; when Lord Dunmore's war broke out he made his escape, and acted as scout to the Earl's army. He served as militia colonel in different Indian campaigns, and was for thirty years a magistrate of the county; he was a man of fine presence, but of jealous, ambitious, overbearing temper. He combined with his fondness for Indian and hunter life a strong taste for books, and gradually collected a large library. So keen were the jealousies, bred of ambition, between himself and his cousin William Campbell, they being the two ranking officers of the

---

[1] " Sketch of Mrs. Elizabeth Russell," by her grandson, Thomas L. Preston, Nashville, 1888, p. 29. An interesting pamphlet.

local forces, that they finally agreed to go alternately on the different military expeditions; and thus it happened that Arthur missed the battle of King's Mountain, though he was at the time County Lieutenant.

William Campbell stood next in rank. He was a man of giant strength, standing six feet two inches in height, and straight as a spear-shaft, with fair complexion, red hair, and piercing, light blue eyes. A firm friend and staunch patriot, a tender and loving husband and father, gentle and courteous in ordinary intercourse with his fellows, he was, nevertheless, if angered, subject to fits of raging wrath that impelled him to any deed of violence.[1] He was a true type of the Roundheads of the frontier, the earnest, eager men who pushed the border ever farther westward across the continent. He followed Indians and tories with relentless and undying hatred; for the long list of backwoods virtues did not include pity for either public or private foes. The tories threatened his life and the lives of his friends and families; they were hand in glove with the outlaws who infested the borders, the murderers, horse-thieves, and passers of counterfeit money. He hunted them down with a furious zest, and did his work with merciless thoroughness, firm in the belief that he thus best served the Lord and the nation. One or two of his deeds illustrate admirably the grimness of the times, and the harsh contrast between the kindly relations of the border folks with their friends, and their ferocity towards their foes.

[1] Campbell MSS. Notes, by Gov. David Campbell.

They show how the better backwoodsmen, the up-right, church-going men, who loved their families, did justice to their neighbors, and sincerely tried to serve God, not only waged an unceasing war on the red and white foes of the State and of order, but carried it on with a certain ruthlessness that indicated less a disbelief in, than an utter lack of knowledge of, such a virtue as leniency to enemies.

One Sunday Campbell was returning from church with his wife and some friends, carrying his baby on a pillow in front of his saddle, for they were all mounted. Suddenly a horseman crossed the road close in front of them, and was recognized by one of the party as a noted tory. Upon being challenged, he rode off at full speed. Instantly Campbell handed the baby to a negro slave, struck spur into his horse, and galloping after the fugitive, overtook and captured him. The other men of the party came up a minute later. Several recognized the prisoner as a well-known tory; he was riding a stolen horse; he had on him letters to the British agents among the Cherokees, arranging for an Indian rising. The party of returning church-goers were accustomed to the quick and summary justice of lynch law. With stern gravity they organized themselves into a court. The prisoner was adjudged guilty, and was given but a short shrift; for the horsemen hung him to a sycamore tree before they returned to the road where they had left their families.

On another occasion, while Campbell was in command of a camp of militia, at the time of a Cherokee outbreak, he wrote a letter to his wife, a sister of Patrick Henry, that gives us a glimpse of the way in which he looked at Indians. His letter began, "My dearest Betsy"; in it he spoke of his joy at receiving her "sweet and affectionate letter"; he told how he had finally got the needles and pins she wished, and how pleased a friend had been with the apples she had sent him. He urged her to buy a saddle-horse, of which she had spoken, but to be careful that it did not start nor stumble, which were bad faults, "especially in a woman's hackney." In terms of endearment that showed he had not sunk the lover in the husband, he spoke of his delight at being again in the house where he had for the first time seen her loved face, "from which happy moment he dated the hour of all his bliss," and besought her not to trouble herself too much about him, quoting to her Solomon's account of a good wife, as reminding him always of her; and he ended by commending her to the peculiar care of Heaven. It was a letter that it was an honor to a true man to have written; such a letter as the best of women and wives might be proud to have received. Yet in the middle of it he promised to bring a strange trophy to show his tender and God-fearing spouse. He was speaking of the Indians; how they had murdered men, women, and children near-by, and how they had been beaten back; and he added: "I have now the scalp of one who was killed eight or nine miles from my house about three weeks ago. The first time I go up I shall take it along to let you see it." Evidently it was as natural for him to bring home to his wife and children the scalp of a slain Indian as the skin of a slain deer.[1]

The times were hard, and they called for men of flinty fibre. Those of softer, gentler mould would have failed in the midst of such surroundings. The iron men of the border had a harsh and terrible task allotted them; and though they did it roughly, they did it thoroughly and on the whole well. They may have failed to learn that it is good to be merciful, but at least they knew that it is still better to be just and strong and brave; to see clearly one's rights, and to guard them with a ready hand.

These frontier leaders were generally very jealous of one another. The ordinary backwoodsmen vied together as hunters, axemen, or wrestlers; as they rose to leadership their rivalries grew likewise, and the more ambitious, who desired to become the civil and military chiefs of the community, were sure to find their interests clash. Thus old Evan Shelby distrusted Sevier; Arthur Campbell was jealous of both Sevier and Isaac Shelby; and the two latter bore similar feelings to William Campbell. When a great crisis occurred all these petty envies were sunk; the nobler natures of the men came uppermost; and they joined with unselfish courage, heart and hand, to defend their country in the hour of her extreme need. But when the danger was over the old jealousies cropped out again.

Some one or other of the leaders was almost always employed against the Indians. The Cherokees and Creeks were never absolutely quiet and at peace.

[1] See Preston's pamphlet on Mrs. Russell, pp. 11-18.

After the chastisement inflicted upon the former by the united forces of all the southern backwoodsmen, Indian treaties were held with them,[1] in the spring Troubles. and summer of 1777. The negotiations consumed much time, the delegates from both sides meeting again and again to complete the preliminaries. The credit of the State being low, Isaac Shelby furnished on his own responsibility the goods and provisions needed by the Virginians and Holston people in coming to an agreement with the Otari, or upper Cherokees [2]; and some land was formally ceded to the whites.

But the chief Dragging Canoe would not make peace. Gathering the boldest and most turbulent of the young braves about him, he withdrew to the great whirl in the Tennessee,[3] at the crossing-place of the Creek war parties, when they followed the trail that led to the bend of the Cumberland River. Here he was joined by many Creeks, and also by adventurous and unruly members from almost all the western tribes [4]—Chickasaws, Chocktaws, and Indians from the Ohio. He soon had a great band of red outlaws round him. These freebooters were generally known as the Chickamaugas, and they were the most dangerous and least controllable of all the foes who menaced the western settlements. Many tories and white refugees from border justice joined them, and shared in their misdeeds. Their shifting villages stretched from Chickamauga Creek to Run-

---

[1] See *ante*, Chapter XI. of Vol. I.

[2] Shelby's MS. autobiography, copy in Col. Durrett's library.

[3] Va. State Papers, III., 271 ; the settlers always spoke of it as the " suck " or " whirl."   [4] Shelby MS.

ning Water. Between these places the Tennessee
twists down through the sombre gorges by which
the chains of the Cumberland ranges are riven
in sunder. Some miles below Chickamauga Creek,
near Chattanooga, Lookout Mountain towers aloft
into the clouds ; at its base the river bends round
Moccasin Point, and then rushes through a gap
between Walden's Ridge and the Raccoon Hills.
Then for several miles it foams through the winding
Narrows between jutting cliffs and sheer rock walls,
while in its boulder-strewn bed the swift torrent is
churned into whirlpools, cataracts, and rapids. Near
the Great Crossing, where the war parties and hunting parties were ferried over the river, lies Nick-a-jack
Cave, a vast cavern in the mountain side. Out of it
flows a stream, up which a canoe can paddle two or
three miles into the heart of the mountain. In these
high fastnesses, inaccessible ravines, and gloomy
caverns the Chickamaugas built their towns, and to
them they retired with their prisoners and booty after
every raid on the settlements.

No sooner had the preliminary treaty been agreed
to in the spring of '77 than the Indians again began
their ravages. In fact, there never was any real
peace. After each treaty the settlers would usually
press forward into the Indian lands, and if they failed
to do this the young braves were sure themselves
to give offence by making forays against the whites.
On this occasion the first truce or treaty was promptly
broken by the red men. The young warriors refused
to be bound by the promises of the chiefs and head-
men, and they continued their raids for scalps,

horses, and plunder.   Within a week of the departure of the Indian delegates from the treaty ground
in April, twelve whites were murdered and many
horses stolen.   Robertson, with nine men, followed
one of these marauding parties, killed one Indian, and
retook ten horses ; on his return he was attacked by
a large band of Creeks and Cherokees, and two of
his men were wounded; but he kept hold of the recaptured horses and brought them safely in.[1]   On the
other hand, a white scoundrel killed an Indian on
the treaty ground, in July, the month in which the
treaties were finally completed in due form.   By act
of the Legislature the Holston militia were kept
under arms throughout most of the year, companies
of rangers, under Sevier's command, scouring the
woods and canebrakes, and causing such loss to the
small Indian war parties that they finally almost
ceased their forays.   Bands of these Holston rangers
likewise crossed the mountains by Boon's trail, and
went to the relief of Boonsborough and St. Asaphs,
in Kentucky, then much harassed by the northwestern warriors.[2]   Though they did little or no fighting,
and stayed but a few days, they yet by their presence
brought welcome relief to the hard-pressed Kentuckians.[3]   Kentucky during her earliest and most trying
years received comparatively little help from sorely
beset Virginia ; but the backwoodsmen of the upper
Tennessee valley—on both sides of the boundary—
did her real and lasting service.

[1] Chas. Robertson to Captain-General of North Carolina, April 27, 1777.

[2] See *ante* Chap. I.

[3] Monette (followed by Ramsey and others) hopelessly confuses these small
relief expeditions ; he portrays Logan as a messenger from Boon's Station, is
in error as to the siege of the latter, etc.

In 1778 the militia were disbanded, as the settlements were very little harried ; but as soon as the vigilance of the whites was relaxed the depredations and massacres began again, and soon became worse than ever.   Robertson had been made superintendent of Indian affairs for North Carolina ; and he had taken up his abode among the Cherokees at the town of Chota in the latter half of the year 1777. He succeeded in keeping them comparatively quiet and peaceable during 1778, and until his departure, which took place the following year, when he went to found the settlements on the Cumberland River.

But the Chickamaugas refused to make peace, and in their frequent and harassing forays they were from time to time joined by parties of young braves from all the Cherokee towns that were beyond the reach of Robertson's influence—that is, by all save those in the neighborhood of Chota.   The Chicka- saws and Choctaws likewise gave active support to the king's cause ; the former scouted along the Ohio, the latter sent bands of young warriors to aid the Creeks and Cherokees in their raids against the settlements.[1]

The British agents among the southern Indians had received the letters Hamilton sent them after he took Vincennes ; in these they were urged at once to send out parties against the frontier, and to make ready for a grand stroke in the spring.   In response the chief agent, who was the Scotch captain Cam- eron, a noted royalist leader, wrote to his official superior that the instant he heard of any movement

[1] Haldimand MSS.   Letter of Rainsford and Tait to Hamilton, April 9, 1779.

of the northwestern Indians he would see that it was
backed up, for the Creeks were eager for war, and
the Cherokees likewise were ardently attached to the
British cause; as a proof of the devotion of the latter, he added : " They keep continually killing and
scalping in Virginia, North Carolina, and the frontier
of Georgia, although the rebels are daily threatening
to send in armies from all quarters and extirpate the
whole tribe." [1]   It would certainly be impossible to
desire better proof than that thus furnished by this
royal officer, both of the ferocity of the British policy
towards the frontiersmen, and of the treachery of the
Indians, who so richly deserved the fate that afterwards befell them.

While waiting for the signal from Hamilton,
Cameron organized two Indian expeditions against
the frontier, to aid the movements of the British
army that had already conquered Georgia. A great
body of Creeks, accompanied by the British commis-
saries and most of the white traders (who were, of
course, tories), set out in March to join the king's
forces at Savannah; but when they reached the frontier they scattered out to plunder and ravage. A
body of Americans fell on one of their parties and
crushed it; whereupon the rest returned home in a
fright, save about seventy, who went on and joined
the British. At the same time three hundred Chickamaugas, likewise led by the resident British com-
missaries, started out against the Carolina frontier.
But Robertson, at Chota, received news of the march,

[1] Haldimand MSS. Series B., Vol. 117, p. 131. Letter of Alexander
Cameron, July 15, 1779.

and promptly sent warning to the Holston settlements [1]; and the Holston men, both of Virginia and
North Carolina, decided immediately to send an
expedition against the homes of the war party.
This would not only at once recall them from the
frontier, but would give them a salutary lesson.

Accordingly the backwoods levies gathered on
Clinch River, at the mouth of Big Creek, April
10th, and embarked in pirogues and canoes to de-
scend the Tennessee. There were several hundred
of them [2] under the command of Evan Shelby; Isaac
Shelby having collected the supplies for the expedition by his individual activity and on his personal
credit. The backwoodsmen went down the river so
swiftly that they took the Chickamaugas completely
by surprise, and the few warriors who were left in
the villages fled to the wooded mountains without
offering any resistance. Several Indians were killed [3]
and a number of their towns were burnt, together
with a great deal of corn; many horses and cattle
were recaptured, and among the spoils were large

[1] *Do.* "A rebel commissioner in Chote being informed of their movements here sent express into Holston river." This "rebel commissioner"
was in all probability Robertson.

[2] State Department MSS. No. 51, Vol. II., p. 17, a letter from the British agents among the Creeks to Lord George Germaine, of July 12, 1779. It
says, "near 300 rebels"; Haywood, whose accounts are derived from oral
tradition, says one thousand. Cameron's letter of July 15th in the Haldimand
MSS. says seven hundred. Some of them were Virginians who had been
designed for Clark's assistance in his Illinois campaign, but who were not
sent him. Shelby made a very clever stroke, but it had no permanent
effect, and it is nonsense to couple it, as has been recently done, with Clark's
campaigns.

[3] Cameron in his letter says four, which is probably near the truth. Haywood says forty, which merely represents the backwoods tradition on the
subject, and is doubtless a great exaggeration.

piles of deer hides, owned by a tory trader. The troops then destroyed their canoes and returned home on foot, killing game for their food; and they spread among the settlements many stories of the beauty of the lands through which they had passed, so that the pioneers became eager to possess them. The Chickamaugas were alarmed and confounded by this sudden stroke; their great war band returned at once to the burned towns, on being informed by swift runners of the destruction that had befallen them. All thoughts of an immediate expedition against the frontier were given up; peace talks were sent to Evan Shelby [1]; and throughout the summer the settlements were but little molested.

Yet all the while they were planning further attacks; at the same time that they sent peace talks to Shelby they sent war talks to the Northwestern Indians, inviting them to join in a great combined movement against the Americans.[2] When the news of Hamilton's capture was brought it wrought a momentary discouragement; but the efforts of the

[1] State Department MSS. No. 71, Vol. I., p. 255, letter of Evan Shelby, June 4, 1779.

[2] Haldimand MSS. Series B., Vol. 117, p. 157. A talk from the Cherokees to the envoy from the Wabash and other Indians, July 12, 1779. One paragraph is interesting : " We cannot forget the talk you brought us some years ago into this Nation, which was to take up the hatchet against the Virginians. We heard and listened to it with great attention, and before the time that was appointed to lift it we took it up and struck the Virginians. Our Nation was alone and surrounded by them. They were numerous and their hatchets were sharp ; and after we had lost some of our best warriors, we were forced to leave our towns and corn to be burnt by them, and now we live in the grass as you see us. But we are not yet conquered, and to convince you that we have not thrown away your talk here are 4 strands of whampums we received from you when you came before as a messenger to our Nation."

British agents were unceasing, and by the end of the year most of the southwestern Indians were again ready to take up the hatchet. The rapid successes of the royal armies in the southern States had turned the Creeks into open antagonists of the Americans, and their war parties were sent out in quick succession, the British agents keeping alive the alliance by a continued series of gifts—for the Creeks were a venal, fickle race whose friendship could not otherwise be permanently kept.[1]

As for the Cherokees, they had not confined themselves to sending the war belt to the northwestern tribes, while professing friendship for the Americans; they had continued in close communication with the British Indian agents, assuring them that their peace negotiations were only shams, intended to blind the settlers, and that they would be soon ready to take up the hatchet.[2] This time Cameron himself marched into the Cherokee country with his company of fifty tories, brutal outlaws, accustomed to savage warfare, and ready to take part in the worst Indian outrages.[3] The ensuing Cherokee war

[1] State Department MSS. Papers Continental Congress. Intercepted Letters, No. 51, Vol. II. Letter of British Agents Messrs. Rainsford, Mitchell, and Macullagh, of July 12, 1779. "The present unanimity of the Creek Nation is no doubt greatly owing to the rapid successes of His Majesty's forces in the Southern provinces, as they have now no cause to apprehend the least danger from the Rebels . . . we have found by experience that without presents the Indians are not to be depended on."

[2] Do., No. 71, Vol. II., p. 189. Letter of David Tait to Oconostota. "I believe what you say about telling lies to the Virginians to be very right."

[3] Do., No. 51, Vol. II. Letter of the three agents. "The Cherokees are now exceedingly well disposed. Mr. Cameron is now among them . . . Captain Cameron has his company of Loyal Refugees with him, who are well qualified for the service they are engaged in. . . . He carried up with him a considerable quantity of presents and ammunition which are absolutely necessary to engage the Indians to go upon service."

was due not to the misdeeds of the settlers—though doubtless a few lawless whites occasionally did wrong to their red neighbors—but to the short-sighted treachery and ferocity of the savages themselves, and especially to the machinations of the tories and British agents. The latter unceasingly incited the Indians to ravage the frontier with torch and scalping knife. They deliberately made the deeds of the torturers and women-killers their own, and this they did with the approbation of the British Government, and to its merited and lasting shame.

Yet by the end of 1779 the inrush of settlers to the Holston regions had been so great that, as with Kentucky, there was never any real danger after this year that the whites would be driven from the land by the red tribes whose hunting-ground it once had been.

CHAPTER IX.

KING'S MOUNTAIN, 1780.

DURING the Revolutionary war the men of the west for the most part took no share in the actual campaigning against the British and Hes- The British sians. Their duty was to conquer and in the South-hold the wooded wilderness that stretched ern States. westward to the Mississippi; and to lay therein the foundations of many future commonwealths. Yet at a crisis in the great struggle for liberty, at one of the darkest hours for the patriot cause, it was given to a band of western men to come to the relief of their brethren of the seaboard and to strike a telling and decisive blow for all America. When the three southern provinces lay crushed and help-less at the feet of Cornwallis, the Holston back-woodsmen suddenly gathered to assail the triumph-ant conqueror. Crossing the mountains that divided them from the beaten and despairing people of the tidewater region, they killed the ablest lieutenant of the British commander, and at a single stroke undid all that he had done.

By the end of 1779 the British had reconquered Georgia. In May, 1780, they captured Charleston, speedily reduced all South Carolina to submission, and then marched into the old North State. Cornwallis, much the ablest of the British generals, was in command over a mixed force of British, Hessian, and loyal American regulars, aided by Irish volunteers and bodies of refugees from Florida. In addition, the friends to the king's cause, who were very numerous in the southernmost States, rose at once on the news of the British successes, and thronged to the royal standards; so that a number of regiments of tory militia were soon embodied. McGillivray, the Creek chief, sent bands of his warriors to assist the British and tories on the frontier, and the Cherokees likewise came to their help. The patriots for the moment abandoned hope, and bowed before their victorious foes.

Cornwallis himself led the main army northward against the American forces. Meanwhile he entrusted to two of his most redoubtable officers the task of scouring the country, raising the loyalists, scattering the patriot troops that were still embodied, and finally crushing out all remaining opposition. These two men were Tarleton the dashing cavalryman, and Ferguson the rifleman, the skilled partisan leader.

Patrick Ferguson, the son of Lord Pitfour, was a Scotch soldier, at this time about thirty-six years Colonel   old, who had been twenty years in the Brit-Ferguson. ish army. He had served with distinction against the French in Germany, had quelled a Carib uprising in the West Indies, and in 1777 was given the command of a company of riflemen in the army opposed to Washington.[1] He played a good part at

---

[1] "Biographical Sketch or Memoir of Lieutenant-Colonel Patrick Ferguson," by Adam Ferguson, LL.D., Edinburgh, 1817, p. 11. The copy was kindly lent me by Mr. Geo. H. Moore of the Lenox Library.

Brandywine and Monmouth. At the former battle he was wounded by an American sharpshooter, and had an opportunity, of which he forbore taking advantage, to himself shoot an American officer of high rank, who unsuspectingly approached the place where he lay hid; he always insisted that the man he thus spared was no less a person than Washington. While suffering from his wound, Sir William Howe disbanded his rifle corps, distributing it among the light companies of the different regiments; and its commander in consequence became an unattached volunteer in the army. But he was too able to be allowed to remain long unemployed. When the British moved to New York he was given the command of several small independent expeditions, and was successful in each case; once, in particular, he surprised and routed Pulaski's legion, committing great havoc with the bayonet, which was always with him a favorite weapon. His energy and valor attracted much attention; and when a British army was sent against Charleston and the South he went along, as a lieutenant-colonel of a recently raised regular regiment, known as the American Volunteers.[1]

Cornwallis speedily found him to be peculiarly fitted for just such service as was needed; for he possessed rare personal qualities. He was of middle height and slender build, with a quiet, serious face and a singularly winning manner; and withal, he was of literally dauntless courage, of hopeful, eager tem-

[1] Though called volunteers they were simply a regular regiment raised in America instead of England; Ferguson's "Memoir" p. 30, etc., always speaks of them as regulars. The British gave an absurd number of titles to their various officers; thus Ferguson was a brigadier-general of militia, lieutenant-colonel of volunteers, a major in the army, etc.

per, and remarkably fertile in shifts and expedients. He was particularly fond of night attacks, surprises, and swift, sudden movements generally, and was unwearied in drilling and disciplining his men. Not only was he an able leader, but he was also a finished horseman, and the best marksman with both pistol and rifle in the British army. Being of quick, inventive mind, he constructed a breech-loading rifle, which he used in battle with deadly effect. This invention had been one of the chief causes of his being brought into prominence in the war against America, for the British officers especially dreaded the American sharpshooters.[1] It would be difficult to imagine a better partisan leader, or one more fitted by his feats of prowess and individual skill, to impress the minds of his followers. Moreover, his courtesy stood him in good stead with the people of the country; he was always kind and civil, and would spend hours in talking affairs over with them and pointing out the mischief of rebelling against their lawful sovereign. He soon became a potent force in winning the doubtful to the British side, and exerted a great influence over the tories; they gathered eagerly to his standard, and he drilled them with patient perseverance.

After the taking of Charleston Ferguson's volunteers and Tarleton's legion, acting separately or together, speedily destroyed the different bodies of patriot soldiers. Their activity and energy was such that the opposing commanders seemed for the time being quite unable to cope with them, and the

[1] Ferguson's " Memoir," p. 11.

American detachments were routed and scattered in quick succession.[1] On one of these occasions, the surprise at Monk's Corners, where the American commander, Huger, was slain, Ferguson's troops again had a chance to show their skill in the use of the bayonet.

Tarleton did his work with brutal ruthlessness; his men plundered and ravaged, maltreated prisoners, outraged women, and hung without mercy all who were suspected of turning from the loyalist to the whig side. His victories were almost always followed by massacres; in particular, when he routed with small loss a certain Captain Buford, his soldiers refused to grant quarter, and mercilessly butchered the beaten Americans.[2]

Ferguson, on the contrary, while quite as valiant and successful a commander, showed a generous heart, and treated the inhabitants of the country fairly well. He was especially incensed at any outrage upon women, punishing the offender with the utmost severity, and as far as possible he spared his conquered foes. Yet even Ferguson's tender mercies must have seemed cruel to the whigs, as may be judged by the following extract from a diary kept by one of his lieutenants[3]: "This day Col. Ferguson got the rear guard in order to do his King and country justice, by protecting friends and widows,

[1] " History of the Campaigns of 1780 and 1781," Lt.-Col. Tarleton, London (1787). See also the "Strictures" thereon, by Roderick Mackenzie, London, same date.

[2] It is worth while remembering that it was not merely the tories who were guilty of gross crimes; the British regulars, including even some of their officers, often behaved with abhorrent brutality.

[3] Diary of Lt. Anthony Allaire, entry for March 24, 1780.

and destroying rebel property; also to collect live stock for the use of the army. All of which we effect as we go by destroying furniture, breaking windows, etc., taking all their horned cattle, horses, mules, sheep, etc., and their negroes to drive them." When such were the authorized proceedings of troops under even the most merciful of the British commanders, it is easy to guess what deeds were done by uncontrolled bodies of stragglers bent on plunder.

When Ferguson moved into the back country of the two Carolinas still worse outrages followed. In the three southernmost of the thirteen rebellious colonies there was a very large tory party.[1] In consequence the struggle in the Carolinas and Georgia took the form of a ferocious civil war. Each side in turn followed up its successes by a series of hangings and confiscations, while the lawless and violent characters fairly revelled in the confusion. Neither side can be held guiltless of many and grave misdeeds ; but for reasons already given the bulk—but by no means the whole—of the criminal and disorderly classes espoused the king's cause in the regions where the struggle was fiercest. They murdered, robbed, or drove off the whigs in their hour of triumph ; and in turn brought down ferocious reprisals on their own heads and on those of their luckless associates.

[1] Gates MSS., *passim*, for July–October, 1780. *E. g.*, letter of Mr. Ramsey, August 9, 1780, describes how " the Scotch are all lying out," the number of tories in the " Drowning Creek region," their resistance to the levy of cattle, etc. In these colonies, as in the middle colonies, the tory party was very strong.

Moreover Cornwallis and his under-officers tried to cow and overawe the inhabitants by executing some of the men whom they deemed the chief and most criminal leaders of the rebellion, especially such as had sworn allegiance and then again taken up arms[1]; of course retaliation in kind followed. Ferguson himself hung some men; and though he did his best to spare the country people, there was much plundering and murdering by his militia.

In June he marched to upper South Carolina, moving to and fro, calling out the loyal militia. They responded enthusiastically, and three or four thousand tories were embodied in different bands. Those who came to Ferguson's own standard were divided into companies and regiments, and taught the rudiments of discipline by himself and his subalterns. He soon had a large but fluctuating force under him; in part composed of good men, loyal adherents of the king (these being very frequently recent arrivals from England, or else Scotch highlanders), in part also of cut-throats, horse-thieves, and desperadoes of all kinds who wished for revenge on the whigs and were eager to plunder them. His own regular force was also mainly composed of Americans, although it contained many Englishmen. His chief subordinates were Lieutenant-Colonels De Peyster[2] and Cruger; the former usually serving under him, the latter commanding at Ninety-Six. They were both New York loyalists, members of

[1] Gates MSS. See Letter from Sumter, August 12th and *passim*, for instances of hanging by express command of the British officers.

[2] A relative of the Detroit commander.

old Knickerbocker families; for in New York many
of the gentry and merchants stood by the king.

Ferguson moved rapidly from place to place,
breaking up the bodies of armed whigs; and the
Ferguson Ap- latter now and then skirmished fiercely
proaches the with similar bands of tories, sometimes
Mountains. one side winning, sometimes the other.
Having reduced South Carolina to submission the
British commander then threatened North Carolina; and Col. McDowell, the commander of the
whig militia in that district, sent across the mountains to the Holston men praying that they would
come to his help. Though suffering continually
from Indian ravages, and momentarily expecting a
formidable inroad, they responded nobly to the call.
Sevier remained to patrol the border and watch the
Cherokees, while Isaac Shelby crossed the mountains with a couple of hundred mounted riflemen,
early in July. The mountain men were joined by
McDowell, with whom they found also a handful of
Georgians and some South Carolinians; who when
their States were subdued had fled northward, resolute to fight their oppressors to the last.

The arrival of the mountain men put new life into
the dispirited whigs. On July 30th a mixed force,
under Shelby and two or three local militia colonels,
captured Thickett's fort, with ninety tories, near the
Pacolet. They then camped at the Cherokee ford of
Broad River, and sent out parties of mounted men to
carry on a guerilla or partisan warfare against detachments, not choosing to face Ferguson's main
body. After a while they moved south to Cedar

Spring.   Here, on the 8th of August, they were set
upon by Ferguson's advanced guard, of dragoons and
mounted riflemen.   These they repulsed, handling
the British rather roughly; but, as Ferguson himself
came up, they fled, and though he pursued them
vigorously he could not overtake them.[1]

On the 18th of the month the mountain men,
assisted as usual by some parties of local militia, all
under their various colonels, performed another feat;
one of those swift, sudden strokes so dear to the
hearts of these rifle-bearing horsemen.   It was of a
kind peculiarly suited to their powers; for they were
brave and hardy, able to thread their way unerringly
through the forests, and fond of surprises; and
though they always fought on foot, they moved on
horseback, and therefore with great celerity.   Their
operations should be carefully studied by all who

[1] Shelby's MS. Autobiography, and the various accounts he wrote of these
affairs in his old age (which Haywood and most of the other local American
historians follow or amplify), certainly greatly exaggerate the British force
and loss, as well as the part Shelby himself played, compared to the Georgia and
Carolina leaders.   The Americans seemed to have outnumbered Ferguson's
advance guard, which was less than two hundred strong, about three to one.
Shelby's account of the Musgrove affair is especially erroneous.   See p. 120
of L. C. Draper's "King's Mountain and Its Heroes" (Cincinnati, 1881).
Mr. Draper has with infinite industry and research gathered all the published
and unpublished accounts and all the traditions concerning the battle; his
book is a mine of information on the subject.   He is generally quite impartial, but some of his conclusions are certainly biassed; and the many traditional statements, as well as those made by very old men concerning events
that took place fifty or sixty years previously, must be received with extreme
caution.   A great many of them should never have been put in the book at
all.   When they take the shape of anecdotes, telling how the British are
overawed by the mere appearance of the Americans on some occasion (as
pp. 94, 95, etc.), they must be discarded at once as absolutely worthless, as
well as ridiculous.   The British and tory accounts, being forced to explain
ultimate defeat, are, if possible, even more untrustworthy, when taken solely
by themselves, than the American.

wish to learn the possibilities of mounted riflemen. Yet they were impatient of discipline or of regular service, and they really had no one commander. The different militia officers combined to perform some definite piece of work, but, like their troops, they were incapable of long-continued campaigns; and there were frequent and bitter quarrels between the several commanders, as well as between the bodies of men they led.

It seems certain that the mountaineers were, as a rule, more formidable fighters than the lowland militia, beside or against whom they battled; and they formed the main strength of the attacking party that left the camp at the Cherokee ford before sunset on the 17th. Ferguson's army was encamped south-west of them, at Fair Forest Shoals; they marched round him, and went straight on, leaving him in their rear. Sometimes they rode through open forest, more often they followed the dim wood roads; their horses pacing or cantering steadily through the night. As the day dawned they reached Musgrove's Ford, on the Enoree, having gone forty miles. Here they hoped to find a detachment of tory militia; but it had been joined by a body of provincial regulars, the united force being probably somewhat more numerous than that of the Americans. The latter were discovered by a patrol, and the British after a short delay marched out to attack them. The Americans in the meantime made good use of their axes, felling trees for a breastwork, and when assailed they beat back and finally completely routed their assailants.[1]

---

[1] Shelby's account of this action, written in his old age, is completely at fault; he not only exaggerates the British force and loss, but he likewise

However, the victory was of little effect, for just as it was won word was brought to Shelby that the day before Cornwallis had met Gates at Camden, and had not only defeated but practically destroyed the American army; and on the very day of the fight on the Enoree, Tarleton surprised Sumter, and scattered his forces to the four winds. The panic among the whigs was tremendous, and the moun- taineers shared it. They knew that Ferguson, angered at the loss of his detachment, would soon be in hot pursuit, and there was no time for delay. The local militia made off in various directions; while Shelby and his men pushed straight for the mountains, crossed them, and returned each man to his own home. Ferguson speedily stamped out the few remaining sparks of rebellion in South Carolina, and crossing the boundary into the North State he there repeated the process. On September 12th he caught McDowell and the only remaining body of militia at Cane Creek, of the Catawba, and beat them thoroughly,[1] the survivors, including their command- er, fleeing over the mountains to take refuge with the Holston men. Except for an occasional small guerilla party there was not a single organized body

greatly overestimates the number of the Americans—always a favorite trick of his. Each of the militia colonels of course claimed the chief share of the glory of the day. Haywood, Ramsey, and even Phelan simply follow Shelby. Draper gives all the different accounts; it is quite impossible to reconcile them; but all admit that the British were defeated.

I have used the word "British"; but though there were some Englishmen and Scotchmen among the tories and provincials, they were mainly loyalist Americans.

[1] Draper apparently endorses the absurd tradition that makes this a whig victory instead of a defeat. It seems certain (see Draper), contrary to the statements of the Tennessee historians, that Sevier had no part in these preliminary operations.

of American troops left south of Gates' broken and dispirited army.

All the southern lands lay at the feet of the conquerors. The British leaders, overbearing and arrogant, held almost unchecked sway throughout the Carolinas and Georgia; and looking northward they made ready for the conquest of Virginia.[1] Their right flank was covered by the waters of the ocean, their left by the high mountain barrier-chains, beyond which stretched the interminable forest; and they had as little thought of danger from one side as from the other.

Suddenly and without warning, the wilderness sent forth a swarm of stalwart and hardy riflemen, of whose very existence the British had hitherto been ignorant.[2] Riders spurring in hot haste brought word to the king's commanders that the backwater men had come over the mountains. The Indian fighters of the frontier, leaving unguarded their homes on the western waters, had crossed by wooded and precipitous defiles, and were pouring down to the help of their brethren of the plains.

The Mountaineers Gather to the Attack.

Ferguson had pushed his victories to the foot of the Smoky and the Yellow mountains. Here he

---

[1] The northern portion of North Carolina was still in possession of the remainder of Gates' army, but they could have been brushed aside without an effort.

[2] "A numerous army now appeared on the frontier drawn from Nolachucky and other settlements beyond the mountains, whose very names had been unknown to us." Lord Rawdon's letter of October 24, 1780. Clarke of Georgia had plundered a convoy of presents intended for the Indians, at Augusta, and the British wrongly supposed this to be likewise the aim of the mountaineers.

learned, perhaps for the first time, that there were a few small settlements beyond the high ranges he saw in his front; and he heard that some of these backwoods mountaineers had already borne arms against him, and were now harboring men who had fled from before his advance. By a prisoner whom he had taken he at once sent them warning to cease their hostilities, and threatened that if they did not desist he would march across the mountains, hang their leaders, put their fighting men to the sword, and waste their settlements with fire. He had been joined by refugee tories from the Watauga, who could have piloted him thither; and perhaps he intended to make his threats good. It seems more likely that he paid little heed to the mountaineers, scorning their power to do him hurt; though he did not regard them with the haughty and ignorant disdain usually felt for such irregulars by the British army officers.

When the Holston men learned that Ferguson had come to the other side of the mountains, and threatened their chiefs with the halter and their homes with the torch, a flame of passionate anger was kindled in all their hearts. They did not wait for his attack; they sallied from their strongholds to meet him. Their crops were garnered, their young men were ready for the march; and though the Otari war bands lowered like thunder-clouds on their southern border, they determined to leave only enough men to keep the savages at bay for the moment, and with the rest to overwhelm Ferguson before he could retreat out of their reach. Hitherto the war with the British had been something afar off; now it had come to their thresholds and their spirits rose to the danger.

Shelby was the first to hear the news. He at once rode down to Sevier's home on the Nolichucky; for they were the two county lieutenants,[1] who had control of all the militia of the district. At Sevier's log-house there was feasting and merry-making, for he had given a barbecue, and a great horse race was to be run, while the backwoods champions tried their skill as marksmen and wrestlers. In the midst of the merry-making Shelby appeared, hot with hard riding, to tell of the British advance, and to urge that the time was ripe for fighting, not feasting. Sevier at once entered heartily into his friend's plan, and agreed to raise his rifle-rangers, and gather the broken and disorganized refugees who had fled across the mountains under McDowell. While this was being done Shelby returned to his home to call out his own militia and to summon the Holston Virginians to his aid. With the latter purpose he sent one of his brothers to Arthur Campbell, the county lieutenant of his neighbors across the border. Arthur at once proceeded to urge the adoption of the plan on his cousin, William Campbell, who had just returned from a short and successful campaign against the tories round the head of the Kanawha, where he had speedily quelled an attempted uprising.

[1] Shelby was regularly commissioned as county lieutenant. Sevier's commission was not sent him until several weeks later; but he had long acted as such by the agreement of the settlers, who paid very little heed to the weak and disorganized North Carolina government.

Gates had already sent William Campbell an earnest request to march down with his troops and join
the main army.   This he could not do, as his militia
had only been called out to put down their own
internal foes, and their time of service had expired.[1]
But the continued advance of the British at last
thoroughly alarmed the Virginians of the mountain
region.   They promptly set about raising a corps of
riflemen,[2] and as soon as this course of action was determined on Campbell was foremost in embodying
all the Holston men who could be spared, intending
to march westward and join any Virginia army
that might be raised to oppose Cornwallis.   While
thus employed he received Shelby's request, and,
for answer, at first sent word that he could not
change his plans; but on receiving a second and
more urgent message he agreed to come as desired.[3]

The appointed meeting-place was at the Sycamore
Shoals of the Watauga.   There the riflemen gathered
on the 25th of September, Campbell bringing four
hundred men, Sevier and Shelby two hundred and

[1] Gates MSS. Letter of William Campbell, Sept. 6, 1780. He evidently
at the time failed to appreciate the pressing danger ; but he ended by saying
that " if the Indians were not harassing their frontier," and a corps of riflemen were formed, he would do all in his power to forward them to Gates.

[2] Gates MSS. Letter of William Preston, Sept. 18, 1780. The corps
was destined to join Gates, as Preston says ; hence Campbell's reluctance to
go with Shelby and Sevier. There were to be from five hundred to one
thousand men. See letter of Wm. Davidson, Sept. 18, 1780.

[3] Shelby's MS. Autobiography.   Campbell MSS., especially MS. letters
of Col. Arthur Campbell of Sept. 3, 1810, Oct. 18, 1810, etc. ; MS. notes
on Sevier in Tenn. Hist. Soc.   The latter consist of memoranda by his old
soldiers, who were with him in the battle ; many of their statements are to
be received cautiously, but there seems no reason to doubt their account of
his receiving the news while giving a great barbecue. Shelby is certainly entitled to the credit of planning and starting the campaign against Ferguson.

forty each, while the refugees under McDowell amounted to about one hundred and sixty. With Shelby came his two brothers, one of whom was afterwards slightly wounded at King's Mountain; while Sevier had in his regiment no less than six relations of his own name, his two sons being privates, and his two brothers captains. One of the latter was mortally wounded in the battle.

To raise money for provisions Sevier and Shelby were obliged to take, on their individual guaranties, the funds in the entry-taker's offices that had been received from the sale of lands. They amounted in all to nearly thirteen thousand dollars, every dollar of which they afterward refunded.

On the 26th [1] they began the march, over a thousand strong, most of them mounted on swift, wiry **The March to the Battle.** horses. They were led by leaders they trusted, they were wonted to Indian warfare, they were skilled as horsemen and marksmen, they knew how to face every kind of danger, hardship, and privation. Their fringed and tasselled hunting-shirts were girded in by bead-worked belts, and the trappings of their horses were stained red and yellow. On their heads they wore caps of coon-skin or mink-skin, with the tails hanging down, or else felt hats, in each of which was thrust a buck-tail or a sprig of evergreen. Every

[1] " State of the proceedings of the western army from Sept. 25, 1780, to the reduction of Major Ferguson and the army under his command," signed by Campbell, Shelby, and Cleavland. The official report ; it is in the Gates MSS. in the N. Y. Hist. Society. It was published complete at the time, except the tabulated statement of loss, which has never been printed ; I give it further on.

man carried a small-bore rifle, a tomahawk, and a scalping-knife.   A very few of the officers had swords,
and there was not a bayonet nor a tent in the army.[1]
Before leaving their camping-ground at the Sycamore
Shoals they gathered in an open grove to hear a
stern old Presbyterian preacher[2] invoke on the
enterprise the blessing of Jehovah. Leaning on their
long rifles, they stood in rings round the black-
frocked minister, a grim and wild congregation, who
listened in silence to his words of burning zeal as he
called on them to stand stoutly in the battle and to
smite their foes with the sword of the Lord and of
Gideon.

The army marched along Doe River, driving their
beef cattle with them, and camped that night at the
" Resting-Place," under Shelving Rock, beyond Crab
Orchard.   Next morning they started late, and went
up the pass between Roan and Yellow mountains.
The table-land on the top was deep in snow.[3]   Here
two tories who were in Sevier's band deserted and
fled to warn Ferguson ; and the troops, on learning
of the desertion, abandoned their purpose of following the direct route, and turned to the left, taking a
more northerly trail.   It was of so difficult a character that Shelby afterwards described it as " the worst
route ever followed by an army of horsemen." [4]
That afternoon they partly descended the east side

[1] Gen. Wm. Lenoir's account, prepared for Judge A. D. Murphy's intended history of North Carolina.   Lenoir was a private in the battle.

[2] Rev. Samuel Doak.   Draper, 176.   A tradition, but probably truthful,
being based on the statements of Sevier and Shelby's soldiers in their old
age.   It is the kind of an incident that tradition will often faithfully preserve.

[3] Diary of Ensign Robert Campbell.   [4] Shelby MS.

of the range, camping in Elk Hollow, near Roaring
Run.   The following day they went down through
the ravines and across the spurs by a stony and precipitous path, in the midst of magnificent scenery,
and camped at the mouth of Grassy Creek.   On the
29th they crossed the Blue Ridge at Gillespie's Gap,
and saw afar off, in the mountain coves and rich
valleys of the upper Catawba, the advanced settlements of the Carolina pioneers,—for hitherto they
had gone through an uninhabited waste.   The mountaineers, fresh from their bleak and rugged hills,
gazed with delight on the soft and fertile beauty of
the landscape.   That night they camped on the North
Fork of the Catawba, and next day they went down
the river to Quaker Meadows, McDowell's home.

At this point they were joined by three hundred
and fifty North Carolina militia from the counties of
Wilkes and Surrey, who were creeping along through
the woods hoping to fall in with some party going
to harass the enemy.[1]   They were under Col. Benjamin Cleavland, a mighty hunter and Indian fighter,
and an adventurous wanderer in the wilderness.   He
was an uneducated backwoodsman, famous for his
great size, and his skill with the rifle, no less than
for the curious mixture of courage, rough good-
humor, and brutality in his character.   He bore a
ferocious hatred to the royalists, and in the course

[1] Shelby MS. Autobiography.   See also Gates MSS.   Letter of Wm.
Davidson, Sept. 14, 1780.   Davidson had foreseen that there would be a
fight between the western militia and Ferguson, and he had sent word to his
militia subordinates to join any force—as McDowell's—that might go against
the British leader.   The alarm caused by the latter had prevented the militia
from joining Davidson himself.

of the vindictive civil war carried on between the
whigs and tories in North Carolina he suffered much.
In return he persecuted his public and private foes
with ruthless ferocity, hanging and mutilating any
tories against whom the neighboring whigs chose to
bear evidence. As the fortunes of the war veered
about he himself received many injuries. His goods
were destroyed, and his friends and relations were
killed or had their ears cropped off. Such deeds
often repeated roused to a fury of revenge his fierce
and passionate nature, to which every principle of
self-control was foreign. He had no hope of redress,
save in his own strength and courage, and on every
favorable opportunity he hastened to take more
than ample vengeance. Admitting all the wrongs
he suffered, it still remains true that many of
his acts of brutality were past excuse. His wife
was a worthy helpmeet. Once, in his absence, a
tory horse-thief was brought to their home, and
after some discussion the captors, Cleavland's sons,
turned to their mother, who was placidly going on
with her ordinary domestic avocations, to know
what they should do with the prisoner. Taking
from her mouth the corn-cob pipe she had been
smoking, she coolly sentenced him to be hung, and
hung he was without further delay or scruple.[1] Yet
Cleavland was a good friend and neighbor, devoted
to his country, and also a staunch Presbyterian.[2]

The tories were already on the alert. Some of
them had been harassing Cleavland, and they had
ambushed his advance guard, and shot his brother,

[1] Draper, 448.   [2] Allaire's Diary, entry for October 29th.

crippling him for life. But they did not dare try to arrest the progress of so formidable a body of men as had been gathered together at Quaker Meadows; and contented themselves with sending repeated warnings to Ferguson.

On October 1st the combined forces marched past Pilot Mountain, and camped near the heads of Cane and Silver creeks. Hitherto each colonel had commanded his own men, there being no general head, and every morning and evening the colonels had met in concert to decide the day's movements. The whole expedition was one of volunteers, the agreement between the officers and the obedience rendered them by the soldiers simply depending on their own free-will; there was no legal authority on which to go, for the commanders had called out the militia without any instructions from the executives of their several States.[1] Disorders had naturally broken out. The men of the different companies felt some rivalry towards one another; and those of bad character, sure to be found in any such gathering, could not be properly controlled. Some of Cleavland's and McDowell's people were very unruly; and a few of the Watauga troops also behaved badly, plundering both whigs and tories, and even starting to drive the stolen stock back across the mountains.[2]

At so important a crisis the good-sense and sincere patriotism of the men in command made them sink all personal and local rivalries. On the 2d of October they all gathered to see what could be done

[1] Gates MSS. Letter of Campbell, Shelby, Cleavland, etc., Oct. 4, 1780.
[2] Deposition of Col. Matthew Willoughby (who was in the fight), April 30, 1823, *Richmond Enquirer*, May 9, 1823.

to stop the disorders and give the army a single head; for it was thought that in a day or two they would close in with Ferguson. They were in Col. Charles McDowell's district, and he was the senior officer; but the others distrusted his activity and judgment, and were not willing that he should command. To solve the difficulty Shelby proposed that supreme command should be given to Col. Campbell, who had brought the largest body of men with him, and who was a Virginian, whereas the other four colonels were North Carolinians.[1] Meanwhile McDowell should go to Gates' army to get a general to command them, leaving his men under the charge of his brother Joseph, who was a major. This proposition was at once agreed to; and its adoption did much to ensure the subsequent success. Shelby not only acted wisely, but magnanimously; for he was himself of superior rank to Campbell, and moreover was a proud, ambitious man, desirous of military glory.

The army had been joined by two or three squads of partisans, including some refugee Georgians. They were about to receive a larger reinforcement; for at this time several small guerilla bands of North and South Carolina whigs were encamped at Flint Hill, some distance west of the encampment of the mountain men. These Flint Hill bands numbered about four hundred men all told, under the leadership of various militia colonels—Hill, Lacey, Williams, Graham, and Hambright.[2] Hill and Lacey

---

[1] Though by birth three were Virginians, and one, Shelby, a Marylander. All were Presbyterians. McDowell, like Campbell, was of Irish descent; Cleavland of English, Shelby of Welsh, and Sevier of French Huguenot. The families of the first two had originally settled in Pennsylvania.

[2] Hambright was a Pennsylvania German, the father of eighteen children.

were two of Sumter's lieutenants, and had under
them some of his men; Williams,[1] who was also a
South Carolinian, claimed command of them because
he had just been commissioned a brigadier-general
of militia. His own force was very small, and he
did not wish to attack Ferguson, but to march southwards to Ninety-Six. Sumter's men, who were
more numerous, were eager to join the mountaineers,
and entirely refused to submit to Williams. A hot
quarrel, almost resulting in a fight, ensued; Hill and
Lacey accusing Williams of being bent merely on
plundering the wealthy tories and of desiring to
avoid a battle with the British. Their imputation
on his courage was certainly unjust; but they were
probably quite right when they accused him of a
desire to rob and plunder the tories. A succession
of such quarrels speedily turned this assemblage of
militia into an armed and warlike rabble. Fortunately Hill and Lacey prevailed, word was sent to the
mountaineers, and the Flint Hill bands marched in
loose order to join them at the Cowpens.[2]

The mountain army had again begun its march
on the afternoon of the third day of the month. Be-

Hill, who was suffering from a severe wound, was unfit to take an active
part in the King's Mountain fight. His MS. narrative of the campaign is
largely quoted by Draper.

[1] Bancroft gives Williams an altogether undeserved prominence. As he
had a commission as brigadier-general, some of the British thought he was
in supreme command at King's Mountain; in a recent magazine article
Gen. De Peyster again sets forth his claims. In reality he only had a small
subordinate or independent command, and had no share whatever in con-
ducting the campaign, and very little in the actual battle, though he behaved with much courage and was killed.

[2] Gates MSS. Letter of Gen. Wm. Davidson, Oct. 3, 1780. Also Hill's
Narrative.

fore starting the colonels summoned their men, told
them the nature and danger of the service, and asked
such as were unwilling to go farther to step to the
rear ; but not a man did so.   Then Shelby made
them a short speech, well adapted to such a levy.
He told them when they encountered the enemy not
to wait for the word of command, but each to " be
his own officer," and do all he could, sheltering himself as far as possible, and not to throw away a
chance; if they came on the British in the woods
they were " to give them Indian play," and advance
from tree to tree, pressing the enemy unceasingly.
He ended by promising them that their officers would
shrink from no danger, but would lead them everywhere, and, in their turn, they must be on the alert
and obey orders.

When they set out their uncertainty as to Ferguson's movements caused them to go slowly, their
scouts sometimes skirmishing with lurking tories.
They reached the mouth of Cane Creek, near Gilbert
Town, on October 4th.   With the partisans that had
joined them they then numbered fifteen hundred men.
McDowell left them at this point to go to Gates with
the request for the appointment of a general to command them.[1] For some days the men had been living

[1] Gates MSS. (in New York Hist. Soc.).   It is possible that Campbell was
not chosen chief commander until this time ; Ensign Robert Campbell's account (MSS. in Tenn. Hist. Soc.) explicitly states this to be the case.   The
Shelby MS. and the official report make the date the 1st or 2d.   One letter
in the Gates MSS. has apparently escaped all notice from historians and in-
vestigators ; it is the document which McDowell bore with him to Gates.   It
is dated " Oct. 4th, 1780, near Gilbert town," and is signed by Cleavland,
Shelby, Sevier, Campbell, Andrew Hampton, and J. Winston.   It begins:
" We have collected at this place 1500 good men drawn from the counties of

on the ears of green corn which they plucked from the fields, but at this camping-place they slaughtered some beeves and made a feast.

The mountaineers had hoped to catch Ferguson at Gilbert Town, but they found that he had fled towards the northeast, so they followed after him. Many of their horses were crippled and exhausted, and many of the footmen footsore and weary; and the next day they were able to go but a dozen miles to the ford of Green River.

That evening Campbell and his fellow-officers held a council to decide what course was best to follow. Lacey, riding over from the militia companies who were marching from Flint Hill, had just reached their camp; he told them the direction in which Ferguson had fled, and at the same time appointed the Cowpens as the meeting-place for their respective forces. Their whole army was so jaded that the

Surrey, Wilkes, Burk, Washington, and Sullivan counties (*sic*) in this State and Washington County in Virginia." It says that they expect to be joined in a few days by Clark of Ga. and Williams of S. C. with one thousand men (in reality Clark, who had nearly six hundred troops, never met them) ; asks for a general ; says they have great need of ammunition, and remarks on the fact of their "troops being all militia, and but little acquainted with discipline." It was this document that gave the first impression to contemporaries that the battle was fought by fifteen hundred Americans. Thus General Davidson's letter of Oct. 10th to Gates, giving him the news of the victory, has served as a basis for most subsequent writers about the numbers. He got his particulars from one of Sumter's men, who was in the fight ; but he evidently mixed them up in his mind, for he speaks of Williams, Lacey, and their companions as joining the others at Gilbert Town, instead of the Cowpens ; makes the total number three thousand, whereas, by the official report of October 4th, Campbell's party only numbered fifteen hundred, and Williams, Lacey, etc., had but four hundred, or nineteen hundred in all ; says that sixteen hundred good horses were chosen out, evidently confusing this with the number at Gilbert Town ; credits Ferguson with fourteen hundred men, and puts the American loss at only twenty killed.

leaders knew they could not possibly urge it on fast enough to overtake Ferguson, and the flight of the latter made them feel all the more confident that they could beat him, and extremely reluctant that he should get away. In consequence they determined to take seven or eight hundred of the least tired, best armed, and best mounted men, and push rapidly after their foe, picking up on the way any militia they met, and leaving the other half of their army to follow as fast as it could.

At daybreak on the morning of the sixth the picked men set out, about seven hundred and fifty in number.[1] In the afternoon they passed by several large bands of tories, who had assembled to join Ferguson; but the Holston men were resolute in their determination to strike at the latter, and would not be diverted from it, nor waste time by following their lesser enemies.

Riding all day they reached the Cowpens when the sun had already set, a few minutes after the arrival of the Flint Hill militia under Lacey, Hill, and Williams. The tired troops were speedily engaged in skinning beeves for their supper, roasting them by the blazing camp-fires; and fifty acres of corn, belonging to the rich tory who owned the Cowpens, materially helped the meal. Meanwhile a council was held, in which all the leading officers,

[1] MS. narrative of Ensign Robert Campbell (see also Draper, 221) says seven hundred; and about fifty of the footmen who were in good training followed so quickly after them that they were able to take part in the battle. Lenoir says the number was only five or six hundred. The modern accounts generally fail to notice this Green River weeding out of the weak men, or confuse it with what took place at the Cowpens; hence many of them greatly exaggerate the number of Americans who fought in the battle.

save Williams, took part. Campbell was confirmed as commander-in-chief, and it was decided to once more choose the freshest soldiers, and fall on Ferguson before he could either retreat or be reinforced. The officers went round, picking out the best men, the best rifles, and the best horses. Shortly after nine o'clock the choice had been made, and nine hundred and ten [1] picked riflemen, well mounted, rode out of the circle of flickering firelight, and began their night journey. A few determined footmen followed, going almost as fast as the horse, and actually reached the battle-field in season to do their share of the fighting.

All this time Ferguson had not been idle. He first heard of the advance of the backwoodsmen on **Ferguson Makes Ready.** September 30th, from the two tories who deserted Sevier on Yellow Mountain. He had furloughed many of his loyalists, as all formidable resistance seemed at an end ; and he now sent out messengers in every direction to recall them to his standard. Meanwhile he fell slowly back from the foot-hills, so that he might not have to face the

---

[1] The official report says nine hundred ; Shelby, in all his earlier narratives, nine hundred and ten ; Hill, nine hundred and thirty-three. The last authority is important because he was one of the four hundred men who joined the mountaineers at the Cowpens, and his testimony confirms the explicit declaration of the official report that the nine hundred men who fought in the battle were chosen after the junction with Williams, Lacey, and Hill. A few late narratives, including that of Shelby in his old age, make the choice take place before the junction, and the total number then amount to thirteen hundred ; evidently the choice at the Cowpens is by these authors confused with the choice at Green River. Shelby's memory when he was old was certainly very treacherous ; in similar fashion he, as has been seen, exaggerated greatly his numbers at the Enoree. On the other hand, Robert Campbell puts the number at only seven hundred, and Lenoir between six and seven hundred. Both of these thus err in the opposite direction.

mountaineers until he had time to gather his own troops. He instantly wrote for reinforcements to Cruger, at Ninety-Six. Cruger had just returned from routing the Georgian Colonel Clark, who was besieging Augusta. In the chase a number of Americans were captured, and thirteen were hung. The British and tories interpreted the already sufficiently severe instructions of their commander-in-chief with the utmost liberality, even the officers chronicling the hanging with exultant pleasure, as pointing out the true way by which to end the war.[1]

Cruger, in his answer to Ferguson, explained that he did not have the number of militia regiments with which he was credited; and he did not seem to quite take in the gravity of the situation,[2] expressing his pleasure at hearing how strongly the loyalists of North Carolina had rallied to Ferguson's support, and speaking of the hope he had felt that the North Carolina tories would by themselves have proved "equal to the mountain lads." However, he promptly set about forwarding the reinforcements that were demanded; but before they could reach the scene of action the fate of the campaign had been decided.

Ferguson had not waited for outside help. He threw himself into the work of rallying the people of the plains, who were largely loyalists,[3] against the over-mountain men, appealing not only to their royalist sentiments, but to their strong local prejudices,

[1] Draper, p. 201, quotes a printed letter from a British officer to this effect.

[2] Probably Ferguson himself failed to do so at this time.

[3] Gates MSS. Letter of Davidson, September 14th, speaks of the large number of tories in the counties where Ferguson was operating.

and to the dread many of them felt for the wild border fighters. On the 1st of October he sent out a proclamation, of which copies were scattered broadcast among the loyalists. It was instinct with the fiery energy of the writer, and well suited to goad into action the rough tories, and the doubtful men, to whom it was addressed. He told them that the Back Water men had crossed the mountains, with chieftains at their head who would surely grant mercy to none who had been loyal to the king. He called on them to grasp their arms on the moment and run to his standard, if they desired to live and bear the name of men; to rally without delay, unless they wished to be eaten up by the incoming horde of cruel barbarians, to be themselves robbed and murdered, and to see their daughters and wives abused by the dregs of mankind. In ending, he told them scornfully that if they chose to be spat [1] upon and degraded forever by a set of mongrels, to say so at once, that their women might turn their backs on them and look out for real men to protect them.

Hoping to be joined by Cruger's regiments, as well as by his own furloughed men, and the neighboring tories, he gradually drew off from the mountains, doubling and turning, so as to hide his route and puzzle his pursuers. Exaggerated reports of the increase in the number of his foes were brought to him, and, as he saw how slowly they marched, he sent repeated messages to Cornwallis, asking for reinforcements; promising speedily to "finish the

---

[1] The word actually used was still stronger.

business," if three or four hundred soldiers, part dragoons, were given him, for the Americans were certainly making their "last push in this quarter."[1] He was not willing to leave the many loyal inhabitants of the district to the vengeance of the whigs[2]; and his hopes of reinforcements were well founded. Every day furloughed men rejoined him, and bands of loyalists came into camp; and he was in momentary expectation of help from Cornwallis or Cruger. It will be remembered that the mountaineers on their last march passed several tory bands. One of these alone, near the Cowpens, was said to have contained six hundred men; and in a day or two they would all have joined Ferguson. If the whigs had come on in a body, as there was every reason to expect, Ferguson would have been given the one thing he needed—time; and he would certainly have been too strong for his opponents. His defeat was due to the sudden push of the mountain chieftains; to their long, swift ride from the ford of Green River, at the head of their picked horse-riflemen.

The British were still in the dark as to the exact neighborhood from which their foes—the "swarm of backwoodsmen," as Tarleton called them[3]—really came. It was generally supposed that they were in part from Kentucky, and that Boon himself was among the number.[4] However, Ferguson probably

[1] See letter quoted by Tarleton.

[2] Ferguson's "Memoir," p. 32.

[3] "Tarleton's Campaigns," p. 169.

[4] British historians to the present day repeat this. Even Lecky, in his "History of England," speaks of the backwoodsmen as in part from Kentucky. Having pointed out this trivial fault in Lecky's work, it would be ungracious not to allude to the general justice and impartiality of its

cared very little who they were; and keeping, as he supposed, a safe distance away from them, he halted at King's Mountain in South Carolina on the evening of October 6th, pitching his camp on a steep, narrow hill just south of the North Carolina boundary. The King's Mountain range itself is about sixteen miles in length, extending in a southwesterly course from one State into the other. The stony, half isolated ridge on which Ferguson camped was some six or seven hundred yards long and half as broad from base to base, or two thirds that distance on top. The steep sides were clad with a growth of open woods, including both saplings and big timber. Ferguson parked his baggage wagons along the northeastern part of the mountain. The next day he did not move; he was as near to the army of Cornwallis at Charlotte as to the mountaineers, and he thought it safe to remain where he was. He deemed the position one of great strength, as indeed it would have been, if assailed in the ordinary European fashion; and he was confident that even if the rebels attacked him, he could readily beat them back. But as General Lee, "Light-Horse Harry," afterwards remarked, the hill was much easier assaulted with the rifle than defended with the bayonet.

The backwoodsmen, on leaving the camp at the Cowpens, marched slowly through the night, which

accounts of these revolutionary campaigns—they are very much more trust-worthy than Bancroft's, for instance. Lecky scarcely gives the right color to the struggle in the south; but when Bancroft treats of it, it is not too much to say that he puts the contest between the whigs and the British and tories in a decidedly false light. Lecky fails to do justice to Washington's military ability, however; and overrates the French assistance.

was dark and drizzly; many of the men got scattered in the woods, but joined their commands in the morning—the morning of October 7th. The troops bore down to the southward, a little out of the straight route, to avoid any patrol parties; and at sunrise they splashed across the Cherokee Ford.[1] Throughout the forenoon the rain continued but the troops pushed steadily onwards without halting,[2] wrapping their blankets and the skirts of their hunting-shirts round their gun-locks, to keep them dry. Some horses gave out, but their riders, like the thirty or forty footmen who had followed from the Cowpens, struggled onwards and were in time for the battle. When near King's Mountain they captured two tories, and from them learned Ferguson's exact position; that "he was on a ridge between two branches,"[3] where some deer hunters had camped the previous fall. These deer hunters were now with the oncoming backwoodsmen, and declared that they knew the ground well. Without halting, Campbell and the other colonels rode forward together, and agreed to surround the hill, so that their men might fire upwards without risk of hurting one another. It was a bold plan; for they knew their foes probably outnumbered them; but they were very confident of their own prowess, and were anxious to strike a crippling blow. From one or

---

[1] "Am. Pioneer," II., 67. An account of one of the soldiers, Benj. Sharp, written in his old age; full of contradictions of every kind (he for instance forgets they joined Williams at the Cowpens); it cannot be taken as an authority, but supplies some interesting details.

[2] Late in life Shelby asserted that this steadiness in pushing on was due to his own influence. The other accounts do not bear him out.

[3] *I. e.*, brooks.

two other captured tories, and from a staunch whig friend, they learned the exact disposition of the British and loyalist force, and were told that their noted leader wore a light, parti-colored hunting-shirt; and he was forthwith doomed to be a special target for the backwoods rifles. When within a mile of the hill a halt was called, and after a hasty council of the different colonels—in which Williams did not take part,—the final arrangements were made, and the men, who had been marching in loose order, were formed in line of battle. They then rode forward in absolute silence, and when close to the west slope of the battle-hill, beyond King's Creek, drew rein and dismounted. They tied their horses to trees, and fastened their great coats and blankets to the saddles, for the rain had cleared away. A few of the officers remained mounted. The countersign of the day was "Buford," the name of the colonel whose troops Tarleton had defeated and butchered. The final order was for each man to look carefully at the priming of his rifle, and then to go into battle and fight till he died.

The foes were now face to face. On the one side were the American backwoodsmen, under their **The Battle.** own leaders, armed in their own manner, and fighting after their own fashion, for the freedom and the future of America; on the opposite side were other Americans—the loyalists, led by British officers, armed and trained in the British fashion, and fighting on behalf of the empire of Britain and the majesty of the monarchy. The Americans numbered, all told, about nine

hundred and fifty men.[1]   The British forces were
composed in bulk of the Carolina loyalists—troops
similar to the Americans who joined the mountaineers at Quaker Meadows and the Cowpens [2];
the difference being that besides these low-land
militia, there were arrayed on one side the men
from the Holston, Watauga, and Nolichucky, and
on the other the loyalist regulars.   Ferguson had,
all told, between nine hundred and a thousand

[1] Nine hundred and ten horsemen (possibly nine hundred, or perhaps nine
hundred and thirty-three) started out ; and the footmen who kept up were
certainly less than fifty in number.   There is really no question as to the
American numbers ; yet a variety of reasons have conspired to cause them to
be generally greatly overstated, even by American historians.   Even Phelan
gives them fifteen hundred men, following the ordinary accounts.   At the
time, many outsiders supposed that all the militia who were at the Cowpens
fought in the battle ; but this is not asserted by any one who knew the facts.
General J. Watts DePeyster, in the *Mag. of Am. Hist.* for 1880,—" The
Affair at King's Mountain,"—gives the extreme tory view.   He puts the
number of the Americans at from thirteen hundred to nineteen hundred.
His account, however, is only based on Shelby's later narratives, told thirty
years after the event, and these are all that need be considered.   When
Shelby grew old, he greatly exaggerated the numbers on both sides in all
the fights in which he had taken part.   In his account of King's Mountain,
he speaks of Williams and the four hundred Flint Hill men joining the
attacking body *after*, not *before*, the nine hundred and ten picked men
started.   But his earlier accounts, including the official report which he
signed, explicitly contradict this.   The question is thus purely as to the time
of the junction ; as to whether it was after or before this that the body of
nine hundred actual fighters was picked out.   Shelby's later report contains
the grossest self-contradictions.   Thus it enumerates the companies which
fought the battle in detail, the result running up several hundred more than
the total he gives.   The early and official accounts are in every way more
worthy of credence ; but the point is settled beyond dispute by Hill's narrative.   Hill was one of the four hundred men with Williams, and he expressly states that after the junction at the Cowpens the force, from both
commands, that started out numbered nine hundred and thirty-three.   The
question is thus definitely settled.   Most of the later accounts simply follow
the statements Shelby made in his old age.

[2] There were many instances of brothers and cousins in the opposing ranks
at King's Mountain ; a proof of the similarity in the character of the forces.

troops, a hundred and twenty or thirty of them being the regulars or " American Volunteers," the remainder tory militia.[1] The forces were very nearly equal in number. What difference there was, was probably in favor of the British and tories. There was not a bayonet in the American army, whereas Ferguson trusted much to this weapon. All his volunteers and regulars were expert in its use, and with his usual ingenuity he had trained several of his loyalist companies in a similar manner, improvising bayonets out of their hunting-knives. The loyalists whom he had had with him for some time were well drilled. The North Carolina regiment was weaker on this point, as it was composed of recruits who had joined him but recently.[2]

[1] The American official account says that they captured the British provision returns, according to which their force amounted to eleven hundred and twenty-five men. It further reports, of the regulars nineteen killed, thirty-five wounded and left on the ground as unable to march, and seventy-eight captured ; of the tories two hundred and six killed, one hundred and twenty-eight wounded and left on the ground unable to march, and six hundred and forty-eight captured. The number of tories killed must be greatly exaggerated. Allaire, in his diary, says Ferguson had only eight hundred men, but almost in the same sentence enumerates nine hundred and six, giving of the regulars nineteen killed, thirty-three wounded, and sixty-four captured (one hundred and sixteen in all, instead of one hundred and thirty-two, as in the American account), and of the tories one hundred killed, ninety wounded, and " about " six hundred captured. This does not take account of those who escaped. From Ramsey and De Peyster down most writers assert that every single individual on the defeated side were killed or taken ; but in Colonel Chesney's admirable " Military Biography " there is given the autobiography or memoir of a South Carolina loyalist who was in the battle. His account of the battle is meagre and unimportant, but he expressly states that at the close he and a number of others escaped through the American lines by putting sprigs of white paper in their caps, as some of the whig militia did—for the militia had no uniforms, and were dressed alike on both sides. A certain number of men who escaped must thus be added.

[2] There were undoubtedly very many horse-thieves, murderers, and rogues of every kind with Ferguson, but equally undoubtedly the bulk of his troops

The Americans were discovered by their foes
when only a quarter of a mile away. They had
formed their forces as they marched. The right
centre was composed of Campbell's troops; the left
centre of Shelby's. These two bodies separated
slightly so as to come up opposite sides of the narrow
southwestern spur of the mountain. The right
wing was led by Sevier, with his own and McDow-

were loyalists from principle, and men of good standing, especially those
from the seaboard. Many of the worst tory bandits did not rally to him,
preferring to plunder on their own account. The American army itself was
by no means free from scoundrels. Most American writers belittle the character of Ferguson's force, and sneer at the courage of the tories, although
entirely unable to adduce any proof of their statements, the evidence being
the other way. Apparently they are unconscious of the fact that they thus
wofully diminish the credit to be given to the victors. It may be questioned if there ever was a braver or finer body of riflemen than the nine hundred who surrounded and killed or captured a superior body of well posted,
well led, and courageous men, in part also well drilled, on King's Mountain.
The whole world now recognizes how completely the patriots were in the
right; but it is especially incumbent on American historians to fairly portray
the acts and character of the tories, doing justice to them as well as to the
whigs, and condemning them only when they deserve it. In studying the
Revolutionary war in the Southern States, I have been struck by the way in
which the American historians alter the facts by relying purely on partisan
accounts, suppressing the innumerable whig excesses and outrages, or else pal-
liating them. They thus really destroy the force of the many grave accusations
which may be truthfully brought against the British and tories. I regret to
say that Bancroft is among the offenders. Hildreth is an honorable exception. Most of the British historians of the same events are even more rancorous and less trustworthy than the American writers; and while fully
admitting the many indefensible outrages committed by the whigs, a long-
continued and impartial examination of accessible records has given me the
belief that in the districts where the civil war was most ferocious, much the
largest number of the criminal class joined the tories, and the misdeeds of
the latter were more numerous than those of the whigs. But the frequency
with which both whigs and tories hung men for changing sides, shows that
quite a number of the people shifted from one party to the other; and so
there must have been many men of exactly the same stamp in both armies.
Much of the nominal changing of sides, however, was due to the needless
and excessive severity of Cornwallis and his lieutenants.

ell's troops.   On the extreme right Major Winston, splitting off from the main body a few minutes before, had led a portion of Cleavland's men by a roundabout route to take the mountain in the rear, and cut off all retreat.   He and his followers " rode like fox-hunters," as was afterwards reported by one of their number who was accustomed to following the buck and the gray fox with horn and hound. They did not dismount until they reached the foot of the mountain, galloping at full speed through the rock-strewn woods ; and they struck exactly the right place, closing up the only gap by which the enemy could have retreated.   The left wing was led by Cleavland.   It contained not only the bulk of his own Wilkes and Surrey men, but also the North and South Carolinians who had joined the army at the Cowpens under the command of Williams, Lacey, Hambright, Chronicle, and others.[1]   The different leaders cheered on their troops by a few last words as they went into the fight ; being especially careful to warn them how to deal with the British bayonet charges.   Campbell had visited each separate band, again requesting every man who felt like flinching not to go into the battle.   He bade them hold on to every inch of ground as long as possible, and when forced back to rally and return at once to the fight. Cleavland gave much the same advice ; telling his men that when once engaged they were not to wait for the word of command, but to do as he did, for he would show them by his example how to fight,

[1] Draper gives a good plan of the battle.   He also gives some pictures of the fighting, in which the backwoodsmen are depicted in full Continental uniform, which probably not a man—certainly very few of them—wore.

and they must then act as their own officers. The
men were to fire quickly, and stand their ground as
long as possible, if necessary sheltering themselves
behind trees. If they could do no better they were
to retreat, but not to run quite off; but to return
and renew the struggle, for they might have better
luck at the next attempt.[1]

So rapid were the movements of the Americans,
and so unexpected the attack, that a loyalist officer,
who had been out reconnoitring, had just brought
word to the British commander that there was no
sign of danger, when the first shots were heard; and
by the time the officer had paraded and posted his
men, the assault had begun, his horse had been
killed, and he himself wounded.[2]

When Ferguson learned that his foes were on him,
he sprang on his horse, his drums beat to arms, and
he instantly made ready for the fight. Though surprised by the unexpected approach of the Americans, he exerted himself with such energy that his
troops were in battle array when the attack began.
The outcrops of slaty rock on the hill-sides made

---

[1] Ramsay ("Revolution in South Carolina"), writing in 1785, gives the
speech verbatim, apparently from Cleavland himself. It is very improbable
that it is verbally correct, but doubtless it represents the spirit of his remarks.

[2] "Essays in Military Biography," Col. Charles Cornwallis Chesney.
London, 1874. On p. 323 begins a memoir of "A Carolina Loyalist in the
Revolutionary War." It is written by the loyalist himself, who was presumably a relation of Col. Chesney's. It was evidently written after the
event, and there are some lapses. Thus he makes the war with the Cherokees take place in 1777, instead of '76. His explanation of Tarleton's defeat at the Cowpens must be accepted with much reserve. At King's
Mountain he says the Americans had fifteen hundred men, instead of twenty-five hundred, of which Allaire speaks. Allaire probably consciously exaggerated the number.

ledges which, together with the boulders strewn on top, served as breastworks for the less disciplined tories; while he in person led his regulars and such of the loyalist companies as were furnished with the hunting-knife bayonets. He hoped to be able to repulse his enemies by himself taking the offensive, with a succession of bayonet charges; a form of attack in which his experience with Pulaski and Huger had given him great confidence.

At three o'clock in the afternoon the firing began, as the Americans drove in the British pickets. The brunt of the battle fell on the American centre, composed of Campbell's and Shelby's men, who sustained the whole fight for nearly ten minutes[1] until the two wings had had time to get into place and surround the enemy. Campbell began the assault, riding on horseback along the line of his riflemen. He ordered them to raise the Indian war-whoop, which they did with a will, and made the woods ring.[2] They then rushed upwards and began to fire, each on his own account; while their war cries echoed along the hill-side. Ferguson's men on the summit responded with heavy volley firing, and then charged, cheering lustily. The mountain was covered with smoke and flame, and seemed to thunder.[3]

[1] Campbell MSS. Letter of Col. Wm. Campbell, Oct. 10, 1780, says 10 minutes: the official report (Gates MSS.) says 5 minutes.

[2] *Richmond Enquirer* (Nov. 12, 1822 and May 9, 1823) certificates of King's Mountain survivors—of James Crow, May 6, 1813; David Beattie, May 4, 1813, etc., etc. All the different commanders claimed the honor of beginning the battle in after-life; the official report decides it in favor of Campbell and Shelby, the former being the first actually engaged, as is acknowledged by Shelby in his letter to Arthur Campbell on October 12, 1780.

[3] Haywood, 71; doubtless he uses the language of one of the actors.

Ferguson's troops advanced steadily, their officers riding at their head, with their swords flashing; and the mountaineers, who had no bayonets, could not withstand the shock. They fled down the hill-side, and being sinewy, nimble men, swift of foot, they were not overtaken, save a few of sullen temper, who would not retreat and were bayoneted. One of their officers, a tall backwoodsman, six feet in height, was cut down by Lieutenant Allaire, a New York loyalist, as the latter rode at the head of his platoon. No sooner had the British charge spent itself than Campbell, who was riding midway between the enemy and his own men, called out to the latter in a voice of thunder to rally and return to the fight, and in a minute or two they were all climbing the hill again, going from tree to tree, and shooting at the soldiers on the summit. Campbell's horse, exhausted by the breakneck galloping hither and thither over the slope, gave out; he then led the men on foot, his voice hoarse with shouting, his face blackened with powder; for he was always in the front of the battle and nearest the enemy.

No sooner had Ferguson returned from his charge on Campbell than he found Shelby's men swarming up to the attack on the other side. Shelby himself was at their head. He had refused to let his people return the dropping fire of the tory skirmishers until they were close up. Ferguson promptly charged his new foes and drove them down the hill-side; but the instant he stopped, Shelby, who had been in the thick of the fight, closest to the British, brought his marksmen back, and they came up nearer than ever, and with a deadlier fire.[1] While Ferguson's bayonet-men—both regulars and militia—charged to and fro, the rest of the loyalists kept up a heavy fire from behind the rocks on the hill-top. The battle raged in every part, for the Americans had by this time surrounded their foes, and they advanced rapidly under cover of the woods. They inflicted much more damage than they suffered, for they were scattered out while the royalist troops were close together, and moreover, were continually taken in flank. Ferguson, conspicuous from his hunting-shirt,[2] rode hither and thither with reckless bravery, his sword in his left hand—for he had never entirely regained the use of his wounded right—while he made his presence known by the shrill, ear-piercing notes of a silver whistle which he always carried. Whenever the British and tories charged with the bayonet, under Ferguson, De Peyster, or some of their lieutenants, the mountaineers were forced back down the hill; but the instant the red lines halted and returned to the summit, the stubborn riflemen followed close behind, and from every tree and boulder continued their irregular and destructive fire. The peculiar feature of the battle was the success with which, after every retreat, Campbell, Shelby, Sevier, and Cleavland rallied their followers on the instant; the great point was to prevent the men from becoming panic-stricken when forced to flee. The pealing volleys of mus-

[1] Shelby MS.

[2] The "Carolina Loyalist" speaks as if the hunting-shirt were put on for disguise; he says Ferguson was recognized, "although wearing a hunting-shirt."

ketry at short intervals drowned the incessant clat-
ter of the less noisy but more deadly backwoods
rifles. The wild whoops of the mountain men, the
cheering of the loyalists, the shouts of the officers,
and the cries of the wounded mingled with the reports of the firearms, and shrill above the din rose
the calling of the silver whistle. Wherever its
notes were heard the wavering British line came on,
and the Americans were forced back. Ferguson
dashed from point to point, to repel the attacks of
his foes, which were made with ever-increasing fury.
Two horses were killed under him;[1] but he continued to lead the charging parties; slashing and
hewing with his sword until it was broken off at the
hilt. At last, as he rode full speed against a part
of Sevier's men, who had almost gained the hill
crest, he became a fair mark for the vengeful backwoods riflemen. Several of them fired together and
he fell suddenly from his horse, pierced by half a
dozen bullets almost at the same instant. The gallant British leader was dead, while his foot yet
hung in the stirrup.[2]

The silver whistle was now silent, but the dis-

[1] Ferguson's "Memoir," p. 32.

[2] The "South Carolina Loyalist" says he was killed just as he had slain
Col. Williams "with his left hand." Ramsey, on the other side, represents
Col. Williams as being shot while dashing forward to kill Ferguson. Williams certainly was not killed by Ferguson himself ; and in all probability the
latter was slain earlier in the action and in an entirely different part of the
line. The "Loyalist" is also in error as to Cleavland's regiment being the
first that was charged. There is no ground whatever for the statement that
Ferguson was trying to escape when shot ; nor was there any attempt at a
charge of horsemen, made in due form. The battle was purely one of footmen and the attempt to show an effort at a cavalry charge at the end is a
simple absurdity.

heartened loyalists were rallied by De Peyster, who bravely continued the fight.[1]   It is said that he himself led one of the charges which were at this time made on Cleavland's line; the "South Fork" men from the Catawba, under Hambright and Chronicle, being forced back, Chronicle being killed and Hambright wounded. When the Americans fled they were scarcely a gun's length ahead of their foes; and the instant the latter faced about, the former were rallied by their officers, and again went up the hill. One of the backwoodsmen was in the act of cocking his rifle when a loyalist, dashing at him with the bayonet, pinned his hand to his thigh; the rifle went off, the ball going through the loyalist's body, and the two men fell together.   Hambright, though wounded, was able to sit in the saddle, and continued in the battle. Cleavland had his horse shot under him, and then led his men on foot. As the lines came close together, many of the whigs recognized in the tory ranks their former neighbors, friends, or relatives; and the men taunted and jeered one another with bitter hatred. In more than one instance brother was slain by brother or cousin by cousin. The lowland tories felt an especial dread of the mountaineers; looking with awe and hatred on their tall, gaunt, rawboned figures, their long, matted hair and wild faces. One wounded tory, as he lay watching them, noticed their deadly accuracy of aim, and saw also that the loyalists, firing from the summit, continually overshot their foes.

[1] In his *Hist. Mag.* article Gen. Watts De Peyster clears his namesake's reputation from all charge of cowardice ; but his account of how De Peyster counselled and planned all sorts of expedients that might have saved the loyalists is decidedly mythical.

The British regulars had lost half their number; the remainder had been scattered and exhausted in their successive charges. The bayonet companies of the loyalist militia were in the same plight; and the North Carolina tories, the least disciplined, could no longer be held to their work. Sevier's men gained the summit at the same time with Campbell's and part of Shelby's. The three colonels were heading their troops; and as Sevier saw Shelby, he swore, by God, the British had burned off part of his hair; for it was singed on one side of his head.

When the Holston and Watauga men gained the crest the loyalists broke and fled to the east end of the mountain, among the tents and baggage wagons, where they again formed. But they were huddled together, while their foes surrounded them on every hand. The fighting had lasted an hour; all hope was gone; and De Peyster hoisted a white flag.

In the confusion the firing continued in parts of the lines on both sides. Some of the backwoodsmen did not know what a white flag meant; others disregarded it, savagely calling out, "Give them Buford's play," in allusion to Tarleton's having refused quarter to Buford's troops.[1] Others of the men as they came up began shooting before they learned what had happened; and some tories who had been out foraging returned at this moment, and also opened fire. A number of the loyalists escaped in turmoil, putting badges in their hats like those worn by certain of the American militia, and thus passing in safety through the whig lines.[2] It was at this time, after the white flag had been displayed, that Col. Williams was shot,

[1] Deposition of John Long, in *Enquirer*, as quoted.   [2] Chesney, p. 333.

as he charged a few of the tories who were still firing.
The flag was hoisted again, and white handkerchiefs
were also waved, from guns and ramrods. Shelby,
spurring up to part of their line, ordered the tories to
lay down their arms, which they did.[1] Campbell, at
the same moment, running among his men with his
sword pointed to the ground, called on them for
God's sake to cease firing; and turning to the prisoners he bade the officers rank by themselves, and the
men to take off their hats and sit down. He then
ordered De Peyster to dismount; which the latter
did, and handed his sword to Campbell.[2] The
various British officers likewise surrendered their
swords, to different Americans; many of the militia
commanders who had hitherto only possessed a
tomahawk or scalping-knife thus for the first time
getting possession of one of the coveted weapons.

Almost the entire British and tory force was killed
or captured; the only men who escaped were the few
who got through the American lines by adopting the
whig badges. About three hundred of the loyalists
were killed or disabled; the slightly wounded do
not seem to have been counted.[3] The colonel-
commandant was among the slain; of the four militia

[1] Shelby MS.

[2] Campbell MSS. Letter of General George Rutledge (who was in the
battle, an eye-witness of what he describes), May 27, 1813. But there is
an irreconcilable conflict of testimony as to whether Campbell or Evan
Shelby received De Peyster's sword.

[3] For the loyalist losses, see *ante*, note discussing their numbers. The
"South Carolina Loyalist" says they lost about a third of their number.
It is worthy of note that the actual fighting at King's Mountain bore much
resemblance to that at Majuba Hill a century later; a backwoods levy
was much like a boer commando.

colonels present, two were killed, one wounded,[1] and the other captured—a sufficient proof of the obstinacy of the resistance. The American loss in killed and wounded amounted to less than half, perhaps only a third, that of their foes.[2] Campbell's command suffered more than any other, the loss among the officers being especially great; for it bore the chief part in withstanding the successive bayonet

[1] In some accounts this officer is represented as a major, in some as a colonel ; at any rate he was in command of a small regiment, or fragment of a regiment.

[2] The official report as published gave the American loss as twenty-eight killed and sixty wounded. The original document (in the Gates MSS., N. Y. Hist. Soc.) gives the loss in tabulated form in an appendix, which has not heretofore been published. It is as follows :

RETURN OF KILLED AND WOUNDED.

REGIMENTS.	KILLED.								WOUNDED.								Grand Total.
	Col.	Major.	Capt.	Lieut.	Ensign.	Sergt.	Private.	Total.	Col.	Major.	Capt.	Lieut.	Ensign.	Sergt.	Private.	Total.	
Campbell's			1	2	4		5	12			1	3			17	21	33
McDowell's							4	4							4	4	8
Thomas'							8	8							8	8	8
Cleavland's							8	8		1	2				10	13	21
Shelby's																	
Sevier's							2	2							10	10	12
Hayes'		1						1							3	3	4
Brannon's								1							3	3	3
Col. Williams' . . .	1							1									1
	1	1	1	2	4		19	28		1	3	3			55	62	90

It will be seen that these returns are imperfect. They do not include Shelby's loss ; yet his regiment was alongside of Campbell's, did its full share of the work, and probably suffered as much as Sevier's, for instance. But it is certain that in the hurry not all the killed and wounded were enumerated (compare Draper, pp. 302–304). Hayes', Thomas', and "Brannon's" (Brandon's) commands were some of those joining at the Cowpens. Winston's loss is doubtless included under Cleavland's. It will be seen that Williams' troops could have taken very little part in the action.

charges of the regulars, and the officers had been
forced to expose themselves with the utmost freedom,
in order to rally their men when beaten back.[1]

The mountain-men had done a most notable
deed. They had shown in perfection the best
After the qualities of horse-riflemen. Their hardi-
Victory. hood and perseverance had enabled them
to bear up well under fatigue, exposure, and
scanty food. Their long, swift ride, and the
suddenness of the attack, took their foes completely by surprise. Then, leaving their horses,
they had shown in the actual battle such courage,
marksmanship, and skill in woodland fighting, that
they had not only defeated but captured an equal
number of well-armed, well-led, resolute men, in a
strong position. The victory was of far-reaching
importance, and ranks among the decisive battles of
the Revolution. It was the first great success of the
Americans in the south, the turning-point in the
southern campaign, and it brought cheer to the
patriots throughout the Union. The loyalists of
the Carolinas were utterly cast down, and never
recovered from the blow; and its immediate effect
was to cause Cornwallis to retreat from North Carolina, abandoning his first invasion of that State.[2]

---

[1] It would be quite impossible to take notice of the countless wild
absurdities of the various writers who have given "histories" so-called, of the
battle. One of the most recent of them, Mr. Kirke, having accepted as the
number of the British dead two hundred and twenty-five, and the wounded
one hundred and eighty five, says that the disproportion shows " the wonderful accuracy of the backwoods rifle "—the beauty of the argument being that
it necessarily implies that the backwoodsmen only fired some four hundred
and ten shots. Mr. Kirke's account of the battle having been " won "
owing to a remarkable ride taken by Sevier to rally the men at the critical
moment is, of course, without any historic basis whatever.

[2] " Tarleton's Campaigns," p. 166.

The expedition offered a striking example of the individual initiative so characteristic of the back-woodsmen. It was not ordered by any one author-ity; it was not even sanctioned by the central or State governments. Shelby and Sevier were the two prime movers in getting it up; Campbell exercised the chief command; and the various other leaders, with their men, simply joined the mountaineers, as they happened to hear of them and come across their path. The ties of discipline were of the slightest. The commanders elected their own chief without regard to rank or seniority; in fact the officer[1] who was by rank entitled to the place was hardly given any share in the conduct of the campaign. The authority of the commandant over the other officers, and of the various colonels over their troops, re-sembled rather the control exercised by Indian chiefs over their warriors than the discipline obtaining in a regular army. But the men were splendid individual fighters, who liked and trusted their leaders; and the latter were bold, resolute, energetic, and intelligent.

Cornwallis feared that the mountain men would push on and attack his flank; but there was no such danger. By themselves they were as little likely to assail him in force in the open as Andreas Hofer's Tyrolese—with whom they had many points in com-mon—were to threaten Napoleon on the Danubian plains. Had they been Continental troops, the Brit-ish would have had to deal with a permanent army. But they were only militia[2] after all, however for-

[1] Williams.

[2] The striking nature of the victory and its important consequences must not blind us to the manifold shortcomings of the Revolutionary militia. The mountaineers did well in spite of being militia; but they would have

midable from their patriotic purpose and personal prowess. The backwoods armies were not unlike the armies of the Scotch Highlanders; tumultuous gatherings of hardy and warlike men, greatly to be dreaded under certain circumstances, but incapable of a long campaign, and almost as much demoralized by a victory as by a defeat. Individually or in small groups they were perhaps even more formidable than the Highlanders; but in one important respect they were inferior, for they totally lacked the regimental organization which the clan system gave the Scotch Celts.

The mountaineers had come out to do a certain thing—to kill Ferguson and scatter his troops. They had done it, and now they wished to go home. The little log-huts in which their families lived were in daily danger of Indian attack; and it was absolutely necessary that they should be on hand to protect them. They were, for the most part, very poor men, whose sole sources of livelihood were the stock they kept beyond the mountains. They loved their country greatly, and had shown the sincerity of their patriotism by the spontaneous way in which they risked their lives on this expedition. They had no hope of reward; for they neither expected nor

done far better under another system. The numerous failures of the militia as a whole must be balanced against the few successes of a portion of them. If the States had possessed wisdom enough to back Washington with Continentals, or with volunteers such as those who fought in the Civil War, the Revolutionary contest would have been over in three years. The trust in militia was a perfect curse. Many of the backwoods leaders knew this. The old Indian fighter, Andrew Lewis, about this time wrote to·Gates (see Gates MSS., Sept. 30, 1780), speaking of "the dastardly conduct of the militia," calling them "a set of poltroons," and longing for Continentals.

received any pay, except in liquidated certificates, worth two cents on the dollar. Shelby's share of these, for his services as colonel throughout '80 and '81, was sold by him for " six yards of middling broadcloth "[1]; so it can be readily imagined how little each private got for the King's Mountain expedition.[2]

The day after the battle the Americans fell back towards the mountains, fearing lest, while cumbered by prisoners and wounded, they should be struck by Tarleton or perhaps Cruger. The prisoners were marched along on foot, each carrying one or two muskets, for twelve hundred stand of arms had been captured. The Americans had little to eat, and were very tired; but the plight of the prisoners was pitiable. Hungry, footsore, and heartbroken, they were hurried along by the fierce and boastful victors, who gloried in the vengeance they had taken, and recked little of such a virtue as magnanimity to the fallen. The only surgeon in either force was Ferguson's. He did what he could for the wounded; but that was little enough, for, of course, there were no medical stores whatever. The Americans buried their dead in graves, and carried their wounded along on horse-litters. The wounded loyalists were left on the field, to be cared for by the neighboring people. The conquerors showed neither respect nor sympathy for the leader who had so gallantly fought them.[3]

[1] Shelby's MS. autobiography.

[2] Among these privates was the father of Davy Crockett.

[3] But the accounts of indignity being shown him are not corroborated by Allaire and Ryerson, the two contemporary British authorities, and are probably untrue.

His body and the bodies of his slain followers were cast into two shallow trenches, and loosely covered with stones and earth. The wolves, coming to the carnage, speedily dug up the carcasses, and grew so bold from feasting at will on the dead that they no longer feared the living. For months afterwards King's Mountain was a favorite resort for wolf hunters.

The victory once gained, the bonds of discipline over the troops were forthwith loosened; they had been lax at the best, and only the strain of the imminent battle with the British had kept them tense for the fortnight the mountaineers had been away from their homes. All the men of the different commands were bragging as to their respective merits in the battle, and the feats performed by the different commanders.[1] The general break up of authority, of course, allowed full play to the vicious and criminal characters. Even before the mountaineers came down the unfortunate Carolinas had suffered from the misdeeds of different bodies of ill-disciplined patriot troops,[2] almost as much as from the British and tories. The case was worse now. Many men deserted from the returning army for the especial purpose of plundering the people of the neighborhood, paying small heed which cause the victims had espoused; and parties continually left camp avowedly with this object. Campbell's control was of the slightest; he was forced to entreat rather than command the troops, complaining that they left their friends in "almost a

[1] Certificate of Matthew Willoughby, in *Richmond Enquirer*, as quoted.
[2] Gates MSS., Deposition of John Satty, and others, Sept. 7, 1780; of Wm. Hamilton, Sept. 12th, etc., etc., etc.

worse situation than the enemy would have done," and expressing what was certainly a moderate "wish," that the soldiers would commit no "unnecessary injury" on the inhabitants of the county.[1] Naturally such very mild measures produced little effect in stopping the plundering.

However, Campbell spoke in stronger terms of an even worse set of outrages. The backwoodsmen had little notion of mercy to beaten enemies, and many of them treated the captured loyalists with great brutality, even on the march,[2] Col. Cleavland himself being one of the offenders.[3] Those of their friends and relatives who had fallen into the hands of the tories, or of Cornwallis' regulars, had fared even worse; yet this cannot palliate their conduct. Campbell himself, when in a fit of gusty anger, often did things he must have regretted afterwards; but he was essentially manly, and his soul revolted at the continued persecution of helpless enemies. He issued a sharp manifesto in reference to the way the prisoners were " slaughtered and disturbed," assuring the troops that if it could not be prevented by moderate measures, he would put a stop to it by taking summary vengeance on the offenders.[4] After this the prisoners were, on the whole, well treated. When they met a couple of Continental officers, the latter were very polite, expressing their sympathy for their fate in falling into such hands; for from Washington and Greene down,

---

[1] Campbell's General Orders, Oct. 14th, and Oct. 26th.

[2] " Our captors . . . cutting and striking us in a most savage manner,"— " South Carolina Loyalist."   [3] Allaire's diary, entry of Nov. 1st.

[4] Campbell's General Orders, Oct. 11th.

the Continental troops disliked and distrusted the militia almost as much as the British regulars did the tories.

There was one dark deed of vengeance. It had come to be common for the victors on both sides to hang those whom they regarded as the chief offenders among their conquered opponents. As the different districts were alternately overrun, the unfortunate inhabitants were compelled to swear allegiance in succession to Congress and to king; and then, on whichever side they bore arms, they were branded as traitors. Moreover, the different leaders, both British and American, from Tarleton and Ferguson to Sumter and Marion, often embodied in their own ranks some of their prisoners, and these were of course regarded as deserters by their former comrades. Cornwallis, seconded by Rawdon, had set the example of ordering all men found in the rebel ranks after having sworn allegiance to the king, to be hung; his under-officers executed the command with zeal, and the Americans, of course, retaliated. Ferguson's troops themselves had hung some of their prisoners.[1]

All this was fresh in the minds of the Americans who had just won so decisive a victory. They were accustomed to give full vent to the unbridled fury of their passions; they with difficulty brooked control; they brooded long over their own wrongs, which were many and real, and they were but little impressed by the misdeeds committed in re-

[1] Allaire's Diary, entry for Aug. 20th; also see Aug. 2d. He chronicles these hangings with much complacency, but is, of course, shocked at the "infamous" conduct of the Americans when they do likewise.

turn by their friends. Inflamed by hatred and the thirst for vengeance, they would probably have put to death some of their prisoners in any event; but all doubt was at an end when on their return march they were joined by an officer who had escaped from before Augusta, and who brought word that Cruger's victorious loyalists had hung a dozen of the captured patriots.[1] This news settled the doom of some of the tory prisoners. A week after the battle a number of them were tried, and thirty were condemned to death. Nine, including the only tory colonel who had survived the battle, were hung; then Sevier and Shelby, men of bold, frank nature, could no longer stand the butchery, and peremptorily interfered, saving the remainder.[2] Of the men who were hung, doubtless some were murderers and marauders, who deserved their fate; others, including the unfortunate colonel, were honorable men, executed only because they had taken arms for the cause they deemed right.

Leaving the prisoners in the hands of the lowland militia, the mountaineers returned to their secure fastnesses in the high hill-valleys of the Holston, the Watauga, and the Nolichucky. They had marched well and fought valiantly, and they had gained a great victory; all the little stockaded forts, all the rough log-cabins on the scattered clearings, were jubilant over the triumph. From that moment their three leaders were men of renown. The legislatures of their respective states thanked them publicly and voted them swords for their ser-

[1] Shelby MS.   [2] *Do.*

vices. Campbell, next year, went down to join Greene's army, did gallant work at Guilford Court-house, and then died of camp-fever. Sevier and Shelby had long lives before them.[1]

[1] Thirty years after the battle, when Campbell had long been dead, Shelby and Sevier started a most unfortunate controversy as to his conduct in the battle. They insisted that he had flinched, and that victory was mainly due to them. Doubtless they firmly believed what they said ; for as already stated, the jealousies and rivalries among the backwoods leaders were very strong ; but the burden of proof, after thirty years' silence, rested on them, and they failed to make their statements good—nor was their act a very gracious one. Shelby bore the chief part in the quarrel, Campbell's surviving relatives, of course, defending the dead chieftain. I have carefully examined all the papers in the case, in the Tenn. Historical Society, the Shelby, MSS., and the Campbell MSS., besides the files of the *Richmond Enquirer*, etc.; and it is evident that the accusation was wholly groundless.

Shelby and Sevier rest their case :

1st, on their memory, thirty years after the event, of some remarks of Campbell to them in private after the close of the battle, which they construed as acknowledgments of bad conduct. Against these memories of old men it is safe to set Shelby's explicit testimony, in a letter written six days after the battle (see *Virginia Argus*, Oct. 26, 1810), to the good-conduct of the "gallant commander" (Campbell).

2d, on the fact that Campbell was seen on a black horse in the rear during the fighting ; but a number of men of his regiment swore that he had given his black horse to a servant who sat in the rear, while he himself rode a bay horse in the battle. See their affidavits in the *Enquirer*.

3d, on the testimony of one of Shelby's brothers, who said he saw him in the rear. This is the only piece of positive testimony in the case. Some of Campbell's witnesses (as Matthew Willoughby) swore that this brother of Shelby was a man of bad character, engaged at the time in stealing cattle from both Whigs and Tories.

4th, on the testimony of a number of soldiers who swore they did not see Campbell in the latter part of the battle, nor until some moments after the surrender. Of course, this negative testimony is simply valueless ; in such a hurly burly it would be impossible for the men in each part of the line to see all the commanders, and Campbell very likely did not reach the places where these men were until some time after the surrender. On the other hand, forty officers and soldiers of Campbell's, Sevier's, and Shelby's regiments, headed by General Rutledge, swore that they had seen Campbell valiantly leading throughout the whole battle, and foremost at the surrender. This positive testimony conclusively settles the matter ; it outweighs that of Shelby's brother, the only affirmative witness on the other side. But it is a fair question as to whether Campbell or another of Shelby's brothers received De Peyster's sword.

CHAPTER X.

THE HOLSTON SETTLEMENTS TO THE END OF THE REVOLUTION, 1781-83.

JOHN SEVIER had no sooner returned from doing his share in defeating foes who were of his own race, than he was called on to face another set of enemies, quite as formidable and much more cruel. These were the red warriors, the ancient owners of the soil, who were ever ready to take advantage of any momentary disaster that befell their hereditary and victorious opponents, the invading settlers.

John Sevier.

For many years Sevier was the best Indian fighter on the border. He was far more successful than Clark, for instance, inflicting greater loss on his foes and suffering much less himself, though he never had any thing like Clark's number of soldiers. His mere name was a word of dread to the Cherokees, the Chickamaugas, and the upper Creeks. His success was due to several causes. He wielded great influence over his own followers, whose love for and trust in "Chucky Jack" were absolutely unbounded; for he possessed in the highest degree the virtues most prized on the frontier. He was open-hearted and hospitable, with winning ways towards all, and combined a cool head with a dauntless heart; he loved a battle for its own sake, and was never so much at his ease as when under fire; he was a first-class marksman, and as good a horseman as was to be found on the border. In his campaigns against the Indians he adopted the tactics of his foes, and grafted on them some important improvements of his own. Much of his success was due to his adroit use of scouts or spies. He always chose for these the best woodsmen of the district, men who could endure as much, see as much, and pass through the woods as silently, as the red men themselves. By keeping these scouts well ahead of him, he learned accurately where the war parties were. In the attack itself he invariably used mounted riflemen, men skilled in forest warfare, who rode tough little horses, on which they galloped at speed through the forest. Once in position they did the actual fighting on foot, sheltering themselves carefully behind the tree-trunks. He moved with extreme rapidity and attacked with instantaneous suddenness, using ambushes and surprises wherever practicable. His knowledge of the whereabouts and size of the hostile parties, and the speed of his own movements, generally enabled him to attack with the advantage of numbers greatly on his side.[1] He could then out-

---

[1] The old Tennessee historians, headed by Haywood, base their accounts of the actions on statements made by the pioneers, or some of the pioneers, forty or fifty years after the event; and they do a great deal of bragging about the prowess of the old Indian fighters. The latter did most certainly perform mighty deeds; but often in an entirely different way from that generally recorded; for they faced a foe who on his own ground was infinitely more to be dreaded than the best trained European regulars. Thus Haywood says that after the battle of the Island Flats, the whites were so encouraged that thenceforward they never asked concerning their enemies, "how

flank or partially surround the Indians, while his sudden rush demoralized them; so that, in striking contrast to most other Indian fighters, he inflicted a far greater loss than he received. He never fought a big pitched battle, but, by incessantly harrying and scattering the different war bands, he struck such terror to the hearts of the Indians that he again and again, in a succession of wars, forced them into truces, and for the moment freed the settlements from their ravages. He was almost the only commander on the frontier who ever brought an Indian war, of whatever length, to an end, doing a good deal of damage to his foes and suffering very little himself. Still, he never struck a crushing blow, nor conquered a permanent peace. He never did any thing to equal Clark's campaigns in the Illinois and against Vincennes, and, of course, he cannot for a moment be compared to his rival and successor, grim Old Hickory, the destroyer of the Creeks and the hero of New Orleans.

many are they?" but "where are they?" Of course, this is a mere piece of barbaric boasting. If the whites had really acted on any such theory there would have been a constant succession of disasters like that at the Blue Licks. Sevier's latest biographer, Mr. Kirke, in the "Rear-guard of the Revolution," goes far beyond even the old writers. For instance, on p. 141 he speaks of Sevier's victories being "often" gained over "twenty times his own number" of Indians. As a matter of fact, one of the proofs of Sevier's skill as a commander is that he almost always fought with the advantage of numbers on his side. Not a single instance can be produced where either he or any one else during his lifetime gained a victory over twenty times his number of Indians, unless the sieges are counted. It is necessary to keep in mind the limitations under which Haywood did his work, in order to write truthfully; but a debt of gratitude will always be due him for the history he wrote. Like Marshall's, it is the book of one who himself knew the pioneers, and it has preserved very much of value which would otherwise have been lost. The same holds true of Ramsey.

When the men of the Holston or upper Tennessee valley settlements reached their homes after the King's Mountain expedition, they found them menaced by the Cherokees. Congress had endeavored in vain to persuade the chiefs of this tribe to make a treaty of peace, or at least to remain neutral. The efforts of the British agents to embroil them with the whites were completely successful; and in November the Otari or Overhill warriors began making inroads along the frontier. They did not attack in large bands. A constant succession of small parties moved swiftly through the county, burning cabins, taking scalps, and, above all, stealing horses. As the most effectual way of stopping such inroads, the alarmed and angered settlers resolved to send a formidable retaliatory expedition against the Overhill towns.[1] All the Holston settlements both north and south of the Virginia line joined in sending troops. By the first week in December, 1780, seven hundred mounted riflemen were ready to march, under the joint leadership of Colonel Arthur Campbell and of Sevier, the former being the senior officer. They were to meet at an appointed place on the French Broad.

Sevier's Cherokee Campaigns. (margin note)

Sevier started first, with between two and three hundred of his Watauga and Nolichucky followers. He marched down to the French Broad, but could hear nothing of Campbell. He was on the great war trace of the southern Indians, and his scouts speedily brought him word that they had exchanged

[1] Campbell MSS. Letter of Gov. Thos. Jefferson, Feb. 17, 1781.

shots with a Cherokee war party, on its way to the
settlements, and not far distant on the other side of
the river. He instantly crossed, and made a swift
march towards the would-be marauders, camping on
Boyd's Creek. The scouts were out by sunrise next
morning—December 16th,—and speedily found the
Indian encampment, which the warriors had just
left. On receipt of the news Sevier ordered the
scouts to run on, attack the Indians, and then instantly retreat, so as to draw them into an ambuscade.
Meanwhile the main body followed cautiously after,
the men spread out in a long line, with the wings
advanced; the left wing under Major Jesse Walton,
the right under Major Jonathan Tipton, while Sevier
himself commanded the centre, which advanced along
the trail by which the scouts were to retreat. When
the Indians were drawn into the middle, the two
wings were to close in, when the whole party would
be killed or captured.

The plan worked well. The scouts soon came up
with the warriors, and, after a moment's firing, ran
back, with the Indians in hot pursuit. Sevier's men
lay hid, and, when the leading warriors were close
up, they rose and fired. Walton's wing closed in
promptly; but Tipton was too slow, and the startled Cherokees ran off through the opening he had
left, rushed into a swamp impassable for horsemen,
and scattered out, each man for himself, being soon
beyond pursuit. Nevertheless, Sevier took thirteen
scalps, many weapons, and all their plunder. In
some of their bundles there were proclamations from
Sir Henry Clinton and other British commanders.

The Indians were too surprised and panic-struck to offer any serious resistance, and not a man of Sevier's force was even wounded.[1]

Having thus made a very pretty stroke, Sevier returned to the French Broad, where Campbell joined him on the 22d, with four hundred troops. Among them were a large number of Shelby's men, under the command of Major Joseph Martin. The next day the seven hundred horsemen made a forced march to the Little Tennessee ; and on the 24th crossed it unopposed, making a feint at one ford, while the main body passed rapidly over another. The Indians did not have the numbers to oppose so formidable a body of good fighters, and only ventured on a little very long range and harmless skirmishing with the vanguard. Dividing into two

[1] Campbell MSS. Copy of the official report of Col. Arthur Campbell, Jan. 15, 1781. The accounts of this battle of Boyd's Creek illustrate well the growth of such an affair under the hands of writers who place confidence in all kinds of tradition, especially if they care more for picturesqueness than for accuracy. The contemporary official report is explicit. There were three hundred whites and seventy Indians. Of the latter, thirteen were slain. Campbell's whole report shows a jealousy of Sevier, whom he probably knew well enough was a man of superior ability to himself ; but this jealousy appears mainly in the coloring. He does not change any material fact, and there is no reason for questioning the substantial truth of his statements.

Forty years afterward Haywood writes of the affair, trying to tell simply the truth, but obliged to rely mainly on oral tradition. He speaks of Sevier's troops as only two hundred in number ; and says twenty-eight Indians were killed. He does not speak of the number of the Indians, but from the way he describes Sevier's troops as encircling them, he evidently knew that the white men were more numerous than their foes. His mistake as to the number of Indian dead is easily explicable. The official report gives twenty-nine as the number killed in the entire campaign, and Haywood, as in the Island Flats battle, simply puts the total of several skirmishes into one.

Thirty years later comes Ramsey. He relies on traditions that have grown more circumstantial and less accurate. He gives two accounts of what he calls " one of the best-fought battles in the border war of Tennessee " ; one of these accounts is mainly true ; the other entirely false ; he does not

bodies, the troops destroyed Chota and the other towns up and down the stream, finding in them a welcome supply of provisions. The next day Martin, with a detachment, fell on a party of flying Indians, killed one, and captured seventeen horses loaded with clothing, skins, and the scanty household furniture of the cabins; while another detachment destroyed the part of Chilhowee that was on the nearer side of the river. On the 26th the rest of Chilhowee was burned, three Indians killed, and nine captured. Tipton, with one hundred and fifty men, was sent to attack another town beyond the river; but owing to the fault of their commander,[1] this body failed to get across. The Indian woman, Nancy Ward, who in '76 had given the settlers timely warning of the intended attack by her tribes-

try to reconcile them. He says three whites were wounded, although the official report says that in the whole campaign but one man was killed and two wounded. He reduces Sevier's force to one hundred and seventy men, and calls the Indians " a large body."

Thirty-four years later comes Mr. Kirke, with the " Rear-guard of the Revolution." Out of his inner consciousness he evolves the fact that there were " not less than a thousand " Indians, whom Sevier, at the head of one hundred and seventy men, vanquishes, after a heroic combat, in which Sevier and some others perform a variety of purely imaginary feats. By diminishing the number of the whites, and increasing that of the Indians, he thus makes the relative force of the latter about *twenty-five times as great as it really was*, and converts a clever ambuscade, whereby the whites gave a smart drubbing to a body of Indians one fourth their own number, into a Homeric victory over a host six times as numerous as the conquerors.

This is not a solitary instance; on the contrary it is typical of almost all that is gravely set forth as history by a number of writers on these western border wars, whose books are filled from cover to cover with just such matter. Almost all their statements are partly, and very many are wholly, without foundation.

[1] His " unmilitary behavior," says Campbell. Ramsey makes him one of the (imaginary) wounded at Boyd's Creek. Kirke improves on this by describing him as falling " badly wounded " just as he was about to move his wing forward, and ascribes to his fall the failure of the wing to advance.

men here came into camp. She brought overtures of peace from the chiefs; but to these Campbell and Sevier would not listen, as they wished first to demolish the Hiawassee towns, where the warriors had been especially hostile. Accordingly, they marched thither. On their way there were a couple of skirmishes, in which several Indians were killed and one white man. The latter, whose name was Elliot, was buried in the Tellico town, a cabin being burned down over his grave, that the Indians might not know where it was. The Indians watched the army from the hills. At one point a warrior was seen stationed on a ridge to beat a drum and give signals to the rest; but the spies of the whites stole on him unawares, and shot him. The Hiawassee towns and all the stores of provisions they contained were destroyed, the work being finished on the last day of the year.

On January 1, 1781, the army broke up into detachments which went home by different routes, some additional towns being destroyed. The Indians never ventured to offer the invaders a pitched battle. Many of the war parties were absent on the frontier, and, at the very time their own country was being invaded, they committed ravages in Powell's Valley, along the upper Holston, and on the Kentucky road, near Cumberland Gap. The remaining warriors were cowed by Sevier's first success, and were puzzled by the rapidity with which the troops moved; for the mounted riflemen went at speed wherever they wished, and were not encumbered by baggage, each man taking only his blanket and a wallet of parched corn.

All the country of the Overhill Cherokees was laid waste, a thousand cabins were burned, and fifty thousand bushels of corn destroyed. Twenty-nine warriors in all were killed, and seventeen women and children captured, not including the family of Nancy Ward, who were treated as friends, not prisoners. But one white man was killed and two wounded.[1]

In the burnt towns, and on the dead warriors, were found many letters and proclamations from the

---

[1] Campbell MSS. Arthur Campbell's official report. The figures of the cabins and corn destroyed are probably exaggerated. All the Tennessee historians, down to Phelan, are hopelessly in the dark over this campaign. Haywood actually duplicates it (pp. 63 and 99) recounting it first as occurring in '79, and then with widely changed incidents as happening in '81—making two expeditions. When he falls into such a tremendous initial error, it is not to be wondered at that the details he gives are very untrustworthy. Ramsey corrects Haywood as far as the two separate expeditions are concerned, but he makes a number of reckless statements apparently on no better authority than the traditions current among the border people, sixty or seventy years after the event. These stand on the same foundation with the baseless tale that makes Isaac Shelby take part in the battle of Island Flats. The Tennessee historians treat Sevier as being the chief commander ; but he was certainly under Campbell ; the address they sent out to the Indians is signed by Campbell first, Sevier second, and Martin third. Haywood, followed by Ramsey, says that Sevier marched to the Chickamauga towns, which he destroyed, and then marched down the Coosa to the region of the Cypress Swamps. But Campbell's official report says that the towns "in the neighborhood of Chickamauga and the Town of Cologn, situated on the sources of the Mobile" were *not* destroyed, nor visited, and he carefully enumerates all the towns that the troops burned and the regions they went through. They did not go near Chickamauga nor the Coosa. Unless there is some documentary evidence in favor of the assertions of Haywood and Ramsey they cannot for a moment be taken against the explicit declaration of the official report.

Mr. Kirke merely follows Ramsey, and adds a few flourishes of his own, such as that at the Chickamauga towns "the blood of the slaughtered cattle dyed red the Tennessee" for some twenty miles, and that "the homes of over forty thousand people were laid in ashes." This last estimate is just about ten times too strong, for the only country visited was that of the Overhill Cherokees, and the outside limit for the population of the devastated territory would be some four thousand souls, or a third of the Cherokee tribe, which all told numbered perhaps twelve thousand people.

British agents and commanders, showing that almost every chief in the nation had been carrying on a double game; for the letters covered the periods at which they had been treating with the Americans and earnestly professing their friendship for the latter and their determination to be neutral in the contest then waging. As Campbell wrote in his report to the Virginian governor, no people had ever acted with more foolish duplicity.

Before returning, the three commanders, Campbell, Sevier, and Martin, issued an address to the Otari chiefs and warriors, and sent it by one of their captured braves, who was to deliver it to the head-men.[1] The address set forth what the white troops had done, telling the Indians it was a just punishment for their folly and perfidy in consenting to carry out the wishes of the British agents; it warned them shortly to come in and treat for peace, lest their country should again be visited, and not only laid waste, but conquered and held for all time. Some chiefs came in to talk, and were met at Chota[2]; but though they were anxious for peace they could not restrain the vindictive spirit of the young braves, nor prevent them from harassing the settlements. Nor could the white commanders keep the frontiersmen from themselves settling within the acknowledged boundaries of the Indian territory. They were constantly pressing against the lines, and eagerly

[1] Campbell MSS. Issued at Kai-a-tee, Jan. 4, 1781; the copy sent to Governor Jefferson is dated Feb. 28th.

[2] The Tennessee historians all speak of this as a treaty; and probably a meeting did take place as described; but it led to nothing, and no actual treaty was made until some months later.

burst through at every opening. When the army marched back from burning the Overhill towns, they found that adventurous settlers had followed in its wake, and had already made clearings and built cabins near all the best springs down to the French Broad. People of every rank showed keen desire to encroach on the Indian lands.[1]

The success of this expedition gave much relief to the border, and was hailed with pleasure throughout Virginia[2] and North Carolina. Nevertheless the war continued without a break, bands of warriors from the middle towns coming to the help of their disheartened Overhill brethren. Sevier determined to try one of his swift, sudden strokes against these new foes. Early in March he rode off at the head of a hundred and fifty picked horsemen, resolute to penetrate the hitherto untrodden wilds that shielded the far-off fastnesses where dwelt the Erati. Nothing shows his daring, adventurous nature more clearly than his starting on such an expedition ; and only a man of strong will and much power could have carried it to a successful conclusion. For a hundred and fifty miles he led his horsemen through a mountainous wilderness where there was not so much as a hunter's trail. They wound their way through the deep defiles and among the towering peaks of the Great Smoky Mountains, descending by passes so precipitous that it was with difficulty the men led down them even such sure-footed beasts as their hardy hill-horses. At last they

---

[1] Calendar of Va. State Papers, II., letter of Col. Wm. Christian to Governor of Virginia, April 10, 1781.

[2] State Department MSS., No. 15, Feb. 25, 1781.

burst out of the woods and fell like a thunderbolt on the towns of the Erati, nestling in their high gorges. The Indians were completely taken by surprise; they had never dreamed that they could be attacked in their innermost strongholds, cut off, as they were, from the nearest settlements by vast trackless wastes of woodland and lofty, bald-topped mountain chains. They had warriors enough to overwhelm Sevier's band by sheer force of numbers, but he gave them no time to gather. Falling on their main town, he took it by surprise and stormed it, killing thirty warriors and capturing a large number of women and children. Of these, however, he was able to bring in but twenty, who were especially valuable because they could be exchanged for white captives. He burnt two other towns and three small villages, destroying much provision and capturing two hundred horses. He himself had but one man killed and one wounded. Before the startled warriors could gather to attack him he plunged once more into the wilderness, carrying his prisoners and plunder, and driving the captured horses before him; and so swift were his motions that he got back in safety to the settlements.[1] The length of the journey, the absolutely untravelled nature of the country, which no white man, save perhaps an occasional wandering hunter, had ever

[1] *Do.* Letters of Col. Wm. Christian, April 10, 1781; of Joseph Martin, March 1st; and of Arthur Campbell, March 28th. The accounts vary slightly; for instance, Christian gives him one hundred and eighty, Campbell only one hundred and fifty men. One account says he killed thirty, another twenty Indians. Martin, by the way, speaks bitterly of the militia as men "who do duty at times as their inclination leads them." The incident, brilliant enough anyhow, of course grows a little under Ramsey and Haywood; and Mr. Kirke fairly surpasses himself when he comes to it.

before traversed, the extreme difficulty of the route over the wooded, cliff-scarred mountains, and the strength of the Cherokee towns that were to be attacked, all combined to render the feat most difficult. For its successful performance there was need of courage, hardihood, woodcraft, good judgment, stealth, and great rapidity of motion. It was one of the most brilliant exploits of the border war.

Even after his return Sevier was kept busy pursuing and defeating small bands of plundering savages. In the early summer he made a quick inroad south of the French Broad. At the head of over a hundred hard riders he fell suddenly on the camp of a war party, took a dozen scalps, and scattered the rest of the Indians in every direction. A succession of these blows completely humbled the Cherokees, and they sued for peace; thanks to Sevier's tactics, they had suffered more loss than they had inflicted, an almost unknown thing in these wars with the forest Indians. In midsummer peace was made by a treaty at the Great Island of the Holston.

During the latter half of the year, when danger from the Indians had temporarily ceased, Sevier and Shelby led down bands of mounted riflemen to assist the American forces in the Carolinas and Georgia. They took an honorable share under Marion in some skirmishes against the British and Hessians[1]; but they did not render any special service, and Greene found

End of the War with the British and Tories.

---

[1] Shelby MSS. Of course Shelby paints these skirmishes in very strong colors. Haywood and Ramsey base their accounts purely on his papers.

he could place no reliance on them for the actual stubborn campaigns that broke the strength of the king's armies. They enlisted for very short periods, and when their time was up promptly returned to their mountains, for they were sure to get home-sick and uneasy about their families; and neither the officers nor the soldiers had any proper idea of the value of obedience. Among their own hills and forests and for their own work, they were literally unequalled; and they were ready enough to swoop down from their strongholds, strike some definite blow, or do some single piece of valiant fighting in the low country, and then fall back as quickly as they had come. But they were not particularly suited for a pitched battle in the open, and were quite unfitted to carry on a long campaign.

In one respect the mountain men deserve great credit for their conduct in the Carolinas. As a general thing they held aloof from the plundering. The frightful character of the civil war between the whigs and tories, and the excesses of the British armies, had utterly demoralized the southern States; they were cast into a condition of anarchic disorder,

Ramsey and his followers endeavor to prove that the mountain men did excellently in these 1781 campaigns; but the endeavor is futile. They were good for some one definite stroke, but their shortcomings were manifest the instant a long campaign was attempted; and the comments of the South Carolina historians upon their willingness to leave at unfortunate moments are on the whole just. They behaved somewhat as Stark and the victors at Bennington did when they left the American army before Saratoga; although their conduct was on the whole better than that of Stark's men. They were a brave, hardy, warlike band of irregulars, probably better fighters than any similar force on this continent or elsewhere; but occasional brilliant exceptions must not blind us to the general inefficiency of the Revolutionary militia, and their great inferiority to the Continentals of Washington, Greene, and Wayne. See Appendix.

and the conflicts between the patriots and loyalists degenerated into a bloody scramble for murder and plunder wherein the whigs behaved as badly as ever the tories had done.[1]   Men were shot, houses burned,

[1] In the Clay MSS. there is a letter from Jesse Benton (the father of the great Missouri Senator) to Col. Thos. Hart, of March 23d, 1783, which gives a glimpse of the way in which the tories were treated even after the British had been driven out ; it also shows how soon maltreatment of royalists was turned into general misrule and rioting.   The letter runs, in part, as follows :

"I cannot help mentioning to You an Evil which seems intaild upon the upper part of this State, to wit, Mobbs and commotions amongst the People. I shall give you the particulars of the last Work of this kind which lately happend, & which is not yet settled ; Plunder being the first cause.   The Scoundrels, under the cloak of great Whigs cannot bear the thought of paying the unfortunate Wretches whom Fame and ill will call Tories (though many of them perhaps honest, industrious and useful men) for plunderd property ; but on the other Hand think they together with their Wives and Children (who are now beging for Mercy) ought to be punished to the utmost extremity.   I am sorry that Col. O Neal and his Brother Peter, who have been useful men and whom I am in hopes are pretty clear of plundering, should have a hand in Arbitrary measures at this Day when the Civil Laws might take place.

"One Jacob Graves son of old John of Stinking Quarter, went off & was taken with the British Army, escaped from the Guards, came & surrendered himself to Gen'l Butler, about the middle of Last month & went to his Family upon Parole.   Col. O Neal being informed of this, armed himself with Gun and sword, went to Graves's in a passion, Graves shut the Door, O Neal broke it down, Graves I believe thinking his own Life at stake, took his Brothers Gun which happened to be in the house & shot O Neal through the Breast.

"O Neal has suffered much but is now recovering.   This accident has inflamed and set to work those who were afraid of suffering for their unjust and unwarrantable Deeds, the Ignorant honest men are also willing to take part against their Rulers & I don't know when nor where it is to end, but I wish it was over.   At the Guilford Feb'y Court Peter O Neal & others armed with clubs in the Face of the Court then sitting and in the Court house too, beat some men called Tories so much that their Lives were despaired of, broke up the Court and finally have stopd the civil Laws in that County. Your old Friend Col. Dunn got out at Window, fled in a Fright, took cold and died immediately.   Rowan County Court I am told was also broke up.

"If O Neal should die I fear that a number of the unhappy wretches called Tories will be Murdered, and that a man disposed to do justice dare not interfere, indeed the times seem to imitate the commencement of the Regulators."

horses stolen, and negroes kidnapped; even the unfortunate freedmen of color were hurried off and
sold into slavery.   It was with the utmost difficulty
that a few wise and good commanders, earnest lovers
of their country, like the gallant General Pickens,
were able to put a partial stop to these outrages, and
gather a few brave men to help in overcoming the
foreign foe.   To the honor of the troops under
Sevier and Shelby be it said that they took little
part in these misdeeds.   There were doubtless some
men among them who shared in all the evil of that
turbulent time; but most of these frontier riflemen,
though poor and ignorant, were sincerely patriotic;
they marched to fight the oppressor, to drive out
the stranger, not to ill-treat their own friends and
countrymen.

Towards the end of these campaigns, which marked
the close of the Revolutionary struggle, Shelby was
sent to the North Carolina Legislature, where he
served for a couple of terms.   Then, when peace
was formally declared, he removed to Kentucky,
where he lived ever afterwards.   Sevier stayed in
his home on the Nolichucky, to be thenceforth, while
his life lasted, the leader in peace and war of his
beloved mountaineers.

Early in 1782 fresh difficulties arose with the Indians.   In the war just ended the Cherokees them-
Quarrels   selves had been chiefly to blame.   The
over the   whites were now in their turn the aggres-
Land.   sors, the trouble being, as usual, that they
encroached on lands secured to the red men by
solemn treaty.   The Watauga settlements had been

kept compact by the presence of the neighboring Indians. They had grown steadily but slowly. They extended their domain slightly after every treaty, such treaty being usually though not always the sequel to a successful war; but they never gained any large stretch of territory at once. Had it not been for the presence of the hostile tribes they would have scattered far and wide over the country, and could not have formed any government.

The preceding spring (1781) the land office had been closed, not to be opened until after peace with Great Britain was definitely declared, the utter demoralization of the government bringing the work to a standstill. The rage for land speculation, however, which had continued, even in the stormiest days of the Revolution, grew tenfold in strength after Yorktown, when peace at no distant day was assured. The wealthy land speculators of the seaboard counties made agreements of various sorts with the more prominent frontier leaders in the effort to secure large tracts of good country. The system of surveying was much better than in Kentucky, but it was still by no means perfect, as each man placed his plot wherever he chose, first describing the boundary marks rather vaguely, and leaving an illiterate old hunter to run the lines. Moreover, the intending settler frequently absented himself for several months, or was temporarily chased away by the Indians, while the official record books were most imperfect. In consequence, many conflicts ensued. The frontiersmen settled on any spot of good land they saw fit, and clung to it with defiant tenacity, whether or not it afterwards proved to be on a tract previously granted to some land company or rich private individual who had never been a hundred miles from the sea-coast. Public officials went into these speculations. Thus Major Joseph Martin, while an Indian agent, tried to speculate in Chero- kee lands.[1] Of course the officer's public influence was speedily destroyed when he once undertook such operations ; he could no longer do justice to outsiders. Occasionally the falseness of his position made him unjust to the Indians ; more often it forced him into league with the latter, and made him hostile to the borderers.[2]

Before the end of the Revolution the trouble be- tween the actual settlers and the land speculators became so great that a small subsidiary civil war was threatened. The rough riflemen resolutely declined to leave their clearings, while the titular owners appealed to the authority of the loose land laws, and wished them to be backed up by the armed force of the State.[3]

The government of North Carolina was far too weak to turn out the frontiersmen in favor of the speculators to whom the land had been granted,— often by fraudulent means, or at least for a ridicu- lously small sum of money. Still less could it pre- vent its unruly subjects from trespassing on the In- dian country, or protect them if they were themselves

[1] See Va. State Papers, III., 560.

[2] This is a chief reason why the reports of the Indian agents are so often bitterly hostile towards those of their own color.

[3] See in Durrett MSS. papers relating to Isaac Shelby ; letter of John Tay- lor to Isaac Shelby, June 8, 1782.

threatened by the savages. It could not do justice
as between its own citizens, and it was quite incom-
petent to preserve the peace between them and outsiders.[1]   The borderers were left to work out their
own salvation.

By the beginning of 1782 settlements were being
made south of the French Broad. This alarmed
and irritated the Indians, and they sent   Further
repeated remonstrances to Major Martin,   Indian
who was Indian agent, and also to the   Troubles.
governor of North Carolina.   The latter wrote
Sevier, directing him to drive off the intruding
settlers, and pull down their cabins. Sevier did not
obey.   He took purely the frontier view of the
question, and he had no intention of harassing his
own staunch adherents for the sake of the savages
whom he had so often fought. Nevertheless, the
Cherokees always liked him personally, for he was as
open-handed and free-hearted to them as to every
one else, and treated them to the best he had whenever they came to his house.   He had much justification for his refusal, too, in the fact that the Indians
themselves were always committing outrages. When
the Americans reconquered the southern States many
tories fled to the Cherokee towns, and incited the
savages to hostility ; and the outlying settlements of
the borderers were being burned and plundered by
members of the very tribes whose chiefs were at the
same time writing to the governor to complain of
the white encroachments.[2]

When in April the Cherokees held a friendly talk

[1] Calendar of Va. State Papers, III., p. 213.   [2] *Do.*, p. 4.

with Evan Shelby they admitted that the tories among them and their own evil-disposed young men committed ravages on the whites, but asserted that most of them greatly desired peace, for they were weak and distressed, and had shrunk much in numbers.[1] The trouble was that when they were so absolutely unable to control their own bad characters, it was inevitable that they should become embroiled with the whites.

The worst members of each race committed crimes against the other, and not only did the retaliation often fall on the innocent, but, unfortunately, even the good men were apt to make common cause with the criminals of their own color.   Thus in July the Chickamaugas sent in a talk for peace; but at that very time a band of their young braves made a foray into Powell's valley, killing two settlers and driving off some stock.   They were pursued, one of their number killed, and most of the stock retaken.   In the same month, on the other hand, two friendly Indians, who had a canoe laden with peltry, were murdered on the Holston by a couple of white ruffians, who then attempted to sell the furs.   They were discovered, and the furs taken from them; but to their disgrace be it said, the people round about would not suffer the criminals to be brought to justice.[2]

The mutual outrages continued throughout the summer, and in September they came to a head. The great majority of the Otari of the Overhill towns were still desirous of peace, and after a council of their head-men the chief Old Tassel, of the town of

---

[1] *Do.*, p. 171, April 29, 1782.   [2] *Do.*, pp. 213, 248.

Chota, sent on their behalf a strong appeal to the governors of both Virginia and North Carolina. The document is written with such dignity, and yet in a tone of such curious pathos, that it is worth giving in full, as putting in strongest possible form the Indian side of the case, and as a sample of the best of these Indian " talks."

" A Talk to Colonel Joseph Martin, by the Old Tassell, in Chota, the 25th of September, 1782, in favour of the whole nation. For His Excellency, the Governor of North Carolina. Present, all the chiefs of the friendly towns and a number of young men.

" Brother : I am now going to speak to you. I hope you will listen to me. A string. I intended to come this fall and see you, but there was such confusion in our country, I thought it best for me to stay at home and send my Talks by our friend Colonel Martin, who promised to deliver them safe to you. We are a poor distressed people, that is in great trouble, and we hope our elder brother will take pity on us and do us justice. Your people from Nolichucky are daily pushing us out of our lands. We have no place to hunt on. Your people have built houses within one day's walk of our towns. We don't want to quarrel with our elder brother ; we, therefore, hope our elder brother will not take our lands from us, that the Great Man above gave us. He made you and he made us ; we are all his children, and we hope our elder brother will take pity on us, and not take our lands from us that our father gave us, because he is stronger than we are. We are the first people that ever lived on this land ; it is ours, and why will our elder brother take it from us? It is true, some time past, the people over the great water persuaded some of our young men to do some mischief to our elder brother, which our principal men were sorry for. But you our elder brothers come to our towns and took satisfaction, and then sent for us to come and treat with you, which we did. Then our elder brother promised to have the line run between us agreeable to the first treaty, and all that should be found over the line should be moved off. But it is not done yet. We have done nothing to offend our elder brother since the last treaty, and why should our elder brother want to quarrel with us? We have sent to the Governor of Virginia on the same subject. We hope that between you both, you will take pity on your younger brother, and send Col. Sevier, who is a good man, to have all your people moved off our land. I should say a great deal more, but our friend, Colonel Martin, knows all our grievances, and he can inform you. A string." [1]

The speech is interesting because it shows that the Indians both liked and respected Sevier, their most redoubtable foe; and because it acknowledges that in the previous war the Cherokees themselves had been the wrongdoers. Even Old Tassel had been implicated in the treacherous conduct of the chiefs at that period; but he generally acted very well, and belonged with the large number of his tribesmen who, for no fault of their own, were shamefully misused by the whites.

The white intruders were not removed. No immediate collision followed on this account; but when Old Tassel's talk was forwarded to the governor, small parties of Chickamaugas, assisted by young braves from among the Creeks and Erati, had already begun to commit ravages on the outlying settlements. Two weeks before Old Tassel spoke, on the 11th of

[1] Ramsey, 271. The "strings" of wampum were used to mark periods and to indicate, and act as reminders of, special points in the speech.

September, a family of whites was butchered on Moccasin Creek. The neighbors gathered, pursued the Indians, and recaptured the survivors.[1] Other outrages followed, throughout the month. Sevier as usual came to the rescue of the angered settlers. He gathered a couple of hundred mounted riflemen, and made one of his swift retaliatory inroads. His men were simply volunteers, for there was no money in the country treasury with which to pay them or provide them with food and provisions ; it was their own quarrel, and they furnished their own services free, each bringing his horse, rifle, ammunition, blanket, and wallet of parched corn. Naturally such troops made war purely according to their own ideas, and cared nothing whatever for the commands of those governmental bodies who were theoretically their superiors. They were poor men, staunch patriots, who had suffered much and done all they could during the Revolution[2] ; now, when threatened by the savages they were left to protect themselves, and they did it in their own way. Sevier led his force down through the Overhill towns, doing their people no injury and holding a peace talk with them. They gave him a half breed, John Watts, afterwards one of their chiefs, as guide ; and he marched quickly against some of the Chickamauga towns, where he destroyed the cabins and provision hoards. Afterwards he penetrated to the Coosa, where he burned one or two Creek villages. The inhabitants fled from the towns before he could reach them ; and his own motions

---

[1] Calendar of Va. State Papers, III., p. 317. [2] *Do.*

were so rapid that they could never gather in force strong enough to assail him.[1] Very few Indians were killed, and apparently none of Sevier's people ; a tory, an ex-British sergeant, then living with an Indian squaw, was among the slain.

This foray brought but a short relief to the settlements. On Christmas day three men were killed on the Clinch ; and it was so unusual a season for the war parties to be abroad that the attack caused widespread alarm.[2] Early in the spring of 1783 the ravages began again.[3] Some time before General Wayne had addressed the Creeks and Choctaws, reproaching them with the aid they had given the

[1] The authority for this expedition is Haywood (p. 106) ; Ramsey simply alters one or two unimportant details. Haywood commits so many blunders concerning the early Indian wars that it is only safe to regard his accounts as true in outline ; and even for this outline it is to be wished we had additional authority. Mr. Kirke, in the " Rear-guard," p. 313, puts in an account of a battle on Lookout Mountain, wherein Sevier and his two hundred men defeat " five hundred tories and savages." He does not even hint at his authority for this, unless in a sentence of the preface where he says, " a large part of my material I have derived from what may be termed ' original sources '—old settlers." Of course the statement of an old settler is worthless when it relates to an alleged important event which took place a hundred and five years before, and yet escaped the notice of all contemporary and subsequent historians. In plain truth unless Mr. Kirke can produce something like contemporary—or approximately contemporary—documentary evidence for this mythical battle, it must be set down as pure invention. It is with real reluctance that I speak thus of Mr. Kirke's books. He has done good service in popularizing the study of early western history, and especially in calling attention to the wonderful careers of Sevier and Robertson. Had he laid no claim to historic accuracy I should have been tempted to let his books pass unnoticed ; but in the preface to his " John Sevier " he especially asserts that his writings " may be safely accepted as authentic history." On first reading his book I was surprised and pleased at the information it contained ; when I came to study the subject I was still more surprised and much less pleased at discovering such wholesale inaccuracy—to be perfectly just I should be obliged to use a stronger term. Even a popular history ought to pay at least some little regard to truth.

[2] Calendar of Va. State Papers, III., p. 424.   [3] *Do.*, p. 479.

British, and threatening them with a bloody chastisement if they would not keep the peace.[1]   A threat from Mad Anthony meant something, and the Indians paid at least momentary heed.   Georgia enjoyed a short respite, which, as usual, the more reckless borderers strove to bring to an end by encroaching on the Indian lands, while the State authorities, on the other hand, did their best to stop not only such encroachments, but also all travelling and hunting in the Indian country, and especially the marking of trees. This last operation, as Governor Lyman Hall remarked in his proclamation, gave " Great Offence to the Indians,"[2] who thoroughly understood that the surveys indicated the approaching confiscation of their territory.

Towards the end of 1783 a definite peace was concluded with the Chickasaws, who ever afterwards remained friendly[3]; but the Creeks, while amusing the Georgians by pretending to treat, let their parties of young braves find an outlet for their energies by assailing the Holston and Cumberland settlements.[4] The North Carolina Legislature, becoming impatient, passed a law summarily appropriating certain lands that were claimed by the unfortunate Cherokees. The troubled peace was continually threatened by the actions either of ungovernable frontiersmen or of bloodthirsty and vindictive Indians.[5]   Small parties of scouts were incessantly employed in patrolling the southern border.

Nevertheless, all pressing danger from the Indians

---

[1] State Department MSS. Letters of Washington, No. 152, Vol. XI., Feb. 1, 1782.   [2] Gazette of the State of Georgia, July 10, 1783.
[3] Va. State Papers, III., p. 548.   [4] *Do.*, p. 532.   [5] *Do.*, p. 560.

was over. The Holston settlements throve lustily.
Wagon roads were made, leading into both Virginia

Growth of and North Carolina.   Settlers thronged
the Set- into the country, the roads were well trav-
tlements. elled, and the clearings became very numerous. The villages began to feel safe without stockades, save those on the extreme border, which were
still built in the usual frontier style. The scattering log school-houses and meeting-houses increased
steadily in numbers, and in 1783, Methodism, destined to become the leading and typical creed of the
west, first gained a foothold along the Holston, with
a congregation of seventy-six members.[1]

These people of the upper Tennessee valleys long
continued one in interest as in blood. Whether they
lived north or south of the Virginia or North Carolina boundary, they were more closely united to one
another than they were to the seaboard governments
of which they formed part. Their history is not generally studied as a whole, because one portion of their
territory continued part of Virginia, while the remainder was cut off from North Carolina as the
nucleus of a separate State. But in the time of
their importance, in the first formative period of the
young west, all these Holston settlements must be
treated together, or else their real place in our
history will be totally misunderstood.[2]

[1] "History of Methodism in Tennessee," John B. M'Ferrin (Nashville,
1873), I., 26.

[2] Nothing gives a more fragmentary and twisted view of our history than
to treat it purely by States ; this is the reason that a State history is generally
of so little importance when taken by itself. On the other hand it is of
course true that the fundamental features in our history can only be shown
by giving proper prominence to the individual state life.

The two towns of Abingdon and Jonesboro, respectively north and south of the line, were the centres of activity. In Jonesboro the log **Frontier** court-house, with its clapboard roof, was **Towns.** abandoned, and in its place a twenty-four-foot-square building of hewn logs was put up; it had a shingled roof and plank floors, and contained a justice's bench, a lawyers' and clerk's bar, and a sheriff's box to sit in. The county of Washington was now further subdivided, its southwest portion being erected into the county of Greene, so that there were three counties of North Carolina west of the mountains. The court of the new county consisted of several justices, who appointed their own clerk, sheriff, attorney for the State, entry-taker, surveyer, and registrar. They appropriated money to pay for the use of the log-house where they held sessions, laid a tax of a shilling specie on every hundred pounds for the purpose of erecting public buildings, laid out roads, issued licenses to build mills, and bench warrants to take suspected persons.[1]

Abingdon was a typical little frontier town of the class that immediately succeeded the stockaded hamlets. A public square had been laid out, round which, and down the straggling main street, the few buildings were scattered; all were of logs, from the court house and small jail down. There were three or four taverns. The two best were respectively houses of entertainment for those who were fond of

---

[1] Ramsey, 277. The North Carolina Legislature, in 1783, passed an act giving Henderson two hundred thousand acres, and appointed Joseph Martin Indian agent, arranged for a treaty with the Cherokees, and provided that any good men should be allowed to trade with the Indians.

their brandy, and for the temperate. There were a blacksmith shop and a couple of stores.[1] The traders brought their goods from Alexandria, Baltimore, or even Philadelphia, and made a handsome profit. The lower taverns were scenes of drunken frolic, often ending in free fights. There was no constable, and the sheriff, when called to quell a disturbance, summoned as a posse those of the bystanders whom he deemed friendly to the cause of law and order. There were many strangers passing through; and the better class of these were welcome at the rambling log-houses of the neighboring backwoods gentry, who often themselves rode into the taverns to learn from the travellers what was happening in the great world beyond the mountains. Court-day was a great occasion; all the neighborhood flocked in to gossip, lounge, race horses, and fight. Of course in such gatherings there were always certain privileged characters. At Abingdon these were to be found in the persons of a hunter named Edward Callahan, and his wife Sukey. As regularly as court-day came round they appeared, Sukey driving a cart laden with pies, cakes, and drinkables, while Edward, whose rolls of furs and deer hides were also in the cart, stalked at its tail on foot, in full hunter's dress, with rifle, powder-horn, and bullet-bag, while his fine, well-taught hunting-dog followed at his heels. Sukey would halt in the middle of the street, make an awning for herself and begin business, while Edward strolled off to see about selling his

---

[1] One was "kept by two Irishmen named Daniel and Manasses Freil" (*sic ;* the names look very much more German than Irish).

peltries.   Sukey never would take out a license, and so was often in trouble for selling liquor.   The judges were strict in proceeding against offenders—and even stricter against the unfortunate tories—but they had a humorous liking for Sukey, which was shared by the various grand juries.   By means of some excuse or other she was always let off, and in return showed great gratitude to such of her benefactors as came near her mountain cabin.[1]

Court-day was apt to close with much hard drinking; for the backwoodsmen of every degree dearly loved whiskey.

[1] Campbell MSS. ; an account of the " Town of Abingdon," by David Campbell, who " first saw it in 1782."

CHAPTER XI.

ROBERTSON had no share in the glory of King's Mountain, and no part in the subsequent career of James Robertson. the men who won it; for, at the time, he was doing his allotted work, a work of at least equal importance, in a different field. The year before the mountaineers faced Ferguson, the man who had done more than any one in founding the settlements from which the victors came, had once more gone into the wilderness to build a new and even more typical frontier commonwealth, the westernmost of any yet founded by the backwoodsmen.

Robertson had been for ten years a leader among the Holston and Watauga people. He had at different times played the foremost part in organizing the civil government and in repelling outside attack. He had been particularly successful in his dealings with the Indians, and by his missions to them had managed to keep the peace unbroken on more than one occasion when a war would have been disastrous to the whites. He was prosperous and successful in his private affairs; nevertheless, in 1779, the restless craving for change and adventure surged so strongly in his breast that it once more drove him forth to wander in the forest. In the true border temper he determined to abandon the home he had made, and to seek out a new one hundreds of miles farther in the heart of the hunting-grounds of the red warriors.

The point pitched upon was the beautiful country lying along the great bend of the Cumberland. Many adventurous settlers were anxious to accompany Robertson, and, like him, to take their wives and children with them into the new land. It was agreed that a small party of explorers should go first in the early spring, to plant corn, that the families might have it to eat when they followed in the fall.

The spot was already well known to hunters. Who had first visited it cannot be said; though tradition has kept the names of several among the many who at times halted there while on their wanderings.[1] Old Kasper Mans- **The Cumberland Country.** ker and others had made hunting trips thither for ten years past; and they had sometimes met the creole trappers from the Illinois. When Mansker first went to the Bluffs,[2] in 1769, the buffaloes were more numerous than he had ever seen them before; the ground literally shook under the gallop of the mighty herds, they crowded in dense throngs round

---

[1] One Stone or Stoner, perhaps Boon's old associate, is the first whose name is given in the books. But in both Kentucky and Tennessee it is idle to try to find out exactly who the first explorers were. They were unlettered woodsmen; it is only by chance that some of their names have been kept and others lost; the point to be remembered is that many hunters were wandering over the land at the same time, that they drifted to many different places, and that now and then an accident preserved the name of some hunter and of some place he visited.

[2] The locality where Nashborough was built, was sometimes spoken of as the Bluffs, and sometimes as the French Lick.

the licks, and the forest resounded with their grunting bellows. He and other woodsmen came back there off and on, hunting and trapping, and living in huts made of buffalo hides; just such huts as the hunters dwelt in on the Little Missouri and Powder rivers as late as 1883, except that the plainsmen generally made dug-outs in the sides of the buttes and used the hides only for the roofs and fronts. So the place was well known, and the reports of the hunters had made many settlers eager to visit it, though as yet no regular path led thither. In 1778 the first permanent settler arrived in the person of a hunter named Spencer, who spent the following winter entirely alone in this remote wilderness, living in a hollow sycamore-tree. Spencer was a giant in his day, a man huge in body and limb, all whose life had been spent in the wilderness. He came to the bend of the Cumberland from Kentucky in the early spring, being in search of good land on which to settle. Other hunters were with him, and they stayed some time. A creole trapper from the Wabash was then living in a cabin on the south side of the river. He did not meet the new-comers; but one day he saw the huge moccasin tracks of Spencer, and on the following morning the party passed close by his cabin in chase of a wounded buffalo, halloing and shouting as they dashed through the underwood. Whether he thought them Indians, or whether, as is more likely, he shared the fear and dislike felt by most of the creoles for the American backwoodsmen, cannot be said; but certainly he left his cabin, swam the river, and plunging into the forest, straightway fled to his kinsfolk on

the banks of the Wabash. Spencer was soon left by
his companions; though one of them stayed with
him a short time, helping him to plant a field of
corn. Then this man, too, wished to return. He
had lost his hunting-knife; so Spencer went with
him to the barrens of Kentucky, put him on the
right path, and breaking his own knife, gave his
departing friend a piece of the metal. The undaunted old hunter himself returned to the banks of the
Cumberland, and sojourned throughout the fall and
winter in the neighborhood of the little clearing on
which he had raised the corn crop; a strange, huge,
solitary man, self-reliant, unflinching, cut off from
all his fellows by endless leagues of shadowy forest.
Thus he dwelt alone in the vast dim wastes, wandering whithersoever he listed through the depths of the
melancholy and wintry woods, sleeping by his camp-
fire or in the hollow tree-trunk, ever ready to do
battle against brute or human foe—a stark and
sombre harbinger of the oncoming civilization.

Spencer's figure, seen through the mist that
shrouds early western history, is striking and pictu-
resque in itself; yet its chief interest lies in the fact
that he was but a type of many other men whose
lives were no less lonely and dangerous. He had no
qualities to make him a leader when settlements
sprang up around him. To the end of his days he
remained a solitary hunter and Indian fighter, spurn-
ing restraint and comfort, and seeking the strong excitement of danger to give zest to his life. Even in
the time of the greatest peril from the savages he
would not stay shut up in the forts, but continued

his roving, wandering life, trusting to his own quick
senses, wonderful strength, and iron nerves. He
even continued to lie out at night, kindling a fire,
and then lying down to sleep far from it.[1]

Early in the year 1779 a leader of men came to
the place where the old hunter had roamed and
Robertson killed game; and with the new-comer came
Travels those who were to possess the land. Rob-
Thither. ertson left the Watauga settlements soon
after the spring opened,[2] with eight companions, one
of them a negro. He followed Boon's trace,—the Wilderness Road,—through Cumberland Gap, and across
the Cumberland River. Then he struck off southwest through the wilderness, lightening his labor by
taking the broad, well-beaten buffalo trails whenever
they led in his direction; they were very distinct
near the pools and springs, and especially going to
and from the licks. The adventurers reached the
bend of the Cumberland without mishap, and fixed
on the neighborhood of the Bluff, the ground near
the French Lick, as that best suited for their purpose; and they planted a field of corn on the site of
the future forted village of Nashborough. A few
days after their arrival they were joined by another

[1] *Southwestern Monthly*, Nashville, 1852, vol. II. General Hall's narrative.
[2] It is very difficult to reconcile the dates of these early movements; even
the contemporary documents are often a little vague, while Haywood, Ramsey, and Putnam are frequently months out of the way. Apparently Robertson stayed as commissioner in Chota until February or March, 1779, when
he gave warning of the intended raid of the Chickamaugas, and immediately afterwards came back to the settlements and started out for the
Cumberland, before Shelby left on his Chickamauga expedition. But it is
possible that he had left Chota before, and that another man was there as
commissioner at the time of the Chickamauga raid which was followed by
Shelby's counter-stroke.

batch of hunter-settlers, who had come out under the leadership of Kasper Mansker.

As soon as the corn was planted and cabins put up, most of the intending settlers returned to their old homes to bring out their families, leaving three of their number " to keep the buffaloes out of the corn." [1] Robertson himself first went north through the wilderness to see George Rogers Clark in Illinois, to purchase cabin-rights from him. This act gives an insight into at least some of the motives that influenced the adventurers. Doubtless they were impelled largely by sheer restlessness and love of change and excitement [2]; and these motives would probably have induced them to act as they did, even had there been no others. But another and most powerful spring of action was the desire to gain land —not merely land for settlement, but land for speculative purposes. Wild land was then so abundant that the quantity literally seemed inexhaustible ; and it was absolutely valueless until settled. Our forefathers may well be pardoned for failing to see that it was of more importance to have it owned in small lots by actual settlers than to have it filled up quickly under a system of huge grants to individuals or corporations. Many wise and good men honestly believed that they would benefit the country at the same time that they enriched themselves by acquiring vast tracts of virgin wilderness, and then proceeding to people them. There was a rage for land speculation and land companies of every kind.

[1] Haywood, 83.

[2] Phelan, p. 111, fails to do justice to these motives, while very properly insisting on what earlier historians ignored, the intense desire for land speculation.

The private correspondence of almost all the public men of the period, from Washington, Madison, and Gouverneur Morris down, is full of the subject. Innumerable people of position and influence dreamed of acquiring untold wealth in this manner. Almost every man of note was actually or potentially a land speculator; and in turn almost every prominent pioneer from Clark and Boon to Shelby and Robertson was either himself one of the speculators or an agent for those who were. Many people did not understand the laws on the subject, or hoped to evade them; and the hope was as strong in the breast of the hunter, who made a "tomahawk claim" by blazing a few trees, and sold it for a small sum to a newcomer, as in that of the well-to-do schemer, who bought an Indian title for a song, and then got what he could from all outsiders who came in to dwell on the land.

This speculative spirit was a powerful stimulus to the settlement not only of Kentucky, but of middle Tennessee. Henderson's claim included the Cumberland country, and when North Carolina annulled his rights, she promised him a large but indefinitely located piece of land in their place. He tried to undersell the state in the land market, and undoubtedly his offers had been among the main causes that induced Robertson and his associates to go to the Cumberland when they did. But at the time it was uncertain whether Cumberland lay in Virginia or North Carolina, as the line was not run by the surveyors until the following spring; and Robertson went up to see Clark, because it was rumored that the latter had the disposal of Virginia "cabin-rights"; under which each man could, for a small sum, purchase a thousand acres, on condition of building a cabin and raising a crop. However, as it turned out, he might have spared himself the journey, for the settlement proved to be well within the Carolina boundary.

In the fall very many men came out to the new settlement, guided thither by Robertson and Mansker; the former persuading a number who were bound to Kentucky to come to the Cumberland instead. Among them were **Many Settlers Join Him.** two or three of the Long Hunters, whose wanderings had done so much to make the country known. Robertson's especial partner was a man named John Donelson. The latter went by water and took a large party of immigrants, including all the women and children, down the Tennessee, and thence up the Ohio and Cumberland to the Bluff or French Lick.[1] Among them were Robertson's entire family, and Donelson's daughter Rachel, the future wife of Andrew Jackson, who missed by so narrow a margin being mistress of the White House. Robertson, meanwhile, was to lead the rest of the men by land, so that they should get there first and make ready for the coming of their families.

Robertson's party started in the fall, being both preceded and followed by other companies of settlers, some of whom were accompanied by their wives

[1] The plan was that Robertson should meet this party at the Muscle Shoals, and that they should go from thence overland; but owing to the severity of the winter, Robertson could not get to the shoals.

and children. Cold weather of extraordinary severity set in during November; for this was the famous "hard winter" of '79–80, during which the Kentucky settlers suffered so much. They were not molested by Indians, and reached the Bluff about Christmas. The river was frozen solid, and they all crossed the ice in a body; when in mid-stream the ice jarred, and—judging from the report—the jar or crack must have gone miles up and down the stream; but the ice only settled a little and did not break. By January first there were over two hundred people scattered on both sides of the river. In Robertson's company was a man named John Rains, who brought with him twenty-one horned cattle and seventeen horses; the only cattle and horses which any of the immigrants succeeded in bringing to the Cumberland. But he was not the only man who had made the attempt. One of the immigrants who went in Donelson's flotilla, Daniel Dunham by name, offered his brother John, who went by land, £100 to drive along his horses and cattle. John accepted, and tried his best to fulfil his share of the bargain; but he was seemingly neither a very expert woodsman nor yet a good stock hand. There is no form of labor more arduous and dispiriting than driving unruly and unbroken stock along a faint forest or mountain trail, especially in bad weather; and this the would-be drover speedily found out. The animals would not follow the trail; they incessantly broke away from it, got lost, scattered in the brush, and stampeded at night. Finally the unfortunate John, being, as he expressed it, nearly "driven mad by the drove," abandoned them all in the wilderness.[1]

The settlers who came by water passed through much greater peril and hardship. By a stroke of good fortune the journal kept by Donel- son, the leader of the expedition, has been preserved.[2] As with all the other recorded wanderings and explorations of these backwoods adventurers, it must be remembered that while this trip was remarkable in itself, it is especially noteworthy because, out of many such, it is the only one of which we have a full account. The adventures that befell Donelson's company differed in degree, but not in kind, from those that befell the many similar flotillas that followed or preceded him. From the time that settlers first came to the upper Tennessee valley occasional hardy hunters had floated down the stream in pirogues, or hollowed out tree-trunks. Before the Revolution a few restless emigrants had adopted this method of reaching Natchez; some of them made the long and perilous trip in safety, others were killed by the Chickamaugas or else foundered in the whirlpools, or on the shoals. The spring before Donelson started, a party of men,

Voyage of the "Adventure."

[1] MSS. on "Dunham Pioneers," in Nashville Hist. Society. Daniel, a veteran stockman, was very angry when he heard what had happened.

[2] Original MS. "Journal of Voyage intended by God's permission in the good boat *Adventure* from Fort Patrick Henry of Holston River to the French Salt Springs on Cumberland River, kept by John Donelson." An abstract, with some traditional statements interwoven, is given by Haywood; the journal itself, with some inaccuracies, and the name of the writer misspelt by Ramsey; and in much better and fuller shape by A. N. Putnam in his "History of Middle Tennessee." I follow the original, in the Nashville Historical Society.

women, and children, in forty canoes or pirogues, went down the Tennessee to settle in the newly conquered Illinois country, and skirmished with the Cherokees or their way.[1]

Donelson's flotilla, after being joined by a number of other boats, especially at the mouth of the Clinch, consisted of some thirty craft, all told—flat-boats, dug-outs, and canoes. There were probably two or three hundred people, perhaps many more, in the company; among them, as the journal records, "James Robertson's lady and children," the latter to the number of five. The chief boat, the flag-ship of the flotilla, was the *Adventure*, a great scow, in which there were over thirty men, besides the families of some of them.

They embarked at Holston, Long Island, on De-

---

[1] State Department MSS., No. 51, Vol. II., p. 45 :

" JAMES COLBERT TO CHAS. STUART.

" CHICKASAW NATION, May 25, 1779.

" SIR,—I was this day informed that there is forty large Cannoes loaded with men women and children passed by here down the Cherokee River who on their way down they took a Dellaway Indian prisoner & kept him till they found out what Nation he was of—they told him they had come from Long Island and were on their way to Illinois with an intent to settle—Sir I have some reason to think they are a party of Rebels My reason is this after they let the Dellaway Indian at liberty they met with some Cherokees whom they endeavoured to decoy, but finding they would not be decoyed they fired on them but they all made their Escape with the Loss of their arms and ammunition and one fellow wounded, who arrived yesterday. The Dellaway informs me that Lieut. Governor Hamilton is defeated and himself taken prisoner," etc.

It is curious that none of the Tennessee annalists have noticed the departure of this expedition ; very, very few of the deeds and wanderings of the old frontiersmen have been recorded ; and in consequence historians are apt to regard these few as being exceptional, instead of typical. Donelson was merely one of a hundred leaders of flotillas that went down the western rivers at this time.

cember 22d, but falling water and heavy frosts detained them two months, and the voyage did not really begin until they left Cloud Creek on February 27, 1780. The first ten days were uneventful. The *Adventure* spent an afternoon and night on a shoal, until the water fortunately rose, and, all the men getting out, the clumsy scow was floated off. Another boat was driven on the point of an island and sunk, her crew being nearly drowned; whereupon the rest of the flotilla put to shore, the sunken boat was raised and bailed out, and most of her cargo recovered. At one landing-place a man went out to hunt, and got lost, not being taken up again for three days, though "many guns were fired to fetch him in," and the four-pounder on the *Adventure* was discharged for the same purpose. A negro became "much frosted in his feet and legs, of which he died." Where the river was wide a strong wind and high sea forced the whole flotilla to lay to, for the sake of the smaller craft. This happened on March 7th, just before coming to the uppermost Chickamauga town; and that night, the wife of one Ephraim Peyton, who had himself gone with Robertson, overland, was delivered of a child. She was in a boat whose owner was named Jonathan Jennings.

The next morning they soon came to an Indian village on the south shore. The Indians made signs of friendliness, and two men started toward them in a canoe which the *Adventure* had in tow, while the flotilla drew up on the opposite side of the river. But a half-breed and some Indians jumping into a pirogue paddled out to meet the two messengers

and advised them to return to their comrades, which
they did. Several canoes then came off from the
shore to the flotilla. The Indians who were in
them seemed friendly and were pleased with the
presents they received; but while these were being
distributed the whites saw a number of other canoes
putting off, loaded with armed warriors, painted
black and red. The half-breed instantly told the
Indians round about to paddle to the shore, and
warned the whites to push off at once, at the same
time giving them some instructions about the river.
The armed Indians went down along the shore for
some time as if to intercept them; but at last they
were seemingly left behind.

In a short time another Indian village was reached,
where the warriors tried in vain to lure the whites
ashore; and as the boats were hugging the opposite
bank, they were suddenly fired at by a party in ambush, and one man slain. Immediately afterwards a
much more serious tragedy occurred. There was
with the flotilla a boat containing twenty-eight men,
women, and children, among whom small-pox had
broken out. To guard against infection, it was
agreed that it should keep well in the rear; being
warned each night by the sound of a horn when it
was time to go into camp. As this forlorn boat-load
of unfortunates came along, far behind the others,
the Indians, seeing its defenceless position, sallied out
in their canoes, and butchered or captured all who
were aboard. Their cries were distinctly heard by
the rearmost of the other craft, who could not stem
the current and come to their rescue. But a dreadful

retribution fell on the Indians; for they were in-
fected with the disease of their victims, and for some
months virulent small-pox raged among many of the
bands of Creeks and Cherokees. When stricken by
the disease, the savages first went into the sweat-
houses, and when heated to madness, plunged into
the cool streams, and so perished in multitudes.

When the boats entered the Narrows they had
lost sight of the Indians on shore, and thought they
had left them behind. A man, who was in a canoe,
had gone aboard one of the larger boats with his
family, for the sake of safety while passing through
the rough water. His canoe was towed alongside,
and in the rapids it was overturned, and the cargo
lost. The rest of the company, pitying his distress
over the loss of all his worldly goods, landed, to see
if they could not help him recover some of his
property. Just as they got out on the shore to walk
back, the Indians suddenly appeared almost over
them, on the high cliffs opposite, and began to fire,
causing a hurried retreat to the boats. For some
distance the Indians lined the bluffs, firing from the
heights into the boats below. Yet only four people
were wounded, and they not dangerously. One of
them was a girl named Nancy Gower. When, by
the sudden onslaught of the Indians, the crew of the
boat in which she was were thrown into dismay, she
took the helm and steered, exposed to the fire of the
savages. A ball went through the upper part of one
of her thighs, but she neither flinched nor uttered
any cry; and it was not known that she was
wounded until, after the danger was past, her

mother saw the blood soaking through her clothes. She recovered, married one of the frontiersmen, and lived for fifty years afterwards, long enough to see all the wilderness filled with flourishing and populous States.

One of the clumsy craft, however, did not share the good fortune that befell the rest, in escaping with so little loss and damage. Jonathan Jennings' boat, in which was Mrs. Peyton, with her new-born baby, struck on a rock at the upper end of the whirl, the swift current rendering it impossible for the others to go to his assistance; and they drifted by, leaving him to his fate. The Indians soon turned their whole attention to him, and from the bluffs opened a most galling fire upon the disabled boat. He returned it as well as he could, keeping them somewhat in check, for he was a most excellent marksman. At the same time he directed his two negroes, a man and woman, his nearly grown son, and a young man who was with him, to lighten the boat by throwing his goods into the river. Before this was done, the negro man, the son, and the other young man most basely jumped into the river, and swam ashore. It is satisfactory to record that at least two of the three dastards met the fate they deserved. The negro was killed in the water, and the other two captured, one of them being afterwards burned at the stake, while the other, it is said, was ultimately released. Meanwhile Mrs. Jennings, assisted by the negro woman and Mrs. Peyton, actually succeeded in shoving the lightened boat off the rock, though their clothes were cut in many places by the bullets; and they rapidly drifted out of danger. The poor little baby was killed in the hurry and confusion; but its mother, not eighteen hours from child-bed, in spite of the cold, wet, and exertion, kept in good health. Sailing by night as well as day, they caught up with the rest of the flotilla before dawn on the second morning afterwards, the men being roused from their watch-fires by the cries of "help poor Jennings," as the wretched and worn-out survivors in the disabled boat caught the first glimpse of the lights on shore.

Having successfully run the gauntlet of the Chickamauga banditti, the flotilla was not again molested by the Indians, save once when the boats that drifted near shore were fired on by a roving war party, and five men wounded. They ran over the great Muscle Shoals in about three hours without accident, though the boats scraped on the bottom here and there. The swift, broken water surged into high waves, and roared through the piles of driftwood that covered the points of the small islands, round which the currents ran in every direction; and those among the men who were unused to river-work were much relieved when they found themselves in safety. One night, after the fires had been kindled, the tired travellers were alarmed by the barking of the dogs. Fearing that Indians were near by, they hastily got into the boats and crossed to camp on the opposite shore. In the morning two of them returned to pick up some things that had been left; they found that the alarm had been false, for the utensils that had been overlooked in the confusion were undisturbed, and a negro who had been left behind in the hurry was still sleeping quietly by the camp-fires.

On the 20th of the month they reached the Ohio. Some of the boats then left for Natchez, and others for the Illinois country; while the remainder turned their prows up stream, to stem the rapid current—a task for which they were but ill-suited. The work was very hard, the provisions were nearly gone, and the crews were almost worn out by hunger and fatigue. On the 24th they entered the mouth of the Cumberland. The *Adventure*, the heaviest of all the craft, got much help from a small square-sail that was set in the bow.

Two days afterwards the hungry party killed some buffalo, and feasted on the lean meat, and the next day they shot a swan " which was very delicious," as Donelson recorded. Their meal was exhausted and they could make no more bread; but buffalo were plenty, and they hunted them steadily for their meat; and they also made what some of them called " Shawnee salad" from a kind of green herb that grew in the bottoms.

On the last day of the month they met Col. Richard Henderson, who had just come out and was running the line between Virginia and North Carolina. The crews were so exhausted that the progress of the boats became very slow, and it was not until April 24th that they reached the Big Salt Lick, and found Robertson awaiting them. The long, toilsome, and perilous voyage had been brought to a safe end.

There were then probably nearly five hundred settlers on the Cumberland, one half of them being able-bodied men in the prime of life.[1]   The central station, the capitol of the little community, was that at the Bluff, where Robertson built a little stockaded hamlet and called it Nashborough[2]; it was of the usual type of small frontier forted town.   Other stations were scattered along both sides of the river; some were stockades, others merely block-houses, with the yard and garden enclosed by stout palings. As with all similar border forts or stations, these were sometimes called by the name of the founder; more rarely they were named with reference to some natural object, such as the river, ford, or hill by which they were, or commemorated some deed, or the name of a man the frontiersmen held in honor; and occasionally they afforded true instances of clan-settlement and clan-nomenclature, several kindred families of the same name building a village which grew to be called after them.   Among these Cumberland stations was Mansker's (usually called Kasper's or Gaspers—he was not particular how his name was spelled), Stone River, Bledsoe's, Freeland's, Eatons', Clover-Bottom, and Fort Union.

As the country where they had settled belonged to no tribe of Indians, some of the people thought they would not be molested, and, being eager to take up the best lands, scattered out to live on separate claims.   Robertson warned them that they would soon suffer from the savages; and his words speed-

[1] Two hundred and fifty-six names are subscribed to the compact of government; and in addition there were the women, children, the few slaves, and such men as did not sign.

[2] After A. Nash; he was the governor of North Carolina; where he did all he could on the patriot side.   See Gates MSS. Sept. 7, 1780.

ily came true—whereupon the outlying cabins were deserted and all gathered within the stockades. In April roving parties of Delawares, Chickasaws, and Choctaws began to harass the settlement. As in Kentucky, so on the banks of the Cumberland, the Indians were the first to begin the conflict. The lands on which the whites settled were uninhabited, and were claimed as hunting-grounds by many hostile tribes; so that it is certain that no one tribe had any real title to them.

True to their customs and traditions, and to their race-capacity for self-rule, the settlers determined **Formation** forthwith to organize some kind of govern-**of a Gov-** ment under which justice might be done **ernment.** among themselves, and protection afforded against outside attack. Not only had the Indians begun their ravages, but turbulent and disorderly whites were also causing trouble. Robertson, who had been so largely instrumental in founding the Watauga settlement, and giving it laws, naturally took the lead in organizing this, the second community which he had caused to spring up in the wilderness. He summoned a meeting of delegates from the various stations, to be held at Nashborough;[1] Henderson being foremost in advocating the adoption of the plan.

In fact, Henderson, the treaty-maker and land-speculator, whose purchase first gave the whites clear color of title to the valleys of the Kentucky and Cumberland, played somewhat the same part,

[1] It is to Putnam that we owe the publication of the compact of government, and the full details of the methods and proceedings by which it was organized and carried on. See "History of Middle Tennessee," pp. 84–103.

though on a smaller scale, in the settlement made by Robertson as in that made by Boon. He and the Virginian commissioner Walker, had surveyed the boundary line and found that the Cumberland settlements were well to the south of it. He then claimed the soil as his under the Cherokee deed; and disposed of it to the settlers who contracted to pay ten dollars a thousand acres. This was but a fraction of the State price, so the settlers were all eager to hold under Henderson's deed; one of the causes of their coming out had been the chance of getting land so cheap. But Henderson's claim was annulled by the legislature, and the satisfaction-piece of 200,000 acres allotted him was laid off elsewhere; so his contracts with the settlers came to nothing, and they eventually got title in the usual way from North Carolina. They suffered no loss in the matter, for they had merely given Henderson promises to pay when his title was made good.

The settlers, by their representatives, met together at Nashborough, and on May 1, 1780, entered into articles of agreement or a compact of government. It was doubtless drawn up by Robertson, with perhaps the help of Henderson, and was modelled upon what may be called the "constitution" of Watauga, with some hints from that of Transylvania.[1] The

---

[1] Phelan, the first historian who really grasped what this movement meant, and to what it was due, gives rather too much weight to the part Henderson played. Henderson certainly at this time did not aspire to form a new State on the Cumberland; the compact especially provided for the speedy admission of Cumberland as a county of North Carolina. The marked difference between the Transylvania and the Cumberland " constitutions," and the close agreement of the latter with the Watauga articles, assuredly point to Robertson as the chief author.

settlers ratified the deeds of their delegates on May 13th, when they signed the articles, binding themselves to obey them to the number of two hundred and fifty-six men. The signers practically guaranteed one another their rights in the land, and their personal security against wrong-doers; those who did not sign were treated as having no rights whatever— a proper and necessary measure as it was essential that the naturally lawless elements should be forced to acknowledge some kind of authority.

The compact provided that the affairs of the community should be administered by a Court or Committee of twelve Judges, Triers or General Arbitrators, to be elected in the different stations by vote of all the freemen in them who were over twenty-one years of age. Three of the Triers were to come from Nashborough, two from Mansker's, two from Bledsoe's, and one from each of five other named stations.[1] Whenever the freemen of any station were dissatisfied with their Triers, they could at once call a new election, at which others might be chosen in their stead. The Triers had no salaries, but the Clerk of the Court was allowed some very small fees, just enough to pay for the pens, ink, and paper, all of them scarce commodities.[2] The Court had jurisdiction in all cases of conflict over land titles; a land office being established and an entry taker appointed.

[1] Putnam speaks of these men as " notables "; apparently they called themselves as above. Putnam's book contains much very valuable information ; but it is written in most curious style and he interlards it with outside matter ; much that he puts in quotation marks is apparently his own material. It is difficult to make out whether his " tribunal of notables " is his own expression or a quotation, but apparently it is the former.

[2] Haywood, 126.

Over half of the compact was devoted to the rules of
the land office. The Court, acting by a majority of
its members, was to have jurisdiction for the recovery of debt or damages, and to be allowed to tax
costs. Three Triers were competent to make a Court
to decide a case where the debt or damage was a
hundred dollars or less; and there was no appeal from
their decision. For a larger sum an appeal lay to
the whole Court. The Court appointed whomsoever
it pleased to see decisions executed. It had power to
punish all offences against the peace of the community, all misdemeanors and criminal acts, provided
only that its decisions did not go so far as to affect
the life of the criminal. If the misdeed of the
accused was such as to be dangerous to the State, or
one "for which the benefit of clergy was taken away
by law," he was to be bound and sent under guard
to some place where he could be legally dealt with.
The Court levied fines, payable in money or provisions, entered up judgments and awarded executions,
and granted letters of administration upon estates of
deceased persons, and took bonds " payable to the
chairman of the Committee." The expenses were to
be paid proportionately by the various settlers. It
was provided, in view of the Indian incursions, that
the militia officers elected at the various stations
should have power to call out the militia when they
deemed it necessary to repel or pursue the enemy.
They were also given power to fine such men as dis-
obeyed them, and to impress horses if need be; if
damaged, the horses were to be paid for by the
people of the station in the proportion the Court

might direct. It was expressly declared that the compact was designed as a "temporary method of restraining the licentious"; that the settlement did not desire to be exempt from the ratable share of the expense for the Revolutionary war, and earnestly asked that North Carolina would immediately make it part of the State, erecting it into a county. Robertson was elected chairman of the Court, and colonel of the militia, being thus made both civil and military commandant of the settlement. In common with the other Triers he undertook the solemnization of marriages; and these were always held legal, which was fortunate, as it was a young and vigorous community, of which the members were much given to early wedlock.

Thus a little commonwealth, a self-governing state, was created. It was an absolute democracy, the majority of freemen of full age in each stockade having power in every respect, and being able not only to elect, but to dismiss their delegates at any moment. Their own good sense and a feeling of fair play could be depended upon to protect the rights of the minority, especially as a minority of such men would certainly not tolerate any thing even remotely resembling tyranny. They had formed a representative government in which the legislative and judicial functions were not separated, and were even to a large extent combined with the executive. They had proceeded in an eminently practical manner, having modelled their system on what was to them the familiar governmental unit of the county with its county court and county militia officers. They made the changes that their peculiar position required, grafting the elective and representative systems on the one they adopted, and of course enlarging the scope of the court's action. Their compact was thus in some sort an unconscious reproduction of the laws and customs of the old-time court-leet, profoundly modified to suit the peculiar needs of backwoods life, the intensely democratic temper of the pioneers and above all the military necessities of their existence. They had certain theories of liberty and justice ; but they were too shrewd and hard-headed to try to build up a government on an entirely new foundation, when they had ready to hand materials with which they were familiar. They knew by experience the workings of the county system; all they did was to alter the immediate channel from which the court drew its powers, and to adapt the representation to the needs of a community where constant warfare obliged the settlers to gather in little groups, which served as natural units.

When the settlers first came to the country they found no Indians living in it, no signs of cultivation or cleared land, and nothing to show that for ages past it had been inhabited. It was a vast plain, covered with woods and canebrakes, through which the wild herds had beaten out broad trails. The only open places were the licks, sometimes as large as corn-fields, where the hoofs of the game had trodden the ground bare of vegetation, and channelled its surface with winding seams and gullies. It is even doubtful if the spot of bare ground which Mansker

called an "old field" or sometimes a "Chickasaw
old field" was not merely one of these licks. Buffalo, deer, and bear abounded; elk, wolves, and pan-
thers were plentiful.

Yet there were many signs that in long by-gone
times a numerous population had dwelt in the land.
Round every spring were many graves, built in a
peculiar way, and covered eight or ten inches deep
by mould. In some places there were earth-covered
foundations of ancient walls and embankments that
enclosed spaces of eight or ten acres. The Indians
knew as little as the whites about these long-van-
ished mound-builders, and were utterly ignorant of
the race to which they had belonged.[1]

For some months the whites who first arrived
dwelt in peace. But in the spring, hunting and war
Indian parties from various tribes began to harass
Hostilities. the settlers. Unquestionably the savages
felt jealous of the white hunters, who were killing
and driving away the game, precisely as they all felt
jealous of one another, and for the same reason.
The Chickasaws in particular, were much irritated
by the fort Clark had built at Iron Bank, on the
Mississippi. But the most powerful motive for the
attacks was doubtless simply the desire for scalps
and plunder. They gathered from different quarters to assail the colonists, just as the wild beasts
gathered to prey on the tame herds.

The Indians began to commit murders, kill the
stock, and drive off the horses in April, and their

---

[1] Haywood. At present it is believed that the mound-builders were Indians. Haywood is the authority for the early Indian wars of the Cumberland settlement, Putnam supplying some information.

ravages continued unceasingly throughout the year. Among the slain was a son of Robertson, and also the unfortunate Jonathan Jennings, the man who had suffered such loss when his boat was passing the whirl of the Tennessee River. The settlers were shot as they worked on their clearings, gathered the corn crops, or ventured outside the walls of the stockades. Hunters were killed as they stooped to drink at the springs, or lay in wait at the licks. They were lured up to the Indians by imitations of the gobbling of a turkey or the cries of wild beasts. They were regularly stalked as they still-hunted the game, or were ambushed as they returned with their horses laden with meat. The inhabitants of one station were all either killed or captured. Robertson led pursuing parties after one or two of the bands, and recovered some plunder; and once or twice small marauding parties were met and scattered, with some loss, by the hunters. But, on the whole, very little could be done at first to parry or revenge the strokes of the Indians.[1]

Horses and cattle had been brought into the new settlement in some number during the year; but the savages killed or drove off most of them, shooting

---

[1] Putnam, p. 107, talks as if the settlers were utterly unused to Indian warfare, saying that until the first murder occurred, in this spring, " few, if any " of them had ever gazed on the victim of scalping-knife and tomahawk. This is a curiously absurd statement. Many of the settlers were veteran Indian fighters. Almost all of them had been born and brought up on the frontier, amid a succession of Indian wars. It is, unfortunately, exceedingly difficult in Putnam's book to distinguish the really valuable authentic information it contains from the interwoven tissue of matter written solely to suit his theory of dramatic effect. He puts in with equal gravity the " Articles of Agreement " and purely fictitious conversations, jokes, and the like. (See pp. 126, 144, and *passim.*)

the hogs and horned stock, and stealing the riding animals. The loss of the milch cows in particular, was severely felt by the women. Moreover, there were heavy freshets, flooding the low bottoms on which the corn had been planted, and destroying most of the crop.

These accumulated disasters wrought the greatest discouragement among the settlers. Many left the country, and most of the remainder, when midsummer was past, began to urge that they should all go back in a body to the old settlements. The panic became very great. One by one the stockades were deserted, until finally all the settlers who remained were gathered in Nashborough and Freelands.[1] The Cumberland country would have been abandoned to the Indians, had Robertson not shown himself to be exactly the man for whom the crisis called.

Robertson was not a dashing, brilliant Indian fighter and popular frontier leader, like Sevier. He had rather the qualities of Boon, with the difference that he was less a wandering hunter and explorer, and better fitted to be head of a settled community. He was far-seeing, tranquil, resolute, unshaken by misfortune and disaster; a most trustworthy man, with a certain severe fortitude of temper. All people naturally turned to him in time of panic, when the ordinarily bold and daring became cowed and confused. The straits to which the settlers were reduced, and their wild clamor for immediate flight, the danger from the Indians, the death of his own

---

[1] By some accounts there were also a few settlers left in Eaton's Station; and Mansker's was rarely entirely deserted for any length of time.

son all combined failed to make him waver one instant in his purpose. He strongly urged on the
settlers the danger of flight through the wilderness.
He did not attempt to make light of the perils that
confronted them if they remained, but he asked
them to ponder well if the beauty and fertility of
the land did not warrant some risk being run to
hold it, now that it was won. They were at last in
a fair country fitted for the homes of their children.
Now was the time to keep it. If they abandoned it,
they would lose all the advantages they had gained,
and would be forced to suffer the like losses and
privations if they ever wished to retake possession of
it or of any similar tract of land. He, at least, would
not turn back, but would stay to the bitter end.

His words and his steadfast bearing gave heart
to the settlers, and they no longer thought of flight.
As their corn had failed them they got their food
from the woods. Some gathered quantities of wal-
nuts, hickory-nuts, and shelbarks, and the hunters
wrought havoc among the vast herds of game. During the early winter one party of twenty men that
went up Caney Fork on a short trip, killed one hundred and five bears, seventy-five buffaloes, and eighty-
seven deer, and brought the flesh and hides back to
the stockades in canoes; so that through the winter
there was no lack of jerked and smoke-dried meat.

The hunters were very accurate marksmen; game
was plenty, and not shy, and so they got up close
and rarely wasted a shot. Moreover, their small-
bore rifles took very little powder—in fact the
need of excessive economy in the use of ammunition

when on their long hunting-trips was one of the chief reasons for the use of small bores. They therefore used comparatively little ammunition. Nevertheless, by the beginning of winter both powder and bullets began to fail. In this emergency Robertson again came to the front to rescue the settlement he had founded and preserved. He was accustomed to making long, solitary journeys through the forest, unmindful of the Indians; he had been one of the first to come from North Carolina to Watauga; he had repeatedly been on perilous missions to the Cherokees; he had the previous year gone north to the Illinois country to meet Clark. He now announced that he would himself go to Kentucky and bring back the needed ammunition; and at once set forth on his journey, across the long stretches of snow-powdered barrens, and desolate, Indian-haunted woodland.

CHAPTER XII.

THE CUMBERLAND SETTLEMENTS TO THE CLOSE OF THE REVOLUTION, 1781-1783.

ROBERTSON passed unharmed through the wilderness to Kentucky. There he procured plenty of powder, and without delay set out on his return journey to the Cumberland. As before, he travelled alone through the frozen woods, trusting solely to his own sharp senses for his safety.

In the evening of January 15, 1781, he reached Freeland's station, and was joyfully received by the inmates. They supped late, and then sat Attack on up for some time, talking over many mat- Freeland's. ters. When they went to bed all were tired, and neglected to take the usual precautions against surprise; moreover, at that season they did not fear molestation. They slept heavily, none keeping watch. Robertson alone was wakeful and suspicious; and even during his light slumbers his keen and long-trained senses were on the alert.

At midnight all was still. The moon shone brightly down on the square block-houses and stockaded yard of the lonely little frontier fort; its rays lit up the clearing, and by contrast darkened the black shadow of the surrounding forest. None of the sleepers within the log-walls dreamed of danger. Yet their peril was imminent. An Indian war band was lurking near by, and was on the point of making an effort to carry Freeland's station by an attack in the darkness. In the dead of the night the attempt was made. One by one the warriors left the protection of the tangled wood-growth, slipped silently across the open space, and crouched under the heavy timber pickets of the palisades, until all had gathered together. Though the gate was fastened with a strong bar and chain, the dextrous savages finally contrived to open it.

In so doing they made a slight noise, which caught Robertson's quick ear, as he lay on his buffalo-hide pallet. Jumping up he saw the gate open, and dusky figures gliding into the yard with stealthy swiftness. At his cry of "Indians," and the report of his piece, the settlers sprang up, every man grasping the loaded arm by which he slept. From each log cabin the rifles cracked and flashed; and though the Indians were actually in the yard they had no cover, and the sudden and unexpected resistance caused them to hurry out much faster than they had come in. Robertson shot one of their number, and they in return killed a white man who sprang out-of-doors at the first alarm. When they were driven out the gate was closed after them; but they fired through the loopholes; especially into one of the block-houses, where the chinks had not been filled with mud, as in the others. They thus killed a negro, and wounded one or two other men; yet they were soon driven off. Robertson's return had been at a most opportune moment. As so often before and afterwards, he had saved the settlement from destruction.

Other bands of Indians joined the war party, and they continued to hover about the stations, daily inflicting loss and damage on the settlers. They burned down the cabins and fences, drove off the stock and killed the hunters, the women and children who ventured outside the walls, and the men who had gone back to their deserted stockades.[1]

On the 2d day of April another effort was made by a formidable war party to get possession of one of the two remaining stations—Free- Attack land's and Nashborough—and thus, at a on Nash- stroke, drive the whites from the Cumber- borough. land district. This time Nashborough was the point aimed at.

A large body[2] of Cherokees approached the fort in the night, lying hid in the bushes, divided into two parties. In the morning three of them came near, fired at the fort, and ran off towards where the smaller party lay ambushed, in a thicket

[1] Haywood says they burned "immense quantities of corn"; as Putnam points out, the settlers could have had very little corn to burn. Haywood is the best authority for the Indian fighting in the Cumberland district during '80, '81, and '82. Putnam supplies some details learned from Mrs. Robertson in her old age. The accounts are derived mainly from the statements of old settlers; but the Robertsons seem always to have kept papers, which served to check off the oral statements. For all the important facts there is good authority. The annals are filled with name after name of men who were killed by the Indians. The dates, and even the names, may be misplaced in many of these instances; but this is really a matter of no consequence, for their only interest is to show the nature of the harassing Indian warfare, and the kind of adventure then common.

[2] How large it is impossible to say. One or two recent accounts make wild guesses, calling it 1,000; but this is sheer nonsense; it is more likely to have been 100.

through which ran a little "branch." Instantly twenty men mounted their horses and galloped after the decoys. As they overtook the fugitives they saw the Indians hid in the creek-bottom, and dismounted to fight, turning their horses loose. A smart interchange of shots followed, the whites having, if any thing, rather the best of it, when the other and larger body of Indians rose from their hiding-place, in a clump of cedars, and running down, formed between the combatants and the fort, intending to run into the latter, mixed with the fleeing riflemen. The only chance of the hemmed-in whites was to turn and try to force their way back through their far more numerous foes. This was a desperate venture, for their pieces were all discharged, and there was no time to reload them; but they were helped by two unexpected circumstances. Their horses had taken flight at the firing, and ran off towards the fort, passing to one side of the intervening line of Indians; and many of the latter, eager for such booty, ran off to catch them. Meanwhile, the remaining men in the fort saw what had happened, and made ready for defense, while all the women likewise snatched up guns or axes, and stood by loopholes and gate. The dogs in the fort were also taking a keen interest in what was going on. They were stout, powerful animals, some being hounds and others watch dogs, but all accustomed to contests with wild beasts; and by instinct and training they mortally hated Indians. Seeing the line of savages drawn up between the fort and their masters, they

promptly sallied out and made a most furious onset
upon their astonished foes. Taking advantage of
this most opportune diversion, the whites ran
through the lines and got into the fort, the Indians
being completely occupied in defending themselves
from the dogs. Five of the whites were killed, and
they carried two wounded men into the fort. Another man, when almost in safety, was shot, and fell
with a broken thigh; but he had reloaded his gun
as he ran, and he killed his assailant as the latter
ran up to scalp him. The people from the fort
then, by firing their rifles, kept his foes at bay until
he could be rescued; and he soon recovered from his
hurt. Yet another man was overtaken almost under
the walls, the Indian punching him in the shoulder
with the gun as he pulled the trigger; but the gun
snapped, and a hunter ran out of the fort and shot
the Indian. The gates were closed, and the whites
all ready; so the Indians abandoned their effort and
drew off. They had taken five scalps and a number
of horses; but they had failed in their main object,
and the whites had taken two scalps, besides killing
and wounding others of the red men, who were carried off by their comrades.

After the failure of this attempt the Indians did
not, for some years, make any formidable attack on
any of the larger stations. Though the most dangerous of all foes on their own ground, their extreme caution and dislike of suffering punishment
prevented them from ever making really determined
efforts to carry a fort openly by storm; moreover,
these stockades were really very defensible against

men unprovided with artillery, and there is no reason for supposing that any troops could have carried them by fair charging, without suffering altogether disproportionate loss. The red tribes acted in relation to the Cumberland settlements exactly as they had previously done towards those on the Kentucky and Watauga. They harassed the settlers from the outset; but they did not wake up to the necessity for a formidable and combined campaign against them until it was too late for such a campaign to succeed. If, at the first, any one of these communities had been forced to withstand the shock of such Indian armies as were afterwards brought against it, it would, of necessity, have been abandoned.

Throughout '81 and '82 the Cumberland settlers were worried beyond description by a succession of Indian Hostilities. small war parties. In the first of these years they raised no corn; in the second they made a few crops on fields they had cleared in 1780. No man's life was safe for an hour, whether he hunted, looked up strayed stock, went to the spring for water, or tilled the fields. If two men were together, one always watched while the other worked, ate, or drank; and they sat down back to back, or, if there were several, in a ring, facing outwards, like a covey of quail. The Indians were especially fond of stealing the horses; the whites pursued them in bands, and occasionally pitched battles were fought, with loss on both sides, and apparently as often resulting in the favor of one party as of the other. The most expert Indian fighters naturally became the leaders, being made colonels and captains of the local militia. The position and influence of the officers depended largely on their individual prowess; they were the actual, not titular, leaders of their men. Old Kasper Mansker, one of the most successful, may be taken as a type of the rest. He was ultimately made a colonel, and shared in many expeditions; but he always acted as his own scout, and never would let any of his men ride ahead or abreast of him, preferring to trust to his own eyes and ears and knowledge of forest warfare. The hunters, who were especially exposed to danger, were also the men who inflicted most loss on the Indians, and though many more of the settlers than of their foes were slain, yet the tables were often turned on the latter, even by those who seemed their helpless victims. Thus, once, two lads were watching at a deer lick, when some Indians came to it; each of the boys chose his man, fired, and then fled homewards; coming back with some men they found they had killed two Indians, whose scalps they took.

The eagerness of the Indians to get scalps caused them frequently to scalp their victims before life was extinct; and, as a result, there were numerous instances in which the scalped unfortunate, whether man, woman, or child, was rescued and recovered, living many years. One of these instances is worth giving in the quaint language of the old Tennessee historian, Haywood:

"In the spring of the year 1782 a party of Indians fired upon three persons at French Lick, and broke the arms of John Tucker and Joseph Hendricks, and shot down David Hood, whom they scalped and stamped, as he said, and followed the others towards the fort; the people of the fort came out and repulsed them and saved the wounded men. Supposing the Indians gone, Hood got up softly, wounded and scalped as he was, and began to walk towards the fort on the bluff, when, to his mortification, he saw, standing upon the bank of the creek, a number of Indians, the same who had wounded him before, making sport of his misfortune and mistake. They then fell upon him again, and having given him, in several places, new wounds that were apparently mortal, then left him. He fell into a brush heap in the mow, and next morning was tracked and found by his blood, and was placed as a dead man in one of the out-houses, and was left alone; after some time he recovered, and lived many years."

Many of the settlers were killed, many others left for Kentucky, Illinois, or Natchez, or returned to their old homes among the Alleghanies; and in 1782 the inhabitants, who had steadily dwindled in numbers, became so discouraged that they again mooted the question of abandoning the Cumberland district in a body. Only Robertson's great influence prevented this being done; but by word and example he finally persuaded them to remain. The following spring brought the news of peace with Great Britain. A large inflow of new settlers began with the new year, and though the Indian hostilities still continued, the Cumberland country throve apace, and by the end 1783 the old stations had been rebuilt and many new ones founded. Some of the settlers began to live out on their clearings. Rude little corn-mills and "hominy pounders" were built beside some of the streams. The piles of furs and hides that had accumulated in the stockades were sent back to the coast country on pack-horses. After this year there was never any danger that the settlements would be abandoned.

During the two years of petty but disastrous Indian warfare that followed the attack on Freelands, the harassed and diminishing settlers had been so absorbed in the contest with the outside foe that they had done little towards keeping up their own internal government. When 1783 opened new settlers began to flock in, the Indian hostilities abated, and commissioners arrived from North Carolina under a strong guard, with the purpose of settling the claim of the various settlers[1] and laying off the bounty lands promised to the Continental troops.[2] It therefore became necessary that the Committee or Court of Triers should again be convened, to see that justice was done as between man and man.

The ten men elected from the different stations met at Nashborough on January 7th, Robertson being again made chairman, as well as colonel of the militia, while a proper clerk and sheriff were chosen. Each member took a solemn oath to do equal justice according to the best of his skill and ability. A number of suits between the settlers themselves were disposed of. These related to a variety of subjects. A kettle had been "detained" from Humphrey Hogan; he

Internal Government.

---

[1] Haywood. Six hundred and forty acres were allowed by preëmption claim to each family settled before June 1, 1780; after that date they had to make proper entries in the courts. The salt-licks were to be held as public property.

[2] Isaac Shelby was one of these commissioners.

brought suit, and it was awarded him, the defendant
" and his mother-in-law " being made to pay the cost
of the suit. A hog case, a horse used in hunting, a
piece of cleared ground, a bed which had not been
made according to contract, the ownership of a canoe,
and of a heifer, a " clevis lent and delayed to be returned "—such were some of the cases on which the
judges had to decide. There were occasional slander
suits; for in a small backwoods community there is
always much jealousy and bitter gossip. When suit
was brought for "cattle won at cards," the committee
promptly dismissed the claim as illegal; they evidently had clear ideas as to what was good public
policy. A man making oath that another had threatened his life, the latter was taken and put under
bonds. Another man produced a note of hand for the
payment of two good cows, "against John Sadler";
he "proved his accompt," and procured an attachment against the estate of "Sd. Sadler." When
possible, the Committee compromised the cases, or
advised the parties to adjust matters between themselves. The sheriff executed the various decrees, in
due form; he arrested the men who refused to pay
heed to the judgments of the court, and when necessary took out of their "goods and chattles, lands and
tenements," the damages awarded, and also the costs
and fees. The government was in the hands of men
who were not only law-abiding themselves but also
resolute to see that the law was respected by others.

The committee took cognizance of all affairs concerning the general welfare of the community. They
ordered roads to be built between the different

stations, appointing overseers who had power to "call out hands to work on the same." Besides the embodiment of all the full-grown men as militia,— those of each station under their own captain, lieutenant, and ensign,—a diminutive force of paid regulars was organized; that is, six spies were "kept out to discover the motions of the enemy so long as we shall be able to pay them; each to receive seventy-five bushels of Indian corn per month." They were under the direction of Colonel Robertson, who was head of all the branches of the government. One of the committee's regulations followed an economic principle of doubtful value. Some enterprising individuals, taking advantage of the armed escort accompanying the Carolina commissioners, brought out casks of liquors. The settlers had drunk nothing but water for many months, and they eagerly purchased the liquor, the merchants naturally charging all that the traffic would bear. This struck the committee as a grievance, and they forthwith passed a decree that any person bringing in liquor "from foreign ports," before selling the same, must give bond that they would charge no more than one silver dollar, or its value in merchandise, per quart.

Some of the settlers would not enter the association, preferring a condition of absolute freedom from law. The committee, however, after waiting a proper time, forced these men in by simply serving notice, that thereafter they would be treated as beyond the pale of the law, not entitled to its protection, but amenable to its penalties. A petition was sent to the North Carolina Legislature, asking that the protection of government should be extended to the Cumberland people, and showing that the latter were loyal and orderly, prompt to suppress sedition and lawlessness, faithful to the United States, and hostile to its enemies.[1]   To show their good feeling the committee made every member of the community, who had not already done so, take the oath of abjuration and fidelity.

Until full governmental protection could be secured the commonwealth was forced to act as a little sovereign state, bent on keeping the peace, and yet Affairs with on protecting itself against aggression from Outside the surrounding powers, both red and white. Powers. It was forced to restrain its own citizens, and to enter into quasi-diplomatic relations with its neighbors.   Thus early this year fifteen men, under one Colbert, left the settlements and went down the river in boats, ostensibly to trade with the Indians, but really to plunder the Spaniards on the Mississippi. They were joined by some Chickasaws, and at first met with some success in their piratical attacks, not only on the Spanish trading-boats, but on those of the French creoles, and even the Americans, as well. Finally they were repulsed in an attempt against the Spaniards at Ozark; some were killed, and the rest scattered.[2] Immediately upon learning of these deeds, the Committee of Triers passed stringent resolutions forbidding all persons trading with the Indians until granted a license by the committee, and until they

---

[1] This whole account is taken from Putnam, who has rendered such inestimable service by preserving these records.

[2] Calendar Va. State Papers, III., pp. 469, 527.

had furnished ample security for their good behavior. The committee also wrote a letter to the Spanish governor at New Orleans, disclaiming all responsibility for the piratical misdeeds of Colbert and his gang, and announcing the measures they had taken to prevent any repetition of the same in the future. They laid aside the sum of twenty pounds to pay the expenses of the messengers who carried this letter to the Virginian "agent" at the Illinois, whence it was forwarded to the Spanish Governor.[1]

One of the most difficult questions with which the committee had to deal was that of holding a treaty with the Indians. Commissioners came out from Virginia and North Carolina especially to hold such a treaty[2]; but the settlers declined to allow it until they had themselves decided on its advisability. They feared to bring so many savages together, lest they might commit some outrage, or be themselves subjected to such at the hands of one of the many wronged and reckless whites; and they knew that the Indians would expect many presents, while there was very little indeed to give them. Finally, the committee decided to put the question of treaty or no treaty to the vote of the freemen in the several stations; and by a rather narrow majority it was decided in the affirmative. The committee then made arrangements for holding the treaty in June, some four miles from Nashborough; and strictly prohib-

[1] Putnam, pp. 185, 189, 191.

[2] Donelson, who was one of the men who became discouraged and went to Kentucky, was the Virginian commissioner. Martin was the commissioner from North Carolina. He is sometimes spoken of as if he likewise represented Virginia.

ited the selling of liquor to the savages. At the appointed time many chiefs and warriors of the Chickasaws, Cherokees, and even Creeks appeared. There were various sports, such as ball-games and foot-races ; and the treaty was brought to a satisfactory conclusion.[1] It did not put a complete stop to the Indian outrages, but it greatly diminished them. The Chickasaws thereafter remained friendly ; but, as usual, the Cherokee and Creek chiefs who chose to attend were unable to bind those of their fellows who did not. The whole treaty was, in fact, on both sides, of a merely preliminary nature. The boundaries it arranged were not considered final until confirmed by the treaty of Hopewell a couple of years later.

Robertson meanwhile was delegated by the unanimous vote of the settlers to go to the Assembly of

Establishment of County Government.

North Carolina, and there petition for the establishment of a regular land office at Nashborough, and in other ways advance the interests of the settlers. He was completely successful in his mission. The Cumberland settlements were included in a new county, called Davidson[2] ; and an Inferior Court of Pleas and Common Sessions, vested by the act with extraordinary powers, was established at Nashborough. The four justices of the new court had all been Triers of the old committee, and the scheme of government was practically not very greatly changed,

[1] Putnam, 196.

[2] In honor of General Wm. Davidson, a very gallant and patriotic soldier of North Carolina during the Revolutionary war. The county government was established in October, 1783.

although now resting on an indisputably legal basis. The Cumberland settlers had for years acted as an independent, law-abiding, and orderly commonwealth, and the Court of Triers had shown great firmness and wisdom. It spoke well for the people that they had been able to establish such a government, in which the majority ruled, while the rights of each individual were secured. Robertson deserves the chief credit as both civil and military leader. The committee of which he was a member, had seen that justice was done between man and man, had provided for defense against the outside foe, and had striven to prevent any wrongs being done to neutral or allied powers. When they became magistrates of a county of North Carolina they continued to act on the lines they had already marked out. The increase of population had brought an increase of wealth. The settlers were still frontiersmen, clad in buckskin or homespun, with rawhide moccasins, living in log-cabins, and sleeping under bearskins on beds made of buffalo hides; but as soon as they ventured to live on their clearings the ground was better tilled, corn became abundant, and cattle and hogs increased as the game diminished. Nashborough began to look more like an ordinary little border town.[1]

During this year Robertson carried on some correspondence with the Spanish governor at New Orleans, Don Estevan Miro. This was the beginning of intercourse between the western settlers and

---

[1] The justices built a court-house and jail of hewed logs, the former eighteen feet square, with a lean-to or shed of twelve feet on one side. The contracts for building were let out at vendue to the lowest bidder.

the Spanish officers, an intercourse which was absolutely necessary, though it afterwards led to many

Correspondence with the Spaniards. intrigues and complications. Robertson was obliged to write to Miro not only to disclaim responsibility for the piratical deeds of men like Colbert, but also to protest against the conduct of certain of the Spanish agents among the Creeks and Chickamaugas. No sooner had hostilities ceased with the British than the Spaniards began to incite the savages to take up once more the hatchet they had just dropped,[1] for Spain already recognized in the restless borderers possible and formidable foes.

Miro in answering Robertson assured him that the Spaniards were very friendly to the western settlers, and denied that the Spanish agents were stirring up trouble. He also told him that the harassed Cherokees, weary of ceaseless warfare, had asked permission to settle west of the Mississippi—although they did not carry out their intention. He ended by pressing Robertson and his friends to come down and settle in Spanish territory, guaranteeing them good treatment.[2]

In spite of Miro's fair words the Spanish agents continued to intrigue against the Americans, and especially against the Cumberland people. Yet there was no open break. The Spanish governor was felt to be powerful for both good and evil, and at least a possible friend of the settlers. To many of

[1] Calendar of Va. State Papers, III., 584, 608, etc.

[2] Robertson MSS. As the letter is important I give it in full in the Appendix.

their leaders he showed much favor, and the people as a whole were well impressed by him; and as a compliment to him they ultimately, when the Cumberland counties were separated from those lying to the eastward, united the former under the name of Mero [1] District.

[1] So spelt; but apparently his true name was Miro.

CHAPTER XIII.

WHAT THE WESTERNERS HAD DONE DURING THE REVOLUTION, 1783.

WHEN the first Continental Congress began its sittings the only frontiersmen west of the mountains, and beyond the limits of continuous settlement within the old Thirteen Colonies,[1] were the two or three hundred citizens of the little Watauga commonwealth. When peace was declared with Great Britain the backwoodsmen had spread westward, in groups, almost to the Mississippi, and they had increased in number to some twenty-five thousand souls,[2] of whom a few hundred dwelt in the bend of the Cumberland, while the rest were about equally divided between Kentucky and Holston.

This great westward movement of armed settlers was essentially one of conquest, no less than of colonization. Thronging in with their wives and children, their cattle, and their few household goods, they won and held the land in the teeth of fierce resistance, both from the Indian claimants of the soil and from the

The Winning of the West.

---

[1] This qualification is put in because there were already a few families on the Monongahela, the head of the Kanawha, and the upper Holston ; but they were in close touch with the people behind them.

[2] These figures are simply estimates ; but they are based on careful study and comparison, and though they must be some hundreds, and maybe some thousands, out of the way, are quite near enough for practical purposes.

representatives of a mighty and arrogant European power. The chain of events by which the winning was achieved is perfect; had any link therein snapped it is likely that the final result would have been failure. The wide wanderings of Boon and his fellow hunters made the country known and awakened in the minds of the frontiersmen a keen desire to possess it. The building of the Watauga commonwealth by Robertson and Sevier gave a base of operations, and furnished a model for similar communities to follow. Lord Dunmore's war made the actual settlement possible, for it cowed the northern Indians, and restrained them from seriously molesting Kentucky during its first and most feeble years. Henderson and Boon made their great treaty with the Cherokees in 1775, and then established a permanent colony far beyond all previous settlements, entering into final possession of the new country. The victory over the Cherokees in 1776 made safe the line of communication along the Wilderness road, and secured the chance for further expansion. Clark's campaigns gained the Illinois, or northwestern regions. The growth of Kentucky then became very rapid; and in its turn this, and the steady progress of the Watauga settlements, rendered possible Robertson's successful effort to plant a new community still farther west, on the Cumberland.

The backwoodsmen pressed in on the line of least resistance, first taking possession of the debatable hunting-grounds lying between the Algonquins of the north and the Appalachian confederacies of the south. Then they began to encroach on the actual tribal territories. Every step was accompanied by

The Wars of the Back-woodsmen.
stubborn and bloody fighting with the Indians. The forest tribes were exceedingly formidable opponents; it is not too much to say that they formed a far more serious obstacle to the American advance than would have been offered by an equal number of the best European troops. Their victories over Braddock, Grant, and St. Clair, gained in each case with a smaller force, conclusively proved their superiority, on their own ground, over the best regulars, disciplined and commanded in the ordinary manner. Almost all of the victories, even of the backwoodsmen, were won against inferior numbers of Indians.[1] The red men were fickle of temper, and large bodies could not be kept together for a long campaign, nor, indeed, for more than one special stroke; the only piece of strategy any of their chiefs showed was Cornstalk's march past

---

[1] That the contrary impression prevails is due to the boastful vanity which the backwoodsmen often shared with the Indians, and to the gross ignorance of the average writer concerning these border wars. Many of the accounts in the popular histories are sheer inventions. Thus, in the "Chronicles of Border Warfare," by Alex. S. Withers (Clarksburg, Va., 1831, p. 301), there is an absolutely fictitious account of a feat of the Kentucky Colonel Scott, who is alleged to have avenged St. Clair's defeat by falling on the victorious Indians while they were drunk, and killing two hundred of them. This story has not even a foundation in fact; there was not so much as a skirmish of the sort described. As Mann Butler—a most painstaking and truthful writer—points out, it is made up out of the whole cloth, thirty years after the event; it is a mere invention to soothe the mortified pride of the whites. Gross exaggeration of the Indian numbers and losses prevails even to this day. Mr. Edmund Kirke, for instance, usually makes the absolute or relative numbers of the Indians from five to twenty-five times as great as they really were. Still, it is hard to blame backwoods writers for such slips in the face of the worse misdeeds of the average historian of the Greek and Roman wars with barbarians.

Dunmore to attack Lewis; but their tactics and discipline in the battle itself were admirably adapted
to the very peculiar conditions of forest warfare.
Writers who speak of them as undisciplined, or as
any but most redoubtable antagonists, fall into an
absurd error. An old Indian fighter, who, at the
close of the last century, wrote, from experience, a
good book on the subject, summed up the case very
justly when he said : " I apprehend that the Indian
discipline is as well calculated to answer the purpose
in the woods of America as the British discipline is
in Flanders; and British discipline in the woods is
the way to have men slaughtered, with scarcely any
chance of defending themselves." [1] A comparison
of the two victories gained by the backwoodsmen,
at the Great Kanawha, over the Indians, and
at Kings Mountain over Ferguson's British and
tories, brings out clearly the formidable fighting
capacity of the red men. At the Kanawha the
Americans outnumbered their foes, at King's Mountain they were no more than equal; yet in the
former battle they suffered twice the loss they did
in the latter, inflicted much less damage in return,
and did not gain nearly so decisive a victory.

The Indians were urged on by the British, who
furnished them with arms, ammunition, and provisions, and sometimes also with leaders
and with bands of auxiliary white troops,
French, British, and tories. It was this
that gave to the revolutionary contest its
twofold character, making it on the part of the
Americans a struggle for independence in the east,

*Twofold
Character
of the
Revolution.*

---

[1] Col. Jas. Smith, "An Account," etc., Lexington, Ky., 1799.

and in the west a war of conquest, or rather a war to establish, on behalf of all our people, the right of entry into the fertile and vacant regions beyond the Alleghanies. The grievances of the backwoods-men were not the same as the grievances of the men of the seacoast. The Ohio Valley and the other western lands of the French had been conquered by the British, not the Americans. Great Britain had succeeded to the policy as well as the possessions of her predecessor, and, strange to say, had become al-most equally hostile to the colonists of her own stock. As France had striven for half a century, so England now in her turn strove, to bar out the settlers of English race from the country beyond the Alle-ghanies. The British Crown, Parliament, and people were a unit in wishing to keep woodland and prairie for the sole use of their own merchants, as regions tenanted only by Indian hunters and French trappers and traders. They became the guardians and allies of all the Indian tribes. On the other hand, the Ameri-can backwoodsmen were resolute in their determina-tion to go in and possess the land. The aims of the two sides thus clashed hopelessly. Under all temporary and apparent grounds of quarrel lay this deep-rooted jealousy and incompatibility of interests. Beyond the Alleghanies the Revolution was fundamentally a struggle between England, bent on restricting the growth of the English race, and the Americans, tri-umphantly determined to acquire the right to con-quer the continent.

Had not the backwoodsmen been successful in the various phases of the struggle, we would certainly have been cooped up between the sea and the mountains. If in 1774 and '76 they had been beaten by the Ohio tribes and the Cherokees, the border ravaged, and the settlements stopped or forced back as during what the colonists called Braddock's War,[1] there is every reason to believe that the Alleghanies would have become our western frontier. Similarly, if Clark had failed in his efforts to conquer and hold the Illinois and Vincennes, it is overwhelmingly probable that the Ohio would have been the boundary between the Americans and the British. Before the Revolution began, in 1774, the British Parliament had, by the Quebec Act, declared the country between the Great Lakes and the Ohio to be part of Canada; and under the provisions of this act the British officers continued to do as they had already done—that is, to hold adverse possession of the land, scornfully heedless of the claims of the different colonies. The country was *de facto* part of Canada; the Americans tried to conquer it exactly as they tried to conquer the rest of Canada; the only difference was that Clark succeeded, whereas Arnold and Montgomery failed.

The West Actually Conquered.

Of course the conquest by the backwoodsmen was by no means the sole cause of our acquisition of the west. The sufferings and victories of the westerners would have counted for nothing, had it not been for the success of the American arms in the east, and for the skill of our three treaty-makers at Paris—Jay,

But only Definitely Secured by Diplomacy.

[1] During this Indian war, covering the period from Braddock's to Grant's defeats, Smith, a good authority, estimates that the frontiers were laid waste, and population driven back, over an area nearly three hundred miles long by thirty broad.

Adams, and Franklin, but above all the two former, and especially Jay. On the other hand, it was the actual occupation and holding of the country that gave our diplomats their vantage-ground. When the treaty was made, in 1782, the commissioners of the United States represented a people already holding the whole Ohio Valley, as well as the Illinois. The circumstances of the treaty were peculiar; but here they need to be touched but briefly, and only so far as they affected the western boundaries. The United States, acting together with France and Spain, had just closed a successful war with England; but when the peace negotiations were begun, they speedily found that their allies were, if any thing, more anxious than their enemy to hamper their growth. England, having conceded the grand point of independence, was disposed to be generous, and not to haggle about lesser matters. Spain, on the contrary, was quite as hostile to the new nation as to England. Through her representative, Count Aranda, she predicted the future enormous expansion of the Federal Republic at the expense of Florida, Louisiana, and Mexico, unless it was effectually curbed in its youth. The prophecy has been strikingly fulfilled, and the event has thoroughly justified Spain's fear; for the major part of the present territory of the United States was under Spanish dominion at the close of the Revolutionary war. Spain, therefore, proposed to hem in our growth by giving us the Alleghanies for our western boundary.[1] France was the

[1] At the north this boundary was to follow the upper Ohio, and end towards the foot of Lake Erie. See maps at end of volume.

ally of America; but as between America and Spain, she favored the latter. Moreover, she wished us to remain weak enough to be dependent upon her further good graces. The French court, therefore, proposed that the United States should content themselves with so much of the trans-Alleghany territory as lay round the head-waters of the Tennessee and between the Cumberland and Ohio. This area contained the bulk of the land that was already settled[1]; and the proposal showed how important the French court deemed the fact of actual settlement.

Thus the two allies of America were hostile to her interests. The open foe, England, on the contrary was anxious to conclude a separate treaty, so that she might herself be in better condition to carry on negotiations with France and Spain ; she cared much less to keep the west than she did to keep Gibraltar, and an agreement with the United States about the former left her free to insist on the retention of the latter. Congress, in a spirit of slavish subserviency, had instructed the American commissioners to take no steps without the knowledge and advice of France. Franklin was inclined to obey these instructions; but Jay, supported by Adams, boldly insisted on disregarding them ; and accordingly a separate treaty was negotiated with England. In settling the claims to the western territory, much stress was laid on the old colonial charters ; but underneath all the verbiage it was practically admitted that these charters conferred

---

[1] Excluding only so much of Robertson's settlement as lay south of the Cumberland, and Clark's conquest.

merely inchoate rights, which became complete only after conquest and settlement. The States themselves had already by their actions shown that they admitted this to be the case. Thus North Carolina, when by the creation of Washington County—now the State of Tennessee—she rounded out her boundaries, specified them as running to the Mississippi. As a matter of fact the royal grant, under which alone she could claim the land in question, extended to the Pacific; and the only difference between her rights to the regions east and west of the river was that her people were settling in one, and could not settle in the other. The same was true of Kentucky, and of the west generally; if the States could rightfully claim to run to the Mississippi, they could also rightfully claim to run to the Pacific. The colonial charters were all very well as furnishing color of title; but at bottom the American claim rested on the peculiar kind of colonizing conquest so successfully carried on by the backwoodsmen. When the English took New Amsterdam they claimed it under old charters; but they very well knew that their real right was only that of the strong hand. It was precisely so with the Americans and the Ohio valley. They produced old charters to support their title; but in reality it rested on Clark's conquests and above all on the advance of the backwoods settlements.[1]

[1] Mr. R. A. Hinsdale, in his excellent work on the "Old Northwest" (New York, 1888), seems to me to lay too much stress on the weight which our charter-claims gave us, and too little on the right we had acquired by actual possession. The charter-claims were elaborated with the most wearisome prolixity at the time; but so were the English claims to New Amster-

This view of the case is amply confirmed by a consideration of what was actually acquired under the treaty of peace which closed the Revolutionary struggle. Map-makers down to the present day have almost invariably misrepresented the territorial limits we gained by this treaty. They represent our limits in the west in 1783 as being the Great Lakes, the Mississippi, and the 31st parallel of latitude from the Mississippi to the Chattahoochee;[1] but in reality we did not acquire these limits until a dozen years later, by the treaties of Jay and Pinckney. Two points must be kept in mind : first, that during the war our ally, Spain, had conquered from England that portion of the Gulf coast known as West Florida; and second, that when the treaty was made the United States and Great Britain mutually covenanted to do certain things, some of which were never done. Great Britain agreed to recognize the lakes as our northern boundary, but, on the alleged

dam a century earlier. Conquest gave the true title in each case ; the importance of a claim is often in inverse order to the length at which it is set forth in a diplomatic document. The west was gained by : (1) the westward movement of the backwoodsmen during the Revolution ; (2) the final success of the Continental armies in the east ; (3) the skill of our diplomats at Paris ; failure on any one of these three points would have lost us the west.

Mr. Hinsdale seems to think that Clark's conquest prevented the Illinois from being conquered from the British by the Spaniards ; but this is very doubtful. The British at Detroit would have been far more likely to have conquered the Spaniards at St. Louis ; at any rate there is small probability that they would have been seriously troubled by the latter. The so-called Spanish conquest of St. Joseph was not a conquest at all, but an unimportant plundering raid.

The peace negotiations are best discussed in John Jay's chapter thereon, in the seventh volume of Winsor's '' Narrative and Critical History of North America.'' Sparks' account is fundamentally wrong on several points. Bancroft largely follows him, and therefore repeats and shares his errors.

[1] The map in Mr. Hinsdale's book may be given as a late instance.

ground that we did not fulfil certain of our promises, she declined to fulfil this agreement, and the lake posts remained in her hands until the Jay treaty was ratified. She likewise consented to recognize the 31st parallel as our southern boundary, but by a secret article it was agreed that if by the negotiations she recovered West Florida, then the boundary should run about a hundred miles farther north, ending at the mouth of the Yazoo. The discovery of this secret article aroused great indignation in Spain. As a matter of fact, the disputed territory, the land drained by the Gulf rivers, was not England's to grant, for it had been conquered and was then held by Spain. Nor was it given up to us until we acquired it by Pinckney's masterly diplomacy. The treaty represented a mere promise which in part was not and in part could not be fulfilled. All that it really did was to guarantee us what we already possessed—that is, the Ohio valley and the Illinois, which we had settled and conquered during the years of warfare. Our boundary lines were in reality left very vague. On the north the basin of the Great Lakes remained British; on the south the lands draining into the Gulf remained Spanish, or under Spanish influence. The actual boundaries we acquired can be roughly stated in the north to have followed the divide between the waters of the lake and the waters of the Ohio, and in the south to have run across the heads of the Gulf rivers. Had we remained a loose confederation these boundaries would more probably have shrunk than advanced; we did not overleap them until some years after

Washington had become the head of a real, not merely a titular, nation. The peace of 1783, as far as our western limits were affected, did nothing more than secure us undisturbed possession of lands from which it had proved impossible to oust us. We were in reality given nothing more than we had by our own prowess gained; the inference is strong that we got what we did get only because we had won and held it.

The first duty of the backwoodsmen who thus conquered the west was to institute civil government. Their efforts to overcome and beat back the The Back-Indians went hand in hand with their efforts woods Government to introduce law and order in the primitive ernments. communities they founded; and exactly as they relied purely on themselves in withstanding outside foes, so they likewise built up their social life and their first systems of government with reference simply to their special needs, and without any outside help or direction. The whole character of the westward movement, the methods of warfare, of settlement, and government, were determined by the extreme and defiant individualism of the backwoodsmen, their inborn independence and self-reliance, and their intensely democratic spirit. The west was won and settled by a number of groups of men, all acting independently of one another, but with a common object, and at about the same time. There was no one controlling spirit; it was essentially the movement of a whole free people, not of a single master-mind. There were strong and able leaders, who showed themselves fearless soldiers

and just law-givers, undaunted by danger, resolute
to persevere in the teeth of disaster ; but even these
leaders are most deeply interesting because they
stand foremost among a host of others like them.
There were hundreds of hunters and Indian fighters
like Mansker, Wetzel, Kenton, and Brady; there
were scores of commonwealth founders like Logan,
Todd, Floyd, and Harrod ; there were many adventurous land speculators like Henderson; there were
even plenty of commanders like Shelby and Campbell. These were all men of mark ; some of them exercised a powerful and honorable influence on the
course of events in the west. Above them rise four
greater figures, fit to be called not merely State or
local, but national heroes. Clark, Sevier, Robertson,
and Boon are emphatically American worthies. They
were men of might in their day, born to sway the
minds of others, helpful in shaping the destiny of
the continent. Yet of Clark alone can it be said
that he did a particular piece of work which
without him would have remained undone. Sevier,
Robertson, and Boon only hastened, and did more
perfectly, a work which would have been done by
others had they themselves fallen by the wayside.[1]

[1] Sevier's place would certainly have been taken by some such man as his
chief rival, Tipton. Robertson led his colony to the Cumberland but a few
days before old Mansker led another ; and though without Robertson the settlements would have been temporarily abandoned, they would surely have been
reoccupied. If Henderson had not helped Boon found Kentucky, then
Hart or some other of Henderson's associates would doubtless have done so;
and if Boon had been lacking, his place would probably have been taken by
some such man as Logan. The loss of these men would have been very
serious, but of no one of them can it be said, as of Clark, that he alone could
have done the work he actually did.

Important though they are for their own sakes, they are still more important as types of the men who surrounded them.

The individualism of the backwoodsmen, however, was tempered by a sound common-sense, and capacity for combination. The first hunters might come alone or in couples, but the actual colonization was done not by individuals, but by groups of individuals. The settlers brought their families and belongings either on pack-horses along the forest trails, or in scows down the streams; they settled in palisaded villages, and immediately took steps to provide both a civil and military organization. They were men of facts, not theories; and they showed their usual hard common-sense in making a government. They did not try to invent a new system; they simply took that under which they had grown up, and applied it to their altered conditions. They were most familiar with the government of the county; and therefore they adopted this for the framework of their little independent, self-governing commonwealths of Watauga, Cumberland, and Transylvania.[1]

They were also familiar with the representative system; and accordingly they introduced it into the new communities, the little forted villages serving as natural units of representation. They were already thoroughly democratic, in instinct and principle, and as a matter of course they made the offices elective, and gave full play to the majority. In organizing the militia they kept the old system

[1] The last of these was the most pretentious and short-lived and least characteristic of the three, as Henderson made an abortive effort to graft on it the utterly foreign idea of a proprietary colony.

of county lieutenants, making them elective, not appointive; and they organized the men on the basis of a regiment, the companies representing territorial divisions, each commanded by its own officers, who were thus chosen by the fighting men of the fort or forts in their respective districts. Thus each of the backwoods commonwealths, during its short-lived term of absolute freedom, reproduced as its governmental system that of the old colonial county, increasing the powers of the court, and changing the justices into the elective representatives of an absolute democracy. The civil head, the chairman of the court or committee, was also usually the military head, the colonel-commandant. In fact the military side of the organization rapidly became the most conspicuous, and, at least in certain crises, the most important. There were always some years of desperate warfare during which the entire strength of the little commonwealth was drawn on to resist outside aggression, and during these years the chief function of government was to provide for the griping military needs of the community, and the one pressing duty of its chief was to lead his followers with valor and wisdom in the struggle with the stranger.[1]

[1] My friend, Professor Alexander Johnson, of Princeton, is inclined to regard these frontier county organizations as reproductions of a very primitive type of government indeed, deeming that they were formed primarily for war against outsiders, that their military organization was the essential feature, the real reason for their existence. I can hardly accept this view in its entirety; though fully recognizing the extreme importance of the military side of the little governments, it seems to me that the preservation of order, and especially the necessity for regulating the disposition of the land, were quite as powerful factors in impelling the settlers to act together. It is important to keep in mind the territorial organization of the militia companies and regiments; a county and a regiment, a forted village and a company, were usually coextensive.

These little communities were extremely independent in feeling, not only of the Federal Government, but of their parent States, and even of one another. They had won their positions by their own courage and hardihood; very few State troops and hardly a Continental soldier had appeared west of the Alleghanies. They had heartily sympathized with their several mother colonies when they became the United States, and had manfully played their part in the Revolutionary war. Moreover they were united among themselves by ties of good-will and of services mutually rendered. Kentucky, for instance, had been succored more than once by troops raised among the Watauga Carolinians or the Holston Virginians, and in her turn she had sent needed supplies to the Cumberland. But when the strain of the war was over the separatist spirit asserted itself very strongly. The groups of western settlements not only looked on the Union itself very coldly, but they were also more or less actively hostile to their parent States, and regarded even one another as foreign communities [1]; they considered the Confederation as being literally only a lax league of friendship.

Up to the close of the Revolutionary contest the settlers who were building homes and States beyond the Alleghanies formed a homogeneous backwoods population. The wood-choppers, game hunters, and

---

[1] See in Gardoqui MSS. the letters of George Rogers Clark to Gardoqui, March 15, 1788 ; and of John Sevier to Gardoqui, September 12, 1788 ; and in the Robertson MS. the letter of Robertson to McGillivray, August 3, 1788. It is necessary to allude to the feeling here ; but the separatist and disunion movements did not gather full force until later, and are properly to be considered in connection with post-revolutionary events.

Indian fighters, who dressed and lived alike, were the typical pioneers. They were a shifting people. Character of the Pioneer Population. In every settlement the tide ebbed and flowed. Some of the new-comers would be beaten in the hard struggle for existence, and would drift back to whence they had come. Of those who succeeded some would take root in the land, and others would move still farther into the wilderness. Thus each generation rolled westward, leaving its children at the point where the wave stopped no less than at that where it started. The descendants of the victors of King's Mountain are as likely to be found in the Rockies as in the Alleghanies.

With the close of the war came an enormous increase in the tide of immigration; and many of the new-comers were of a very different stamp from their predecessors. The main current flowed towards Kentucky, and gave an entirely different character to its population. The two typical figures in Kentucky so far had been Clark and Boon, but after the close of the Revolution both of them sank into unimportance, whereas the careers of Sevier and Robertson had only begun. The disappearance of the two former from active life was partly accidental and partly a resultant of the forces that assimilated Kentucky so much more rapidly than Tennessee to the conditions prevailing in the old States. Kentucky was the best known and the most accessible of the western regions; within her own borders she was now comparatively safe from serious Indian invasion, and the tide of immigration naturally flowed thither.

So strong was the current that, within a dozen years, it had completely swamped the original settlers, and had changed Kentucky from a peculiar pioneer and backwoods commonwealth into a State differing no more from Virginia, Pennsylvania, and North Carolina than these differed from one another.

The men who gave the tone to this great flood of new-comers were the gentry from the sea-coast country, the planters, the young lawyers, the men of means who had been impoverished by the long-continued and harassing civil war. Straitened in circumstances, desirous of winning back wealth and position, they cast longing eyes towards the beautiful and fertile country beyond the mountains, deeming it a place that afforded unusual opportunities to the man with capital, no less than to him whose sole trust was in his own adventurous energy.

Most of the gentle folks in Virginia and the Carolinas, the men who lived in great roomy houses on their well-stocked and slave-tilled plantations, had been forced to struggle hard to keep their heads above water during the Revolution. They loyally supported the government, with blood and money; and at the same time they endeavored to save some of their property from the general wreck, and to fittingly educate their girls, and those of their boys who were too young to be in the army. The men of this stamp who now prepared to cast in their lot with the new communities formed an exceptionally valuable class of immigrants; they contributed the very qualities of which the raw settlements stood most in need. They had suffered for no fault of their own; fate had gone hard with them. The fathers had been in the Federal or Provincial congresses; the older sons had served in the Continental line or in the militia. The plantations were occasionally overrun by the enemy; and the general disorder had completed their ruin. Nevertheless, the heads of the families had striven to send the younger sons to school or college. For their daughters they did even more; and throughout the contest, even in its darkest hours, they sent them down to receive the final touches of a lady-like education at some one of the State capitals not at the moment in the hands of the enemy—such as Charleston or Philadelphia. There the young ladies were taught dancing and music, for which, as well as for their frocks and "pink calamanco shoes," their fathers paid enormous sums in depreciated Continental currency.[1]

Even the close of active hostilities, when the British were driven from the Southern States, brought at first but a slight betterment of condition to the struggling people. There was no cash in the land, the paper currency was nearly worthless, every one was heavily in debt, and no one was able to collect what was owing to him. There was much mob violence, and a general relaxation of the bonds of law and order. Even nature turned hostile; a terrible drought shrunk up all the streams until they could not turn the grist-mills, while from the same cause the crops failed almost completely. A hard

[1] Clay MSS. Account of Robert Morris with Miss Elizabeth Hart, during her residence in Philadelphia in 1780–81. The account is so curious that I give it in full in the Appendix.

winter followed, and many cattle and hogs died; so that the well-to-do were brought to the verge of bankruptcy and the poor suffered extreme privations, being forced to go fifty or sixty miles to purchase small quantities of meal and grain at exorbitant prices.[1]

This distress at home inclined many people of means and ambition to try their fortunes in the west: while another and equally powerful motive was the desire to secure great tracts of virgin lands, for possession or speculation. Many distinguished soldiers had been rewarded by successive warrants for unoccupied land, which they entered wherever they chose, until they could claim thousands upon thousands of acres.[2] Sometimes they sold these warrants to outsiders; but whether they remained in the hands of the original holders or not, they served as a great stimulus to the westward movement, and drew many of the representatives of the wealthiest and most influential families in the parent States to the lands on the farther side of the mountains.

At the close of the Revolution, however, the men from the sea-coast region formed but an insignificant portion of the western pioneers. The country beyond the Alleghanies was first won and settled by the backwoodsmen themselves, acting under their own leaders, obeying their own desires, and following their own methods. They were a marked and

[1] Clay MSS. Letters of Jesse Benton, 1782 and '83. See Appendix.
[2] Thus Col. Wm. Christian, for his services in Braddock's and Dunmore's wars and against the Cherokees, received many warrants; he visited Kentucky to enter them, 9,000 acres in all. See "Life of Caleb Wallace," by Wm. H. Whitsitt, Louisville, 1888.

peculiar people. The good and evil traits in their character were such as naturally belonged to a strong, harsh, and homely race, which, with all its shortcomings, was nevertheless bringing a tremendous work to a triumphant conclusion. The backwoodsmen were above all things characteristically American; and it is fitting that the two greatest and most typical of all Americans should have been respectively a sharer and an outcome of their work. Washington himself passed the most important years of his youth heading the westward movement of his people; clad in the traditional dress of the backwoodsmen, in tasselled hunting-shirt and fringed leggings, he led them to battle against the French and Indians, and helped to clear the way for the American advance. The only other man who in the American roll of honor stands by the side of Washington, was born when the distinctive work of the pioneers had ended; and yet he was bone of their bone and flesh of their flesh; for from the loins of this gaunt frontier folk sprang mighty Abraham Lincoln.

APPENDICES.

APPENDICES.

APPENDIX A—TO CHAPTER I.

DURING the early part of this century our more pretentious historians who really did pay some heed to facts and wrote books that—in addition to their mortal dulness—were quite accurate, felt it undignified and beneath them to notice the deeds of mere ignorant Indian fighters. They had lost all power of doing the best work ; for they passed their lives in a circle of small literary men, who shrank from any departure from conventional European standards.

On the other hand, the men who wrote history for the mass of our people, not for the scholars, although they preserved much important matter, had not been educated up to the point of appreciating the value of evidence, and accepted undoubted facts and absurd traditions with equal good faith. Some of them (notably Flint and one or two of Boon's other biographers) evidently scarcely regarded truthfulness and accuracy of statement as being even desirable qualities in a history. Others wished to tell the facts, but lacked all power of discrimination. Certain of their books had a very wide circulation. In some out-of-the-way places they formed, with the almanac, the staple of secular literature. But they did not come under the consideration of trained scholars, so their errors remained uncorrected ; and at this day it is a difficult, and often an impossible task, to tell which of the statements to accept and which to reject.

Many of the earliest writers lived when young among the old companions of the leading pioneers, and long afterwards wrote down from memory the stories the old men had told them. They were themselves often clergymen, and were usually utterly inexperienced in wild backwoods life, in spite of their early surroundings—exactly as to-day any town in the Rocky Mountains is sure to contain some half-educated men as ignorant of mountain and plains life, of Indians and wild beasts, as the veriest lout on an eastern farm. Accordingly they accepted the wildest stories of frontier warfare with a faith that forcibly reminds one of the equally simple credulity displayed by the average classical scholar concerning early Greek and Roman prowess. Many of these primitive historians give accounts of overwhelming Indian numbers and enormous Indian losses, that read as if taken from the books that tell of the Gaulish hosts the Romans conquered, and the Persian hordes the Greeks repelled ; and they are almost as untrustworthy.

Some of the anecdotes they relate are not far removed from the Chinese-like tale—given, if my memory is correct, in Herodotus—of the Athenian soldier, who went into action with a small grapnel or anchor attached by a chain to his waist, that he might tether himself out to resist the shock of the charging foe. A flagrant example is the story which describes how the white man sees an Indian very far off making insulting gestures ; how he forthwith loads his rifle with two bullets— which the narrator evidently thinks will go twice as far and twice as straight as one,—and, taking careful aim, slays his enemy. Like other similar anecdotes, this is told of a good many different frontier heroes ; the historian usually showing a delightful lack of knowledge of what is and what is not possible in hunting, tracking, and fighting. However, the utter ignorance of even the elementary principles of rifle-shooting may not have been absolutely confined to the historians. Any one accustomed to old hunters knows that their theories concerning their own weapons are often rather startling. A year ago last fall I was hunting some miles below my ranch (on the Little Missouri) to lay in the winter stock of meat, and was encamped for a week with an old hunter. We both had 45–75 Winchester rifles ; and I was much amused at his insisting that his gun " shot level " up to two hundred yards—a distance at which the ball really drops considerably over a foot. Yet he killed a good deal of game; so he must either in practice have disregarded his theories, or else he must have always overestimated the distances at which he fired.

The old writers of the simpler sort not only delighted in impossible feats with the rifle, but in equally impossible deeds of strength, tracking and the like; and they were very fond of attributing all the wonderful feats of which they had heard to a single favorite hero, not to speak of composing speeches for him.

It seems—though it ought not to be—necessary to point out to some recent collectors of backwoods anecdotes, the very obvious truths: that with the best intentions in the world the average backwoodsman often has difficulty in describing a confused chain of events exactly as they took place; that when the events are described after a long lapse of years many errors are apt to creep in; and that when they are reported from tradition it is the rarest thing imaginable for the report to be correct.

APPENDIX B—TO CHAPTER II.

(The following account of the first negotiations of the Americans with the Indians near Vincennes is curious as being the report of one of the Indians; but it was evidently colored to suit his hearer, for as a matter of fact the Indians of the Wabash were for the time being awed into quiet, the Piankeshaws sided with the Americans, and none of them dared rise until the British approached.)

(*Haldimand MSS.*, Series B, Vol. 122, p. 219.)

Proceedings of the Rebels at St. Vincennes as related to Lieut Govr. Hamilton by Neegik an Ottawa War Chief sent forward to gain intelligence. Camp at Rocher de Bout 14th Octr. 1778—

On the Rebels first arrival at St. Vincennes they took down the English Flag left there by Lieut. Gen. Abbott, wrapped a large stone in it, and threw it into the Ouabash, saying to the Indians, thus we mean to treat your Father—

Having called the Indians together they laid a War Belt colored red, & a belt colored green before them, telling them that if they delighted in mischief and had no compassion on their wives & children they might take up the red one, if on the contrary they were wise & preferred peace, the green one—

The old Tobacco a chief of the [Piankeshaws] spoke as follows— My brothers—you speak in a manner not to be understood, I never yet saw, nor have I heard from my ancestors that it was customary to place good & bad things in the same dish—You talk to us as if you meant us well, yet you speak of War & peace in the same minute, thus I treat the speeches of such men—on which with a violent kick he spurned their belts from him.

The son of Lagesse, a young Chief of the Pontconattamis of St Joseph spoke next to them.

My Brothers—'Tis because I have listened to the voice of our old men, & because I have regard to our women & children that I have not before now struck my Tomahawk into some of your heads—attend to what I say, I will only go to see in what condition our wives & children are (meaning I will first place them in security) & then you may depend on seeing me again—

The Rebel speaker then said—

You are young men & your youth excuses your ignorances, you would not else talk as you do—Our design is to march thro' your country, & if we find any fires in our way, we shall just tread them out as we walk along & if we meet with any obstacle or barrier we shall remove it with all ease, but the bystanders must take care lest the splinters should scar their faces.

We shall then proceed to Detroit where your father is whom we consider as a Hog put to fatten in a penn, we shall enclose him in his penn, till he be fat, & then we will throw him into the river—We shall draw a reinforcement from the Falls on the Ohio & from thence & the Ilinois send six hundred men to Chicagou—

To this the Indians replied—You that are so brave, what need have you to be reinforced, go to Detroit, you that can put out our fires & so easely remove our barriers.—This we say to you, take care that in attempting to extinguish our fires you do not burn yourselves, & that in breaking down our barriers you do not run splinters into your hands. You may also expect that we shall not suffer a single Frenchman to accompany you to Detroit.

End of the Conference.

APPENDIX C—TO CHAPTER IV.

(From Canadian Archives.)

(*Haldimand MSS.*, Series B, Vol. 122, p. 351.)

(Copy.)

UPPER ST. DUSKI, June 9, 1779.

DEAR SIR,

After much running about, some presents to Chiefs, we had collected at the Mingo Town near 200 Savages chiefly Shawanese—When lo! a runner arrived with accounts of the Shawanese towns being attacked by a body from Kentuck, they burnt five houses, killed one Indian & wounded the Chief badly—lost their own Commander *Heron* or *Herington*—they carried off 30 Horses, were pursued by fifty Shawanese, the Shawanese were beat back with loss of five & six wounded—News flew that all the Towns w re to be attack'd & our little body seperated in an instant past reassembling—confusion still prevails—much counselling—no resolves—many are removing—more for peace.

The Delawares make it dangerous travelling. By this opportunity Davison & Cook return sick—Girty is flying about —McCarty stays with me with some Ottawas—these unsteady Rogues put me out of all patience.—I will go with him in a few days, if nothing material occurs—See the Enemy that I may not be laugh'd at then return.—The Rebels mean I believe to destroy the Villages & corn now up—the method they bring their little armies into the field as follows : Every Family on the Borders receive orders to send according to their strength (one or two men) to the place of Rendezvous at a time appointed (on pain of fine or imprisonment) with fifteen or twenty days Provisions, they immediately receive their ammunition & proceed quickly to action—I am credibly inform'd by various means, that they can raise in that manner three or four thousand in a few days for such excursions—I was obliged to

Kill four more Cattle for the Indians at the Mingo Town—they are always Cooking or Counselling.

I have nothing more to inform you off if anything material occurs, which I really expect in a day or two, I will inform you by Express.

I am &c

HENRY BIRD.

To CAPT. LERNOULT.

(Copy.)

June 12th, UPPER ST. DUSKI.

SIR,

Couriers after Couriers arrive with accounts of the Rebels advancing to destroy the Savage Villages now all their corn is planted—

APPENDIX D—TO CHAPTER IV.

(State Department MSS.; No. 48, Vol. " Memorials &c Inhabitants of Illi-
nois, Kaskaskias and Kentucky.")

The Petition and Prayr. of the people of that Part of Contry [sic] now Claim'd. by the State of Virginia in the Countys of Kaintuckey and Ilinois Humbly Sheweth—That we the leige Subjects of the United States Labour under many Greivences on acount of not being formd. into a Seperate State or the Mind and Will of Congress more fully known respecting us— And we Humbly beg leave to Present to the Honorable Continental Congress our Humble Petition seting forth the Grievences and oppressions we labour under and Pray Congress may Consider Such our greivences and grant us redress

We your Petitioners being situate in a wide Extencive Uncultivated Contry and Exposd. on every side to incursions of the Savage Indians humbly Conceive Ourselves approssed by several acts of the general assembly of Virginia for granting large Grants for waist and unapropriated lands on the Western Waters without Reservation for Cultivating and Settling the same whereby Setling the Contry is Discouraged and the inhabitants are greatly Exposd. to the Saviges by whome our wives and Childring are daly Cruily murdered Notwithstanding our most Humble Petitions Canot Obtain Redress— By an other act we are Taxd. which in our Present Situation we Conceive to be oppresive and unjust being Taxd. with money and grain whilst Enrold and in actual Pay residing in Garrisons. We are Situate from Six Hundred to one Thousand Miles from our Present Seite of Goverment, Whereby Criminals are Suffered to Escape with impunity, Great numbers who ware Ocationaly absent are Deprived of an Opertunity of their Just Rights and Emprovements and here we are Obliged to Prosecute all Apeals, and whillst we remain uncertain whether the unbounded Claim of This Extencive Contry Ought of right to belong to the United States or the State of Virginia, They have by another late act required of us to Sware alegince to the State of Virginia in Particular Notwithstanding we have aredy taken the Oath of alegance to the united States. These are Greivences too Heavy to be born, and we do Humbly Pray that the Continental Congress will Take Proper Methods to form us into a Seperate State or grant us Such Rules and regulations as they in their Wisdoms shall think most Proper, During the Continuance of the Present War and your Petitioners shall ever Pray

May 15th, 1780.

[Signed]   ROBERT TYLER   RICHARD CONNOR
            THOMAS HUGHES   ARCHIBALD MCDONALD
            ABRAHAM VAN METER (and others to the number of 640).

APPENDIX E—TO CHAPTER VII.

(*Haldimand MSS.* Series B, Vol. 123, p. 302.)

SIR,

My Letter of the 22nd & 23rd of July informed you of the reports brought us of the Enemy's motions at that time which was delivered by the Chiefs of the standing Stone Village & confirmed by Belts & Strings of Wampum in so earnest a manner that could not but gain Credit with us. We had upon this occasion the greatest Body of Indians collected to an advantageous peice of ground near the Picawee Village that have been assembled in this Quarter since the commencement of the War & perhaps may never be in higher spirits to engage the

Enemy, when the return of Scouts from the Ohio informed us that the account we had received was false ; this disappointment notwithstanding all our endeavours to keep them together occasioned them to disperse in disgust with each other, the inhabitants of this Country who were the most immediately interested in keeping in a Body ware the first that broke off & though we advanced towards the Ohio with upwards of three hundred Hurons & Lake Indians few of the Delawares, Shawanese or Mingoes followed us. On our arrival at the Ohio we remain'd still in uncertainty with respect to the Enemys motions, & it was thought best from hence to send Scouts to the Falls & that the main Body should advance into the Enemy's Country and endeavour to lead out a party from some of their Forts by which we might be able to gain some certain Intelligence accordingly we crossed the Ohio and arrived the 18th Inst. at one of the Enemys settlements—call'd Bryans Station, but the Indians discovering their numbers prevented their coming out and the Lake Indians finding this rush'd up to the Fort and set several out Houses on fire but at too great a distance to touch the Fort the Wind blowing the Contrary way. the firing continued this day during which time a Party of about twenty of the Enemy approached a part that happened not to be Guarded & about one half of them reached it the rest being drove back by a few Indians who ware near the place, the next morning finding it to no purpose to keep up a fire longer upon the Fort as we were getting men killed, & had already several men wounded which ware to be carried, the Indians determined to retreat & the 20th reached the Blue Licks where we encamp'd near an advantageous Hill and expecting the enemy would pursue determined here to wait for them keeping spies at the Lick who in the morning of the 21st discovered them & at half past 7 o'clock we engaged them & in a short time totally defeated them, we ware not much superior to them in Numbers they being about two hundred picked men from the settlement of Kentucky. Commanded by the Colonels Todd, Trigg, Boon & Todd, with the Majors Harlin, and McGary most of whom fell in the action, from the best inquiry I could make upon the spot there was upwards of one hundred

& forty killed & taken with near an hundred rifles several being thrown into a deep River that ware not recovered. It was said by the Prisoners that a Colonel Logan was expected to join them with one hundred men more we waited upon the ground to-day for him, but seeing there was not much probability of his coming we set off & crossed the ohio the second day after the action. Captain Caldwell & I arrived at this place last night with a design of sending some assistance to those who are bring on the wounded people who are fourteen in number, we had Ten Indians kill'd with Mr. La Bute of the Indian Department who by sparing the life of one of the Enemy & endeavouring to take him Prisoner loss'd his own, to our disappointment we find no Provisions brought forward to this place or likely hood of any for some time, and we have entirely subsisted since we left this on what we got in the Woods, and took from the Enemy. The Prisoners all agree in their account that there is no talk of an Expedition from that Quarter, nor indeed are they able without assistance from the Colonies, & that the Militia of the Country have been employed during the summer in Building the Fort at the Falls, & what they call a Row Galley which has made one trip up the River to the Mouth of the big Miamis & occasioned that alarm that created us so much trouble, she carries one six pounder, six four pounders & two two pounders & Row's eighty oars, she had at the big Bone Lick one hundred men but being chiefly draughts from the Militia many of them left her on different parts of the River. One of the Prisoners mentions the arrival of Boats lately from Fort Pitt & that Letters has pass'd between the Commanding officer of that place & Mr. Clark intimating that preparation is making there for another Expedition into the Indian Country, we have since our arrival heard something of this matter and that the particulars has been forwarded to you, a Detachment of Rangers with a large party of Delawares, & Shawanese are gone that way who will be able to discover the truth of this matter.

I am this day favoured with yours of the 6th Augt. containing the report of Isaac Gians concerning the Cruelties of the Indians. It is true they have made sacrifices to their revenge after the massacre of their women & children some being known to them to be perpetraters of it, but it was done in my absence or before I could reach any of the places to interfere. And I can assure you Sir that there is not a white person here wanting in their duty to represent to the Indians in the strongest terms the highest abhorence of such conduct as well as the bad consequences that may attend it to both them & us being contrary to the rule of carrying on war by Civilized nations, however it is not improbable that Gians may have exaggerated matters greatly being notoriously known for a disaffected person and concerned in sending Prisoners away with Intelligence to the Enemy at the time Captain Bird came out as we ware then informed. I flatter myself that I may by this time have an answer to the Letter I had the honor of writing to the Commandr. in Chief on leaving Detroit. Mr. Elliot is to be the Bearer of this who will be able to give you any farther information necessary respecting matters here.

I am with respect Sir your most obedient & Very Humble Servant

A. McKEE.

SHAWANESE COUNTRY, }
August 28th, 1782. }

Major DE PEYSTER.

APPENDIX F—TO CHAPTER VII.

(*Haldimand MSS.*, Series B, Vol. 123, p. 297.)

Extract of a letter from Captain Caldwell, dated at Wakitamiki, August 26, 1782.

"When I last had the pleasure of writing you, I expected to have struck at Wheeling as I was on my march for that place, but was overtaken by a Messenger from the Shawnese, who informed me that the Enemy was on their march for their Country, which obliged me to turn their way, and to my great mortification found the alarm false & that it was owing to a Gondals coming up to the mouth of Licking Creek, and landing some men upon the South side of the Ohio which when the Indians saw supposed it must be Clark. It would have been a lucky circumstance if they had come on, as I had eleven hundred Indians on the ground, and three hundred within a days march of me. When the Report was contradicted They mostly left us, many of them had left their Towns no way equipped for War, as they expected as well as myself to fight in a few days, notwithstanding I was determined to pay the Enemy a visit with as many Indians as would follow me : accordingly I crossed the Ohio with three hundred Indians & Rangers, and Marched for Bryants Station on Kentuck, and surrounded the Fort the 15th in the morning, & tried to draw 'em out by sending up a small party to try to take a Prisoner and shew themselves, but the Indians were in too great a hurry and the whole shewed too soon—I then saw it was in vain to wait any longer and so drew nigh the Fort. burnt 3 Houses which are part of the Fort but the wind being contrary prevented it having the desired effect Killed upwards of 300 Hogs, 150 Head of Cattle, and a number of Sheep, took a number of Horses, pull'd up and destroy'd their Potatoes, cut down a great deal of their Corn, burn't their Hemp and did other considerable damage—by the Indians exposing themselves too much we had 5 Killed & 2 Wounded.

We retreated the 16th and came as far as Biddle's former Station, when nigh 100 Indians left me, as they went after their things they left at the Forks of Licking, and I took the Road by the blue Licks as it was nigher and the ground more advantageous in case the Enemy should pursue us—got to the Licks on the 17th and encamped.

On the 18th in the morning, one of my party that was watching the Road came in and told me the Enemy was within a mile of us, upon which I drew up to fight them—at ½ past seven they advanced in three Divisions in good order, they had spied some of us and it was the very place they expected to overtake us.—We had but fired one Gun till they gave us a Volley and stood to it very well for some time, 'till we rushed in upon them. when they broke immediately.—We pursued for about two miles, and as the enemy was mostly on horseback, it was in vain to follow further.

We killed and took one hundred and Forty six. Amongst

the killed is Col. Todd the Commandr Col. Boon, Lt. Col. Trigg, Major Harlin who commanded their Infantry, Major Magara and á number more of their officers. Our loss is Monsr. La Bute killed, he died like a warrior fighting Arm to Arm, six Indians killed and ten wounded—The Indians behaved extremely well, and no people could behave better than both Officers & men in general—The Indians I had with me were the Wyandots and Lake Indians—The Wyandots furnished me with what provisions I wanted, and behaved extremely well."

APPENDIX G—TO CHAPTER X.

It has been so habitual among American writers to praise all the deeds, good, bad, and indifferent, of our Revolutionary ancestors, and to belittle and make light of what we have recently done, that most men seem not to know that the Union and Confederate troops in the Civil War fought far more stubbornly and skilfully than did their forefathers at the time of the Revolution. It is impossible to estimate too highly the devoted patriotism and statesmanship of the founders of our national life ; and however high we rank Washington, I am confident that we err, if any thing, in not ranking him high enough, for on the whole the world has never seen a man deserving to be placed above him ; but we certainly have overestimated the actual fighting qualities of the Revolutionary troops, and have never laid enough stress on the folly and jealousy with which the States behaved during the contest. In 1776 the Americans were still in the gristle ; and the feats of arms they then performed do not bear comparison with what they did in the prime of their lusty youth, eighty or ninety years later. The Continentals who had been long drilled by Washington and Greene were most excellent troops ; but they never had a chance to show at their best, because they were always mixed in with a mass of poor soldiers, either militia or just-enlisted regulars.

The resolute determination of the Americans to win, their trust in the justice of their cause, their refusal to be cast down by defeat, the success with which they overran and con-

quered the west at the very time they were struggling for life
or death in the east, the heroic grandeur of their great leader
—for all this they deserve full credit. But the militia who
formed the bulk of the Revolutionary armies did not generally
fight well. Sometimes, as at Bunker's Hill and King's Mountain, they did excellently, and they did better, as a rule, than
similar European bodies—than the Spanish and Portuguese
peasants in 1807–12, for instance. At that time it was believed
that the American militia could not fight at all ; this was a
mistake, and the British paid dearly for making it ; but the
opposite belief, that militia could be generally depended upon,
led to quite as bad blunders, and the politicians of the Jeffer-
sonian school who encouraged the idea made us in our turn
pay dearly for our folly in after years, as at Bladensburg and
along the Niagara frontier in 1812. The Revolutionary war
proved that hastily gathered militia, justly angered and strung
to high purpose, could sometimes whip regulars, a feat
then deemed impossible ; but it lacked very much of prov-
ing that they would usually do this. Moreover, even the stalwart fighters who followed Clark and Sevier, and who did
most important and valorous service, cannot point to any one
such desperate deed of fierce courage as that of the doomed
Texans under Bowie and Davy Crockett in the Alamo.

A very slight comparison of the losses suffered in the battles
of the Revolution with those suffered in the battles of the Civil
War is sufficient to show the superiority of the soldiers who
fought in the latter (and a comparison of the tactics and other
features of the conflicts will make the fact even clearer). No
Revolutionary regiment or brigade suffered such a loss as befell the 1st Minnesota at Gettysburg, where it lost 215 out of
263 men, 82 per cent. ; the 9th Illinois at Shiloh, where it lost
366 out of 578 men, 63 per cent. ; the 1st Maine at Petersburg,
which lost 632 out of 950 men, 67 per cent. ; or Caldwell's
brigade of New York, New Hampshire, and Pennsylvania
troops, which, in Hancock's attack at Fredericksburg, lost 949
out of 1,947 men, 48 per cent. ; or, turning to the Southern
soldiers, such a loss as that of the 1st Texas at Antietam, when
186 out of 226 men fell, 82 per cent. ; or of the 26th North

Carolina, which, at Gettysburg, lost 588 out of 820 men, 72 per cent. ; or the 8th Tennessee, at Murfreesboro, which lost 306 out of 444 men, or 68 per cent. ; or Garnett's brigade of Virginians, which, in Pickett's charge, lost 941 men out of 1,427, or 65 per cent.

There were over a hundred regiments, and not a few brigades, in the Union and Confederate armies, each of which in some one action suffered losses averaging as heavy as the above. The Revolutionary armies cannot show such a roll of honor as this. Still, it is hardly fair to judge them by this comparison, for the Civil War saw the most bloody and desperate fighting that has occurred of late years. None of the European contests since the close of the Napoleonic struggles can be compared to it. Thus the Light Brigade at Balaclava lost only 37 per cent., or 247 men out of 673, while the Guards at Inkermann lost but 45 per cent., or 594 out of 1,331 ; and the heaviest German losses in the Franco-Prussian war were but 49 and 46 per cent., occurring respectively to the Third Westphalian Regiment at Mars-le-Tours, and the Garde-Schutzen battalion at Metz.

These figures are taken from " Regimental Losses in the American Civil War," by Col. Wm. F. Fox, Albany, 1881 ; the loss in each instance includes few or no prisoners, save in the cases of Garnett's brigade and of the Third Westphalian Regiment.

APPENDIX H—TO CHAPTER XII.

(From the *Robertson MSS.*, Vol. I., Letter of Don Miro.)

NEW ORLEANS, the 20th April, 1783.

SIR

I received yours of 29th January last, & am highly pleased in seeing the good intentions of the People of that District, & knowing the falsehood of the report we have heard they are willing to attack their Province. You ought to make the same account of the news you had that the Indians have been excited in their Province against you, since I wrote quite the contrary at different times to Alexander McGillevray to induce him to make peace, & lastly he answered me that he gave his word to the Governor of North Carolina that the Creeks would not trouble again those settlements : notwithstanding after the letter received from you, and other from Brigadier general Daniel Smith Esqr I will writte to him engaging him to be not more troublesome to you.

I have not any connection with Cheroquis & Marcuten, but as they go now & then to Illinois I will give advice to that Commander to induce them to be quiet : in respect to the former in the month of May of last year they asked the permission of settling them selves on the west side of the Mississpi River which is granted & they act accordingly, you plainly see you are quite free from their incursions

I will give the Passeport you ask for your son-in-law, & I will be highly pleased with his coming down to setle in this Province & much more if you, & your family should come along with him, since I can assure you that you will find here your welfare, without being either molested on religious matters or paying any duty & under the circumstances of finding allwais market for your crops which makes every one of the planters settled at Natchez or elsewhere to improve every day, much more so than if they were to purchase the Lands, as they are granted gratis

I wish to be usefull to you being with regard sir

Your most obt. hl. servant

(Dupte.)   ESTEVAN MIRO.

Colonel JAMES ROBERTSON, Esqr.

The duplicity of the Spaniards is well illustrated by the fact that the Gardoqui MSS. give clear proof that they were assisting the Creeks with arms and ammunition at the very time Miro was writing these letters. See the Gardoqui MSS., *passim*, especially Miro's letter of June 28, 1786.

APPENDIX I—TO CHAPTER XIII. From the Clay MSS.

Account of Robert Morris with Miss Betsey Hart, Philadelphia, 1780–81.

Dr.   Miss Harte   IN ACCOUNT CURRENT WITH   ROBERT MORRIS   **Cr.**

[Oldest daughter of Col. Thomas Hart. She married Dr. Richard Pendell.]

Date	Particulars	Continental	Exchange	Specie		
1780 Aug. 29	To cash paid for a Pair of Shoes for you	£ 64 2 6	at 60 for 1 £	1	1	4½
	To a Chest of Sugar delivered Mrs. Brodeau & Porterage . . .	107 15	Do	18	9	3
	To two ps Sheeting Delivered Ditto	116 0	Do	18	12	0
	To Cash paid Wm. McDugall's Bill for one & a half Quarters Tuition at Dancing	223 10	Do	3	12	6
	Paid E. Denaugheys Bill for washing Done for you . . .	95 12 6	Do	1	11	10¾
Dec. 6	To Ditto paid Hannah Estys Bill for making Frocks for you £257 10/ Paid D Denaugheys Bill for Washg . . . £125.12.6	383 2 6	at 75 for 1	5	2	2
29	To Ditto paid for pair of Pink Calemancoi Shoes for you . . .	78 15 0	Do	1	1	0
1781 Feb. 3	To Ditto paid B. Victor your music master for one Quarter Tuition of Music	506 5 0	75 for 1	6	15	0
	To the following Articles delivered Mrs. Brodeau on your Accot. One Firkin of Butter one Box of Candles & a Box of Soap Amounting p Account to	629 1 2	Do	8	7	9
	To Cash paid Mrs. Brodeau in full of her Accot. to October last against you	3856 17 6	Do	51	8	6
	Allowed for Depreciation . . .			£115 3 5	57 13 7	
				£172 17 0		

Received Philad. April 7th 1781 the One hundred and Seventy two Pounds 17/ State Specie being in full the amount of the annexed account for Robt. Morris

£172. 17. State Specie

J. SWANNICK

APPENDIX J—TO CHAPTER XIII.

In the Clay MSS. the letters of Jesse Benton to Col. Hart, of December 4, 1782, and March 22, 1783, paint vividly the general distress in the Carolinas. They are taken up mostly with accounts of bad debts and of endeavors to proceed against various debtors ; they also touch on other subjects.

In the first, of December 4, 1782, Benton writes : " It seems the powers above are combined against us this year. Such a Drouth was never known here [in the upper Carolinas] before ; Corn sells from the stack at 4 & 5/ p. Bushel, Wheat 6 & 8/, Rye the same, Oats 3/ 6 &c &c . . . I have not had Water to keep the Grist Mill Fuling Mill and Oyl Mill at Work before this Week. . . . Johny Rice has gone to Kentuck with his goods to buy Furs, but before he went we talked of your debts and he did not like to be concerned, saying he should gain ill will for no profit ; However I will immediately enforce the Law to recover your Debts . . . the Lands which You had of me would sell as soon as any but this hard year makes many settlers and few buyers. I have heard nothing more of Major Haywoods desire of purchasing & all I ever heard upon the subject was from his son-in-law who now appears very sick of his late purchase of Elegant Buildings. . . . Your Brother Capt. Nat Hart, our worthy and respectable Friend, I doubt is cut off by the Savages at the time and in the manner as first represented, to wit, that he went out to hunt his horses in the month of July or August it is supposed the Indians in Ambuscade between Boonsboro and Knockbuckle, intended to take him Prisonner, but killd his horse and at the same time broke his Thigh, that the savages finding their Prisonner with his Thigh broken was under the necessity of puting him to Death by shooting him through the Heart at so small a Distance as to Powder burn his Flesh. He was Tomhawkd, scalped & lay two Days before he was found and buried. This Account has come by difrent hands & confirmd to Col. Henderson by a Letter from an intimate Friend of his at Kentuck."

This last bit of information is sandwiched in between lamentations over bad debts, concerning which the writer manifested considerably more emotion than over the rather startling fate of Captain Hart.

The second letter contains an account of the " trafficking off " of a wagon and fine pair of Pennsylvania horses, the news that a debt had been partially liquidated by the payment of sixty pounds' worth of rum and sugar, which in turn went to pay workmen, and continues : " The common people are and will be much distressed for want of Bread. I have often heard talk of Famine, but never thought of seeing any thing so much like it as the present times in this part of the Country. Three fourths of the Inhabitants of this country are obliged to purchase their Bread at 50 & 60 miles distance at the common price of 16/ and upwards per barrel. The winter has been very hard upon the live stock & I am convinced that abundance of Hogs and Cattle will die this Spring for want of Food. . . . Cash is now scarcer here than it ever was before. . . . I have been industrious to get the Mills in good repair and have succeeded well, but have rcd. very little benefit from them yet owing intirely to the general failure of a Crop. We have done no Merchant work in the Grist Mill, & she only supplies my Family and workmen with Bread. Rye, the people are glad to eat. Flaxseed the cattle have chiefly eaten though I have got as much of that article as made 180 Gallons of Oyl at 4/ per bushel. The Oyl is in great demand ; I expect two dollars p. Gallon for it at Halifax or Edenton, & perhaps a better price. We were very late in beginning with the Fulling Business ; for want of water. . . . [there are many] Mobbs and commotions among the People."

INDEX TO VOLUMES I. AND II.

All Four Volumes Available in Bison Book Editions

THE WINNING OF THE WEST.

By THEODORE ROOSEVELT.